# Celebrating the Voices of Literacy

THE COLLEGE READING ASSOCIATION

## The Twenty-Third Yearbook
## A Peer Reviewed Publication of
## The College Reading Association
## 2001

### Co-Editors

**Wayne M. Linek**
Texas A&M University-Commerce

**Elizabeth G. Sturtevant**
George Mason University

**Jo Ann R. Dugan**
Clarion University of Pennsylvania

**Patricia E. Linder**
Texas A&M University-Commerce

### Editorial Assistants

**Sujith K. Chithamur**     **Hemanth K. Jaladhi**
Texas A&M University-Commerce

**Eileen McCartin**     **Judith Fontana**
George Mason University

**Meggan Wachob Matson**
Clarion University of Pennsylvania

# COLLEGE READING ASSOCIATION BOARD MEMBERS 2001-2002

# TABLE OF CONTENTS

# ACKNOWLEDGEMENTS

It goes without saying that this volume would not be possible without the authors who devoted much energy and thought toward writing the articles presented here. We are especially grateful for the expertise of the Editorial Review Board members who make possible the review/selection of manuscripts and the CRA Publications Committee, which is chaired by Michael McKenna of Georgia Southern University. We are thankful for the unwavering commitment of the CRA Board of Directors who have supported the editorial team and the publication of the CRA Yearbook year after year.

We feel privileged to have had outstanding editorial assistants who attended to fine details and tracking of the manuscripts. We commend our graduate assistants Sujith K. Chithamur and Hemanth K. Jaladhi at Texas A&M University-Commerce; Eileen McCartin and Judith Fontana at George Mason University; and Meggan Wachob Matson at Clarion University, for their hard work and the long hours they spent reading manuscripts, communicating with reviewers, and communicating with authors. We also appreciate the clerical support provided by our secretarial staff, Frances Norman and Jan Hazelip, at Texas A&M University-Commerce. Finally, we thank Vivian Freeman and Lyndal Burnett, at Texas A&M University-Commerce, for facilitating the printing and production of the Yearbook.

We are eternally grateful for the extensive support provided by our universities. At Texas A&M University-Commerce, we thank President Keith McFarland, Provost and Academic Vice President Vicki Davis, and Dean Jerry Hutton for ongoing financial assistance. We also extend a warm thanks to faculty in the Department of Elementary Education for supporting the publication. At George Mason University, we thank, Dean Jeffrey Gorrell, Senior Associate Dean Martin Ford, President Alan G. Merten, administrators, and faculty of the Graduate School of Education for creating a collaborative academic community. At Clarion University of Pennsylvania, we thank President Diane L. Reinhard and Dean Gail Grejda, for supporting the Yearbook.

We also extend a heartfelt thanks to our families, colleagues, friends, and readers who have supported our professional efforts with encouragement, acknowledgement, and genuine interest.

WML, EGS, JRD, PEL
September, 2001

# Introduction:

## Celebrating The Voices of Literacy
## Looking Back, Looking Forward

We hope you will enjoy this twenty-third edition of the College Reading Association's Yearbook, *Celebrating the Voices of Literacy*. Since this will be our last yearbook as an editorial team we'd like to take time to review and reflect on the nine years of editorial work with CRA.

In 1993, Betty and Wayne were fresh out of the Kent State doctoral program when they applied for the editorship of the yearbook. The first year was a learning experience and in our 1994 yearbook *Pathways for Literacy: Learners Teach and Teachers Learn* we said,

> We appreciate the guidance and support of the CRA Board of Directors and Publications Committee, especially the . . . Publications Chairperson, J. Estill Alexander . . . and we dedicate this book to Nancy D. Padak and Timothy V. Rasinski, both of Kent State University. In 1990, Tim and Nancy took on the challenge of reviving the CRA Yearbook series after a twenty-year gap in publication; they developed it into a respected scholarly work in only four years. The current Yearbook is possible solely because of the groundwork they laid. In a less public role, Nancy and Tim also have spent endless hours over the past 7 years mentoring our personal growth as literacy educators and scholars. From the beginning, they offered both knowledge and friendship, and they have always been cheerfully available on a moment's notice. We hope that our efforts during our term as Yearbook editors reflect some of Tim and Nancy's extraordinary scholarship, persistence, vision, and caring.

In the 1995 yearbook *Generations of Literacy*, the introduction helped to clarify that the term generations included two ideas:

> First, "generations" embraces our "early leaders" . . . Second "generations" highlights the mentoring relationship between students and teachers including the reciprocity implied in . . . learners teach and teachers learn. This year we would like to dedicate this book to future generations of literacy learners, particularly our students who will carry literacy instruction into the twenty-first century. Not only do they love learning but they are struggling to understand how to help others come to love learning. Specifically, we'd like to recognize Kathleen A. J. Mohr. Kit . . . was the Yearbook's first editorial assistant . . . although she was officially the "student," the learning was mutual. Kit and all of our students continue to teach us more "stuff" than we could ever teach them.

In 1996 we introduced the yearbook *Growing Literacy* with the following questions/issues, then dedicated the book to our family members:

What is literacy and how does it grow? Simple-sounding questions, with far from simple answers. Around the globe, educators, parents, authors, newspaper columnists—even politicians—discuss issues related to literacy definitions and literacy growth. These are the "hot topics" in the 1990s. Everyone, it seems, favors "literacy;" few however, can agree on what "literacy" is, much less how to help it develop . . . our family members . . . caring and support has inspired confidence, new journeys, and growth. In their individual ways, each also reminds us that '. . . all work is empty save when there is love' (Gibran, 1923, p.26).

In 1997 Betty and Wayne finished their four-year term as editors and introduced the yearbook *Exploring Literacy* to the members of the College Reading Association with the following sentiments:

Where in the human psyche do we find the catalyst for "Exploring Literacy?" We believe the driving force that provides fuel for individual and collaborative explorations into the nature of literacy is grounded in a stimulating interplay among a variety of factors. Collegial relationships in professional organizations like CRA provide an impetus, a forum, and a means for clarification of, and reflection upon, our explorations into literacy. . . . Throughout our extensive interactions with the CRA officers, board members, and the general membership, we have encountered not only outstanding scholarship and professionalism, but also a genuine kindness and patience. We hope we can give back at least a part of what we have gained.

In 1998 Pat and JoAnn joined the editorial team and we produced *Community and Literacy* with an introduction that recognized:

A community can be as simple as two young children sharing a book or a group of adults performing music on a street corner. Literate communities occur throughout the world and across generations. They inspire us to *want to participate,* and they facilitate our growth as readers, writer, and learners . . . our own literacy communities, wherever they have been or will be in the future. Our families, teachers, students, colleagues, friends—and unknown others—have created communities for our own literate development and have inspired us to create communities for others.

In 1999 we produced two volumes, *History of the College Reading Association: 1958-1998* authored by co-historians historians at that time J. Estill Alexander and Susan L. Strode, and *Advancing the World of Literacy: Moving into the 21st Century.* In our introduction we stated:

As educators we wish to inspire our students to think critically and to construct their own understandings of the world. Yet we must not lose sight of the underlying driving force that motivates us. That is an overwhelming passion for reading, writing, and learning. We really do enjoy our work. If we let our students see our passion, and share with them our enthusiasm for reading and writing, we can make it possible for them to experience the same joy and satisfaction that we do. With that passion in mind, we dedicate this volume of the CRA Yearbook to prospective teachers who will inherit the enormous responsibility of educating children and perpetuating the world of literacy in the new millennium.

In the 2000 Yearbook, *Literacy at a New Horizon* we noted that:
As we anticipate new eras of literacy, we must be mindful of the many centuries of literacy development that brought us to this moment. In this volume many authors have reflected on the heritage of centuries and gazed upon the possibilities of growth in literacy that loom on each day's horizon. The horizons are indeed varied. They depend on the perspective of each reader/scholar . . . We, the ones who have chosen literacy as a life work, recognize these horizons transcend the K-12 or even K-16 levels. Literacy is for life; and literacy is for everyone. When we surge past new horizons, let us remember the lessons of the past as we generate questions for the future. And let us do it together in community with our colleagues, our students, our friends, and our loved ones.

As we review our former book introductions we see that we have come full circle in our understanding and appreciation of literacy. We began with a focus on our teachers/mentors, then moved to our students, then to growth and family, then to support of colleagues and professional organizations, then to communities in all variations, then to future teachers, and finally to a new horizon. In our introduction of *Celebrating the Voices of Literacy* we are coming back to our teachers and mentors. Why? Because in the dawning of this new millennium we have experienced terrorism and tragedy. As we move into this new and uncertain era, we need models of tough yet gentle strength to guide us as we make decisions that impact the future of the human race.

We of the College Reading Association have been blessed with models of kind, gentle, patient mentors who "held our feet to the fire" and helped guide us through uncertainty. We can now call upon these mental models stored in our memories as we try to figure out how to employ literacy in dealing with our losses and begin constructing a new future. Thus, we dedicate our final volume to a person who was a model of gentle strength and perseverance, the late J. Estill Alexander. Estill was the chair of the CRA Publications Committee when we began our editorship. He was the patient guiding force who, with mentors Tim Rasinski and Nancy Padak, helped us develop a quality publication. Estill was also the guiding force behind the Early Leaders series and the person responsible for capturing the history of the College Reading Association. When we lost Estill this past year, we lost the physical presence of a great friend and mentor—but we will never lose his spirit because he lives on in us whenever: we are kind and caring mentors, we balance our emotions with intellect, we persevere and support our colleagues, and we honor history to create our future.

*Estill, we thank you, we miss you, we honor you, we remember you . . .*

WML, EGS, JRD, PEL
September, 2001

# PRESIDENTIAL
# ADDRESS

# LITERACY 2001: WHAT IS AND WHAT SHOULD BE

## 2000 Presidential Address

### Jack Cassidy

Texas A&M University-Corpus Christi

The thought of this particular speech I have found somewhat intimidating—"PRESIDENTIAL ADDRESS." Somehow, with that particular title, you feel some obligation to say something extremely profound and enlightening. The last time that I prepared to give a Presidential Address the venue was in the main arena at the Anaheim Convention Center. Luckily this room is not quite as overpowering.

As I thought back over the CRA Presidential Addresses that I had heard, I was amazed that I could only really remember two of them—Tim Rasinski's two years ago and Nancy Padak's last year. I'm sure part of the reason for this recollection was that those two presentations were the most immediate. However, I soon realized that my primary motivation for the vivid memories of my two predecessors was that I knew I was soon going to be in their shoes. This realization relieved some of my anxiety because I now believed that there were only two people who were going to be paying close attention to my words. They are Maria Valeri-Gold and Jane Matanzo-each of whom will be standing in this spot in the subsequent two years.

Last year, Nancy Padak recounted how she had asked two of the CRA yearbook editors, "What should I talk about?" After some delay, they finally came up with an answer: ". . . about 15 minutes!" (Padak, 2000). I thought that was a very good idea!

My wife, who used to be in public relations, tells me that you should always start a speech with a joke. Unfortunately, I can never remember punch lines of jokes. But, luckily, I remembered that Tim Rasinski had told a joke in his Presidential Address; and, luckily, I had the 1999 CRA Yearbook handy.

There was the joke-printed verbatim! Unfortunately, the joke (which was about a dog), pertained directly to Tim's Presidential Address; but, alas, it had nothing to do with mine. Thus, although I repeated the joke in my address, I'll merely refer my readers to the published version of Tim's speech (Rasinski, 1999.) Thank you Tim Rasinski, for my joke!

My remarks today are going to address the topic *Literacy 2000, What Is and What Should Be!* I'm going to look at some of the topics in literacy instruction that have been a focus of current and positive attention, and some that have been receiving negative or less attention. As many of you know, I do a column each year, now with my wife, but in the past with Judith Wenrich of Millersville University, entitled "What's Hot, What's Not" (Cassidy & Cassidy, 2000/2001; Cassidy & Cassidy, 1999/2000; Cassidy & Cassidy, 1998/1999; Cassidy & Wenrich, 1998; Cassidy & Wenrich, 1997). In addition more in-depth discussions of these issues have also appeared (Cassidy & Wenrich, 1998/99; Cassidy, Brozo, & Cassidy, 2000). In those columns and articles, I compiled a list of topics in literacy education that have/had been receiving attention and then surveyed literacy leaders from around the world asking them if they thought a particular topic was "hot" or "not hot."

When I thought of the idea of a "what's hot" list in early 1996, it seemed like a kind of whimsical piece. After it first appeared in *Reading Today* in early 1997, I was surprised at the reactions that I received. Reporters from several prominent newspapers called asking permission to summarize the results of my survey. During her keynote address at the Boston CRA Convention, Rona Flippo referenced it and subsequently alluded to it in her book *What Do the Experts Say* (Flippo, 1999). And, I received lots of "hate" mail with comments like: "How could you write something like this. You are contributing to the bandwagon effect-already too prevalent in literacy education."

Partially, to relieve some of the "hate" mail, I decided last year to ask my 25 experts not only *what is hot, what is not,* but also *should this topic be hot.* The dichotomy between the two sets of responses proved both interesting and disturbing. In Table One are the topics for 2001, that at least 75% of our 25 literacy experts rated as "*hot*" or "*not hot.*" These are the fourteen very hottest and very coldest from the list of twenty-nine topics presented. Although all the topics were grouped alphabetically in the survey, for convenience I have grouped these fourteen topics into five categories: philosophy/approach; level; content; materials; and assessment.

Probably, there is nothing in Table 1 that is surprising to you. You knew this information without the opinions of these 25 literacy experts. Like me, you are probably disturbed by some of the topics that are receiving current and positive attention and some that are not.

**TABLE 1.**

|  | WHAT'S HOT | WHAT'S NOT |
|---|---|---|
| PHILOSOPHY/<br>APPROACH | • Balanced Reading<br>  Instruction<br>• Research-based Practice<br>• Guided Reading | • Whole Language |
| LEVEL | • Early Intervention | |
| CONTENT | • Phonemic Awareness<br>• Phonics | • Comprehension<br>• Vocabulary<br>• Spelling |
| MATERIALS | • Decodable Text | • Literature/Based<br>  Instruction |
| ASSESSMENT | • High Stakes Assessment | • Portfolio Assessment |

Table Two confirms that the literacy leaders are also disturbed. These are their responses when they were asked "should this topic be hot." Although they were not asked why they said a topic *should be hot or not hot,* some of the experts explained their reasoning.

Sometimes, they felt that too much research attention had already been directed toward a given topic; it was now time to move on. Sometimes, however, they felt that a topic really was important and was not receiving the attention it deserved.

**TABLE 2.**

|  | SHOULD BE HOT | SHOULD NOT BE HOT |
|---|---|---|
| Philosophy/<br>Approach | • Balanced Reading<br>  Instruction<br>• Research-based Practice<br>• Guided Reading | • Whole Language |
| Level | • Early Intervention | |
| Content | • Comprehension<br>• Vocabulary | • Phnemic Awareness<br>• Phonics<br>• Spelling |
| Materials | • Literature-Based<br>  Instruction | • Decodable Text |
| Assessment | • Portfolio Assessment<br>• High-stakes Assessment | |

The fifteen minutes suggested to Nancy Padak by the Yearbook editors does not allow me to discuss all of these topics. However, I would like to mention two: *comprehension* and *vocabulary,* the very essence of what we know as reading. They are not receiving attention in the popular media or in the research community despite the fact that virtually every literacy leader believes they are crucial to what we call READING. There was a time–not too long ago when I felt that these two very important topics were the "hot" topics–receiving the attention they so richly deserved. That time, from 1976 to 1991, roughly corresponded to the 15 years that the Center for the Study of Reading at the University of Illinois was receiving federal funding for its groundbreaking research on comprehension and cognition.

Yesterday, as you listened to our general session speaker, Dr. Sandra Stotsky, Deputy Commissioner of Academic Affairs for the Massachusetts Department of Education, many of you may have disagreed with some of her remarks. However, I doubt if any of you disagreed with her premise about the need to develop vocabulary knowledge in our students. There was a time, in the not too distant past, when this topic was a priority. Books and whole issues of journals were devoted to this issue. Today, discussions of word meaning/vocabulary have virtually disappeared from the professional literature.

## In Summary

My fifteen minutes are just about up. Trends in literacy have existed since the dawn of recorded language and will probably continue to exist. At the advent of the last millennium, silent reading was the "hot" topic. Scribes began separating words to facilitate the silent perusal of text. Prior to that time, oral reading, primarily in church, was thought to be synonymous with reading (Manguel, 1996). In 1900, with the invention of scientific measurement instruments, "researched-based practice" became a *hot* issue (Smith, 1961). Luckily, it is still a focus of attention.

But, perhaps the most important finding of the 2001 survey is the discrepancy between what is not *hot,* and what should be *hot.* With the exception of *whole language* and *spelling,* all aspects of literacy on what's "not hot" list (comprehension, vocabulary, literature-based instruction, and portfolio assessment) were thought by most of those surveyed to be deserving of much greater positive attention. Similarly, several items on the hot list (*phonemic awareness, phonics, and decodable text*) were thought to be receiving too much attention. These disparities between what *is* and what *should be* suggest that literacy practices today have less to do with the informed understanding of experts than with political agendas and media hype.

As pendulums and political winds shift, I hope that in the near future, we—the literacy leaders—will be providing the momentum for those pendulums. We will be determining the literacy agenda. The *hot* topics will be those that *should be* the focus of attention and research. *What is* will be synonymous with *what should be*.

## References

Cassidy, J., Brozo, W. G. & Cassidy, D. (2000). Literacy at the millennium. *Reading Online*. [online serial] Hostname reading.org director: readingonline.org/past/past_indese.asp?HREF=../critical/cassidy/index.html

Cassidy, J., & Cassidy, D. (1998/99). What's hot, what's not for 1999. *Reading Today*, 16(3). pp. 1, 28.

Cassidy, J., & Cassidy, D. (1999/2000). What's hot, what's not for 2000. *Reading Today*, 18(3), pp. 1,18.

Cassidy, J., & Cassidy, D. (2000/2001). What's hot, what's not for 2001. *Reading Today*. 18(3), pp. 1,18.

Cassidy, J., & Wenrich, J. K. (1997). What's hot, what's not for 1997: A look at key topics in reading research and practice. *Reading Today*, 14(4), p. 34.

Cassidy, J., & Wenrich, J. K. (1998). What's hot, what's not for 1998. *Reading Today*, 15(4) p. 128.

Cassidy, J., & Wenrich, J. K. (1998/99). Literacy research and practice: What's hot, what's not and why. *The Reading Teacher* 52(4) p. 402-406.

Flippo, R.F. (1999). *What do the experts say: helping children learn to read.* Portsmouth, NH: Heinemann.

Manguel, A. (1996). A history of reading. New York: Viking.

Padak, N. (2000). Listening to learners. In P. E. Linder, W. M. Linek, E. G. Sturtevant, & J. R. Dugan (Eds.), *Literacy at a new horizon* (pp.2-8). Commerce, TX: College Reading Association.

Rasinski, T. V. (1999). Outside of a dog, a book is a man's best friend. Inside of a dog, it's too dark to read. (With apologies to Groucho Marx). In J. R. Dugan, P. E. Linder, W. M. Linek & E. G. Sturtevant. (Eds.), *Advancing the world of literacy: Moving into the 21st century. Twenty-first yearbook of the College Reading Association.* (pp. 2-6) Commerce, TX: College Reading Association.

Smith, N.B. (1961). What have we accomplished in reading? *Elementary English*, 35, 141-150.

# EARLY
# LEADER

# COLLEGE READING FIFTY YEARS LATER

## Martha Maxwell

University of California-Berkley

*Martha Maxwell was president of the College Reading Association in 1965. She founded reading programs at American University, the University of Maryland and the University of California-Berkeley, and has published five books in the field.*

When I started teaching reading improvement courses in college over 50 years ago, times were different. Streams of servicemen from WWII were returning to civilian life and taking advantage of the GI Bill to enter college. Many had never considered college before and although they were motivated, they were not well prepared. The GI Bill gave them money, tuition, and support services including counseling, reading and study skills courses, and tutoring. Like the returning GI's, I too was unprepared to teach them. Having just completed a master's degree in counseling, I accepted my first job at American University with the provision that I teach an evening course in reading improvement, something I had never done before. Not wanting to jeopardize a job that paid $3000 for 12 months, I didn't say I knew little about reading.

I was fortunate that my thesis director had taught the same course before and offered me his notes. So that's how I started. I'm sure many others who lacked experience faced equally difficult challenges as beginning college reading teachers.

Shortly after starting, the president called me into his office to show me the new reading machine he had bought. It had a sliding shutter that covered the pages of a book and flashing red and green lights. (I don't remember what the lights were for, but you had to tear out the pages to make it work). Anyway he wanted me to set up a reading improvement lab for students whom he felt did not read well enough. We talked about it briefly and I asked, "But what can I use for reading material?" "Don't worry," he replied lifting a stack of papers from his book shelf. They were copies of the *Communist Daily Worker* and this was in Washington DC during the McCarthy era. Faculty were already paranoid about having FBI agents in their classes ready to spring on them if they made a politically incorrect remark. So it was a bit touchy. Somehow I managed to start a reading lab to help students improve their reading speed and comprehension.

Initially most reading courses were taught with a stop watch and a book. For determining comprehension, instructors asked students questions on their reading or had them summarize what they had read. Reading faster was the goal. Later reading textbooks were available with exercises aimed at teaching students basic reading skills such as reading for the main idea, for details, and for inference.

In the fifties and sixties, there was more emphasis on devices to force your eyes faster such as the Controlled Reader, a projector with a sliding shutter that pushed your eyes across the line of print. You could increase the shutter speed and take comprehension quizzes after using the machine. Another device was the tachistoscope that flashed a word or a phrase quickly. I selected a list of words from the beginning sociology textbook and had them photographed to use on the tachistoscope. These were non-technical words like *intrinsic* and *expiate* that helped students improve their vocabulary.

Today, computers offer similar training, and I feel that more teachers now recognize that practice on realistic text book passages is preferable to reading magazine articles.

To be sure in the 40's and 50's, we taught students to use Robinson's SQ3R method in reading their textbooks although few of them followed through as they found it tedious.

## How Do Today's Students Differ?

Today's college students comprise a far higher percentage of US high school graduates than they have in the past. In the 30's, only about 10% of high school graduates went to college, while the figure today is over 60% and, in some areas, up to 75% enter college. Politicians promise that the growth in college enrollment will continue. Thus, while there are many students in college who are well qualified there are also many more who are at-risk, for today 20-30% of entering students are held for developmental courses.

College faculty expect that students have good reading skills. That has not changed but students with poor reading skills still enter. Today's college reading courses typically invest more time and effort in reading college textbooks and difficult material than teachers used in the past. The question remains. How well do our courses work? Can we turn a reluctant reader who doesn't like to read and avoids it whenever possible into a person who likes reading and reads well?

The present trend is to move reading and other developmental courses to the community college. The rationale is that instructors in two-year colleges can do a better job with poor readers.

At the four year college level, learning center (L.C.'s), provide academic support services including reading help for those enrolled in four year colleges usually on an individualized basis. L.C.'s also offer tutoring in different subjects.

We still seem to have a large number of students who have successfully avoided practicing reading in the past although they can decode. Sometimes I feel they are the ones who never successfully made the change from oral to silent reading. They are masters at avoiding reading, assignments. If assigned a book to read in developmental reading, they choose one they have been assigned in high school or they use *Cliff* notes.

I'm not at all sure that our reading programs do much to change them and have not seen studies that show how poor readers were transformed into good ones.

## College Reading Programs Then and Now

Many of today's approaches are not new. When I taught Psychology 1 in the 1950's I gave students questions on each chapter to read and answer. This strategy worked well for poor readers and later became systematized as the Keller plan, a collaborative approach where undergraduate assistants helped students in Psychology 1 and tested them on the questions. Recent studies justify giving developmental students questions to answer on their Psych. 1 text, arguing that at least it ensured that most of them would read the textbook.

William Perry in 1958 tested Harvard freshmen to determine who needed to enroll in their new college remedial reading course. Students were tested, informed of their plight and given the opportunity to volunteer for the reading course. The test involved the following: students were given twenty-two minutes to study 30 pages from a history text on the development of the English state 1066-1272. They were asked to write a short statement about the selection. Only about one percent could do so even though there was a clearly identified section called "Recapitualization" at the end of the chapter.

When tested with multiple-choice questions, they could answer "every sensible question we could ask about the details," according to Perry. So he tried a different approach. He gave them two answers to a history exam question purportedly written by two different students and asked them which got the higher grade. One answer was a chronological reiteration of the text showing an extraordinary memory for dates and kings but no interest in the question nor any intellectual content. This answer might have been given a C- for effort. The second answer was short, gave no details, but dealt with the overall issues and probably received a C+. Those who picked the C- answer as best were encouraged to enroll in the reading course.

Based on Perry's article, which appeared in the *Harvard Educational Review* in 1959, the Harvard reading program became the prototype for university reading programs around the country. Instructors in the Harvard reading program used selections from college textbooks and they developed a speed reading movie based on textbook selections to train eye movements.

Developmental courses seem to work best for older, returning students who have decided on vocational goals and are motivated to succeed in college than for students who are fresh out of high school. Older students are more likely to follow suggestions and do the work asked. Some basic problems still linger. What should the goal be for college reading courses? Do you teach textbook skills or try to try to turn student on to reading in general? Are students really aware of what college teachers expect and require?

In my next job, at the University of Maryland, I taught in a special program for developmental students—only we didn't call them that. It was called the College for Special and Continuation Studies, which admitted students with high school grade averages below "C". Most were former GI's returning to college under the GI Bill. We offered them a college orientation and study skills lecture course their first semester and a reading course their second, and they took a limited number of regular courses, received counseling, advisement and tutoring. If they earned a C average their first year, they were taken "off trial" and transferred to regular college departments. After finding that few made grades above "C" we changed the transfer level to a 2.5 average their first year semester which would enable them to get off trial. That inspired students to work harder. Maryland continues to offer a similar program today.

Then I developed a Reading and Study Skills Program in the University of Maryland Counseling Center. It was open to all students stressed individualized instruction, and trained graduate students from psychology to teach sections, and work with individuals.

## College Reading Associations

In 1965 I was elected president of the College Reading Association. CRA wasn't the oldest college reading association for Oscar Causey had started what became the National Reading Conference in southwest Texas a decade before. But CRA was a much smaller organization than it is now, and its members were primarily from the mid-eastern states. Most of its members were teaching reading courses to college students but a few were professors who taught teachers to teach reading.

In 1967 I studied the demographic characteristics of 278 CRA members and found that 80% of the men and 40% of the women had doctoral degrees. They came from a wide range of backgrounds and from many different universities. Most had degrees in education, psychology/counseling, English, or student personnel. Two were optometrists.

Those holding doctoral degrees worked in jobs titled director, dean, or professor while only 46% of those without doctoral degrees held those titles. Sixty-nine percent of members without doctoral degrees said they had taken a course in reading compared with 60% of those with doctorates and about half of each group reported they had taken a practicum course in reading.

CRA offered valuable inservice training since the average CRA member had less than one year's experience in college reading.

About half of the group were IRA members (62 percent of those without doctorates.) Those with doctorates were more likely to have had experience teaching college undergraduate or graduate courses and have published one or more papers (57%).

I'm sure that things have changed for today CRA has a number of different divisions, which suggests that those who teach reading to college students are in the minority.

Many other associations for those teaching college students have been formed. For example, the College Reading and Learning Association was a western spin-off from CRA in the late sixties.

## Speed Reading

During the 60's and early 70's private reading courses became an important issue to CRA members. Such outfits as Evelyn Wood, Vicore and others were offering expensive speed reading courses on college campuses. VICORE advertised students' the pre-test and post-test scores. One ad described a student who was reading at 200 wpm with 20% comprehension on the pre-test and 1000 wpm with 20% comprehension after the course. (I guess you could say he was spending less time trying to read while still getting little out of it.)

I'm not averse to rapid reading-it's essential for many college courses but the commercial courses tended to stress page turning rather than thinking. The victims of these courses were the students who had low comprehension to begin with or tried to use speed reading techniques inappropriately-for instance on their organic chemistry textbooks.

I complained to the local school superintendent who was considering adopting these programs for high school students and received a letter from a lawyer for the commercial program stating "Cease and desist from interfering with our business at once or we will sue." This didn't stop me but worried other reading professionals when they were told about it.

Let me reiterate, I am not against reading rapidly. In fact I wrote a book on skimming and scanning for college students which contained exercises based on reading freshmen and sophomore college textbooks in different fields (from literature to nursing). Many students who read well still need this kind of training.

In 1968 I moved to UC Berkeley where I headed a reading and study skills program in the Counseling Center and taught education courses. The impetus for beginning a reading program was early Affirmative Action policies and the need to help non-traditional students adjust to college. In the early 70's, I started a campus wide Student Learning Center that helped freshmen and sophomore students in a wide variety of subjects, and provided tutoring and tutor training. At Berkeley, students were assigned lengthy reading homework and needed help in improving their ability to read rapidly with good comprehension. Often an instructor would assign three books to read in a ten-week term so effective skimming and scanning skills were essential.

Some basic problems still remain especially those in regard to speed reading. Although we recognize that students with poor comprehension skills need more than speed training, unfortunately our most popular reading tests fail to distinguish these problems. For example, the Nelson Denny has a self-reported speed score and its comprehension score is not corrected for guessing. Thus students can raise their scores easily by reading faster and guessing at more questions.

## The Future

The development of computer-adaptive testing represents a paradigm shift that promises to alleviate the problems with today's most popular reading tests. The application of artificial intelligence to standardized testing is enabling machines to read and instantly evaluate real-life expository prose faster and more consistently than can human raters. Thus it will eliminate the expensive, labor-intensive, and time consuming process that human scoring involves. In addition, lengthy tests will no longer be necessary to evaluate skills involved in reading for college courses. Speed and time pressure will be replaced by emphasis on reading in context. Today's problems arising from mass testing, inconvenient scheduling, and score inflating test taking strategies will be eliminated by substituting essays, short answer, and other formats for multiple choice items. The tests will then have a stronger influence on the strategies used in teaching students to improve their reading skills.

# RESEARCH
# AWARDS

# THE NATURE OF LITERATURE-BASED ELECTRONIC MAIL COLLABORATIVES BETWEEN FOURTH GRADE STRUGGLING READERS AND PRESERVICE TEACHERS: A MULTIPLE-CASE STUDY

## Christine A. McKeon

Kent State University

## Abstract

*The purpose of this study was to examine the nature of literature-based electronic mail collaboratives between fourth grade struggling readers and preservice teacher partners. The participants dialogued for one semester about literature, and for serial purposes. The participants dialogued for one semester about literature, and for serial purposes. Grounded in sociocultural and motivation theories, four partnerships were analyzed using the constant comparative method (Glaser & Strauss, 1967). A cross-case analysis was also conducted.*

*The major findings revealed that the e-mail collaborative provided the struggling readers with an optimal challenging, student-centered literacy experience. The fourth graders were able to share knowledge about literature, they made decisions and choices, and they took responsibility for their own reading. This combination of factors suggested how the e-mail collaborative emerged as a motivating literacy event for each of the struggling readers.*

"I hate to read, but I love to read e-mail." "I wish [e-mail] went all year . . . now that the e-mail thing is done . . . I have to do papers and work." Two fourth grade below-grade-level reluctant readers who were part of this study candidly made these comments during separate interviews. Additionally, their classroom teachers observed that, although the fourth graders did not typically like to read, they were highly motivated to read the e-mail. Reading practitioners consider struggling readers to be one of their greatest challenges (Baumann, Hoffman, Duffy-Hester, & Ro, 2000) and motivating all children to read is a recurring concern for classroom teachers (Worthy, Moorman, & Turner, 1999). Coupled with these thoughts, is the notion that a wide variety of classroom computer applications seem to motivate children (Leu, 1996; Reinking, McKenna, Labbo, & Kieffer, 1998), including collaboratives in which they can read and write with e-mail partners (Garner & Gillingham, 1996; Moore, 1991). During several pilot studies, I became interested in the motivating nature of e-mail for reluctant readers. My observations became the impetus for this study.

A growing number of literacy studies examine technology applications for those who struggle in reading (Boone & Higgins, 1992; Higgins & Boone, 1990; Higgins, Boone, & Lovitt, 1996; Horney & Anderson-Inman, 1994, 1999; Labbo & Kuhn, 1998; McKenna & Watkins, 1995; McNabb, 1998). While some suggest that technology has the potential to assist those who find reading difficult (McKenna, Reinking, Labbo, & Kieffer, 1999; Topping & McKenna, 1999), others speculate that digital text may open the door to "new electronic learning disabilities" (Cunningham, Many, Carver, Gunderson, & Mosenthal, 2000, p. 69). Further research that examines issues regarding the nature of students' experiences with electronic text for all readers, including those who struggle with reading, is recommended (Leu, 1996; Miller & Olson, 1998; Tao & Reinking, 2000). Case studies, for example, "that delve into the sociocognitive dimensions of students' encounters with particular instructional activities that involve new technologies will provide an important window to view the construction of knowledge in digital environments" (Labbo & Reinking, 1999, p. 489).

Research studies suggest a variety of findings regarding electronic classroom collaboratives. Studies illustrate, for example, that e-mail partnerships can broaden students' perspectives of the world (Baugh & Baugh, 1997; Bruce & Rubin, 1993; Fey, 1997; Garner & Gilllingham, 1996; Manrique & Gardiner, 1995). Other studies demonstrate increased student involvement (Chong, 1998; Ellsworth, 1995; Fowler & Wheeler, 1995; Sturtevant & Padak, 1998), and a number of studies suggest that e-mail can be used as an effective tool for social communication as well as literature response (Curtiss & Curtiss, 1995; Fey, 1994; McKeon, 1999; Moore, 1991, Seme, 1997). In their review of classroom-based e-mail partnerships, Tao and Reinking (2000) suggest that the field of reading will benefit from additional research that specifically examines e-mail from literacy perspectives.

In this study, the e-mail partnerships between the fourth grade below-grade-level readers and preservice teachers emerged as literacy engaging events with text; this multiple-case study offers a new perspective on the nature of e-mail as a motivating literacy experience for struggling readers. The following questions framed the study:

(a) What is the nature of the fourth graders' interactions about the literature; (b) what is the nature of the fourth graders' social interactions with their preservice teacher partners; and (c) what are the fourth graders', their preservice teacher partners', and the classroom teachers' perceptions of the e-mail collaboratives?

## Theoretical Framework
### *Sociocultural Theory*

Sociocultural theory is based on the social nature of learning in particular contexts; learning is a function of the cultural environment in which one masters speaking, listening, and thinking (Bonk & King, 1998; Forman, Minick, & Stone, 1993; Rogoff, 1990; Vygotsky, 1962, 1978)). In school settings, teachers facilitate the social construction of knowledge when they provide students with multiple ways of viewing the world (Honebein, 1996) and foster children's self-awareness, ownership, and voice through social experiences. From a sociocultural perspective, this study focused on how the struggling fourth grade readers socially constructed knowledge about themselves and about the literature that they read with their partners using e-mail.

### *Motivation Theory*

Struggling readers typically do not feel good about themselves as readers and often are not motivated to read (Rasinski & Padak, 2000). Two theories of motivation grounded this study: (a) Deci and Ryan's (1985) theory of self-determination and, (b) Bandura's (1986) notion of self-efficacy. The theory of self-determination suggests that students' natural curiosity energizes their desire to learn (Deci & Ryan, 1985) and that students are motivated by activities that match their needs, desires, and capacities (Deci, 1992.). Moreover, when children are provided with optimal challenging experiences, their engagement with these events leads to intrinsic motivation. In this study the struggling readers found the process of e-mailing to be a challenging, yet highly achievable task that seemed to pique their curiosity. Additionally, self-efficacy is an important factor with respect to motivation. Self-efficacy refers to judgments about how well one can perform or achieve in specific situations. One's belief about one's ability to achieve success is derived from feedback from others, observations of other's success, and verbal persuasion by others (Harter, 1983)."It is partly on the basis of self-beliefs of efficacy that people choose what challenges to undertake, how much effort to expend in the endeavor, and how long to persevere in the face of difficulties" (Bandura, 1989, p. 1180). The preservice teachers in this study provided the struggling readers with positive feedback that appeared to enhance their self-confidence and self-concept as readers and writers; this contributed to an understanding of why e-mail emerged as a motivating literacy event for these children.

## Setting

North School District (all names and places are pseudonyms) was situated in a city of about 16,000 in the Midwest. Redwood, where the study took place, was one of four elementary schools in the district. The socioeconomic level was mixed. Redwood housed grades one through five with four classrooms at each grade level. Each classroom had five computers, a modem with Internet access, e-mail, and a printer.

The university was a liberal arts institution located about 10 miles from the elementary school; enrollment was approximately 1,200. The university was equipped with three computer labs with open-lab hours; the students had access to free e-mail accounts.

## Participants

Using purposeful, intensity sampling (Patton, 1990), a total of four 4th graders were selected mid-semester, during two, 14 week consecutive semesters. They were selected based on teacher judgment with respect to below-grade-level reading ability, observed low motivation for reading, observed high motivation for the project, and parental permission for participation.

"The logic and power of purposeful sampling lies in selecting *information-rich cases* for study in depth" (Patton, 1990, p. 169). An intensity sample "seeks excellent or rich examples of the phenomenon of interest, but not unusual cases" (Patton, p. 171).

### The Elementary Students

Donna was a 10-year-old, Caucasian female who lived with her mother, stepfather, and two younger siblings. She spent alternate weekends with her biological father. Joseph was a 10-year-old, Caucasian male. He lived with his mother and younger brother. His mother consistently expressed concern about his difficulty in school. Michael was a 9-year-old, Caucasian male. He lived with his mother, father, and older brother. William was a 9-year-old, Caucasian male. He lived with his father and younger sister. William's mother abandoned the home when he was in the first grade. According to the classroom teachers, all of the fourth graders were reading significantly below their peers.

Donna used e-mail occasionally at home. This was Joseph's, Michael's, and William's first experience with e-mail. Donna and Joseph e-mailed with their partners during the spring of 1999; Michael and William participated during the fall of 1998.

### The Preservice Teachers

The education students were enrolled in Methods of Reading classes. All of the preservice teachers were Caucasian females. Kris was Donna's partner. She had experience working with at-risk children through a university program. Kathryn was Joseph's partner. She was a non-traditional student and a single parent with three children. Kelley was Michael's partner. She had worked as a day camp counselor and as a tutor. Laura was William's partner. She planned to work with primary children.

Each of the preservice teachers had used e-mail for personal communications. None of them had used e-mail in an educational setting.

### *The Classroom Teachers*

Both teachers were Caucasian females with a bachelor's degree in elementary education. Mrs. Collins taught fourth grade at Redwood for 9 years. She was Donna and Joseph's teacher. Mrs. Collins selected the book, *The Wright Brothers at Kitty Hawk* (Sobol, 1961), because she planned to integrate the content into the social studies curriculum. The book cover indicates that it is written on a fifth grade reading level. Mrs. Smith taught fourth grade at Redwood for 10 years. She was Michael and William's teacher. Mrs. Smith selected the book, *The War with Grandpa* (Smith, 1984), because it fit well with her plans to integrate problem solving into social studies. The book cover indicates that it is written on a 4.5 grade reading level. Both teachers acknowledged that the books that they selected for this project were difficult for students who struggle in reading; however, they wanted the whole class to correspond with the preservice teacher partners about these books because they "fit" with other areas of the curriculum.

Although Mrs. Collins occasionally needed technical assistance, she felt confident using technology in her classroom. Mrs. Smith considered herself a novice in using technology in the classroom but enjoyed the challenge.

## Research Design, Data Collection, and Analysis

This study used a qualitative multiple-case design (Yin, 1994). The data included: (a) an average of 11 weekly e-mail correspondences written by each participant; (b) weekly preservice teacher written reflections about the correspondences; (c) participant interviews, including think-aloud protocol interviews conducted mid-semester with the fourth graders, and exit interviews with each of the participants, and (d) fieldnotes. The weekly correspondences and reflections were collected and read by me during each semester. I wrote comments on the correspondences and/or reflections, returned them to the preservice teachers, and recollected them at the end of each semester. The correspondences and reflections were placed in portfolios that became part of the data collection. I conducted protocol open-ended interviews (Flower & Hayes, 1983) with the fourth graders mid-semester during times set aside by the teachers. As they engaged in corresponding with their partners, the fourth graders were asked to describe the process of accessing, reading, writing, saving, and sending the e-mail. Open-ended interviews with the fourth graders were conducted at the end of each semester in order to understand how they perceived the project, what they learned, and why they appeared to be movitated by the collaborative. Individual interviews were also conducted with the preservice and classroom teachers at the end of each semester in order to understand their perceptions of the project. All of the interviews were tape-recorded. Additionally, fieldnotes were gathered by me during each semester and included ongoing informal observations.

Using a variation of Hunt's (1965) t-units, the correspondences were retyped to reflect units of text that informed each question and that could stand alone. Units were defined as segments that could be "interpretable in the absence of any additional information other than a broad understanding of the context in which the inquiry [was] carried out" (Lincoln & Guba, 1985, p. 345). The segments ranged in length from several words to sentences. Although this study did not focus on the length of the correspondences, I conducted a word count for each correspondence. The interviews were transcribed and the correspondences, reflections, fieldnotes, and interviews were organized as files for each case. By using multiple sources of data, triangulation increased the reliability and validity of the study (Patton, 1990).

After multiple rereadings of the correspondences and in order to address the first two questions, the segments were initially coded as either social talk or book talk. Social talk segments were those that did not refer to the literature; book talk segments did relate to the book or reading the book. The correspondences were reread multiple times in search for patterns. Using inductive case-analysis and the constant comparative method (Glaser & Strauss, 1967), emerging themes were color-coded. After rereading the segments multiple times, subcategories were defined. Social segments were defined and coded as "Personal," thoughts about the student's life unrelated to the story; "General," including greetings and closings, such as "How are you?" and "E-Mail," comments about the project, such as "I can't wait to meet you." Book segments were later refined to reflect reading skills that were coded as "Book Content," information written about the story; "Self," personal connections made to the story; "Predictions," speculations about what would happen in the story; and "Vocabulary," segments that were related to studying words from the story. The interviews, preservice teacher reflections, and fieldnotes were reread multiple times in search of data that supported, or failed to support, the initial phases of the analysis, as well as the participants perceptions of the collaborative. These were coded accordingly. Closure was reached when clear patterns emerged that addressed each question (Lincoln & Guba, 1985).

Two outside readers were trained and coded 20% of the data. The overall interrater reliability was 96%; this added to the credibility of the study. Member checking occurred after a rough draft of each case was written. The purpose of this step was to "test for factual and interpretative accuracy . . . and to provide evidence of credibility" (Lincoln & Guba, 1985, pp. 373-375). A cross-case analysis (Patton, 1990) was conducted in search of similarities and differences among the cases.

## Results

The following sections synthesize the results of each case study including the cross-case analysis. In order to preserve the authentic nature of the fourth graders' correspondences, citations are quoted in their original form. Spelling corrections are included in brackets as needed.

The word count revealed that Donna wrote an average of 122 words per message; Joseph and William typed an average of 72 words per correspondence; Michael's correspondences averaged 54 words. Although all of the fourth graders wrote longer messages as the partnerships developed, this may have been due to additional time allowed for typing and/or improved keyboarding skills. The preservice teachers' correspondences also varied. Kelley wrote an average of 129 words per message; Kris and Laura's correspondences averaged 139 words; Kathryn's correspondences were, by contrast, quite lengthy. She wrote an average of 326 words per message. The tone of the messages between the partners became increasingly friendly as the collaborative progressed.

Table 1 displays the frequencies and percentages of social and book segments for each fourth grader. Donna, Joseph, and William wrote substantially more social segments than book segments. Michael wrote slightly more about the book than he did socially.

**Table 1. Frequencies and Percentages
of the Fourth Graders' Social and Book Segments**

| Fourth Grader | Social Segment | Book Segment | Total |
|---|---|---|---|
| Donna | 166 (82%) | 36 (18%) | 202 (100%) |
| Joseph | 85 (66%) | 44 (34%) | 129 (100%) |
| Michael | 54 (47%) | 60 (53%) | 114 (100%) |
| William | 92 (65%) | 49 (35%) | 141 (100%) |

### *Nature of the Book Segments*

The analysis revealed that the fourth graders demonstrated a variety of reading skills by answering and asking questions about the content of the book, as well as making personal connections to the literature. Donna, for example, explained why Kitty Hawk was a good location for the Wright brothers to fly the airplane, "It is because it has nice flat land" (e-mail, 2-20-99). When asked how she would feel if she encountered problems like the Wright brothers, she responded, "I would fant [faint] if I went through that much trouble" (e-mail, 2-3-99). Two of the fourth graders made predictions. Michael, for example, speculated what would happen at the end of *The War with Grandpa* (Smith, 1984), "At the end I think grandpa will be nice, and give Peter his room back." (e-mail, 11-23-98). Joseph defined vocabulary using the context of the story. On one occasion he wrote, "Cradle means a place of control" (e-mail, 4-14-99). Table 2 displays the frequencies and percentages of reading skills for each fourth grader.

**Table 2. Frequencies and Percentages of Reading Skills for Each Fourth Grader**

|  |  | READING SKILL |  |  |  |
|---|---|---|---|---|---|
| FOURTH GRADER | BOOK CONTENT | SELF | PREDICTION | VOCABULARY | TOTAL |
| Donna | 5 (50%) | 5 (50%) | — | — | 10 (100%) |
| Joseph | 9 (50%) | 3 (17%) | — | 6 (33%) | 18 (100%) |
| Michael | 26 (76%) | 7 (21%) | 1 (3%) | — | 34 (100%) |
| William | 11 (55%) | 7 (35%) | 2 (10%) | — | 20 (100%) |

The fourth graders also made decisions about the process of reading and writing about the book, including the pace at which they read the literature. The results of Donna's case suggested that she found the book component of the collaborative too difficult. She initially shared her thoughts about the story, however her correspondences about the book diminished over time. In early correspondences, she wrote about the characters, plot, and setting. In other correspondences, however, Donna avoided Kris's queries about the book. She wrote, "I need more time to think about the 2nd question" (e-mail, 2-10-99); "can you put it in different words," (e-mail, 2-17-99); and "Next time I will tell you what happened" (e-mail, 3-3-99). Donna was the only fourth grader who did not complete the book. During her exit interview, Donna shared that she did not really like to read and that she would have rather e-mailed "without the book . . . because it was kind of hard to read the book and keep on reading" (interview, 5-19-99). The interviews with Kris (4-20-99) and Mrs. Collins (5-25-99) confirmed that the book component of the collaborative was difficult for Donna.

Joseph finished reading the Wright brothers' book a month before the collaborative ended. Not only did he respond to Kathryn's prompts about the content, but he also took the initiative to ask his partner questions about the book; he, too, paced his own reading. In an early correspondence, Joseph wrote:

> Did you read chapter 3? It is very good. If you read chapter 3 may [maybe] you can answer this. Why did the kite not fly at first? Also how did it get in the air after they tried and try? I have only read chapter 3. Do you like the book? I do. (e-mail, 2-3-99)

During his protocol interview, Joseph shared, " I like to *ask* (emphasis) questions, but I don't like to answer questions . . . I'm not an answer questioner . . . I'm not that great" (interview, 3-11-99). Midsemester, he wrote, "I just finished book Wed. 16 . . . I liked the book a lot. Did you?" (e-mail, 3-17-99). Joseph frequently told Kathryn that he was enjoying the book.

Michael finished reading *The War with Grandpa* (Smith, 1984) a week before the collaborative ended. At the outset, Kelley suggested how far he should read and Michael kept up with the reading. Midway through the collaborative, when she suggested that he could read as far as he wanted, Michael decided to slow down his reading considerably. In one month, he read only two chapters. When Kelley resumed requests that he read particular chapters and wrote encouraging comments about his reading, Michael's pace increased dramatically. He reported, "I've bin reading a lot. I'am on chapter 20" (e-mail, 11-18-98). In his next correspondence, he wrote, "Now I am on chapter 27" (e-mail, 11-23-98). Michael also frequently told Kelley that he was enjoying the book. During the exit interview, he shared, "I know it was a good book" (interview, 12-15-98). Additionally, Michael chose to construct questions in a true-false format for Kelley. Kelley did not frame her questions this way; this was Michael's decision. For example, in one correspondence, he wrote, "True of [or] false Peter thought the note was a bad idea to declare war" (e-mail, 11-2-98); in another, he wrote, "true or false Grandpa was frightened when he saw the note" (e-mail, 11-18-98). Kelley's reflections and interview confirmed that the book was a positive component of the collaborative for Michael. Mrs. Collins characterized Michael as a shy student and suggested that "it gave him a safe environment to say things [about the book]" (interview, 12-8-98).

William completed the book with his partner and independently chose to begin another book with Laura. He read *The War with Grandpa* (Smith, 1984) at his own pace and initiated the idea to question Laura about the book. In an early correspondence, he wrote, "I'm going to ak [ask] you a qestion: What does Peter do when his grandpa moves in? And don't forget to anwer thes qestion's!" (e-mail, 10-22-98). Although Laura requested that he read specific chapters, William consistently reported that he had already read further. Several weeks before the collaborative ended, William wrote, "What chapter are you on in the book I'm on the last chapter" (11-16-98), and in his next correspondence he shared, "I'm finishid" (e-mail, 11-16-98). Mrs. Smith and Laura confirmed that the book component of the collaborative was positive for William. His teacher expressed amazement that William completed the book and took the initiative to select another one. Laura shared, "I think he's becoming more confident . . . I think it's like boosting his ego . . . he told me he doesn't like to read, and he said he's liking *this* reading" (interview, 12-2-98.)

### Nature of the Social Interactions

The fourth graders corresponded about personal topics including school, family, friends, and events that seemed to be important to them. With respect to school, they wrote about content they were learning in social studies. They also made positive comments about the e-mail collaborative. For example, Donna wrote, "I just love righting to you" (e-mail, 4-21-99) and they wrote general comments such as William's, "now how are you doing?" (e-mail, 11-19-98), as well as greetings and closings. Table 3 displays the frequencies and percentages of the fourth graders' social segments.

### Table 3. Frequencies and Percentages of the Fourth Graders' Social Segments

| FOURTH GRADER | SOCIAL SEGMENT | | | |
| | E-MAIL | GENERAL | PERSONAL | TOTAL |
| --- | --- | --- | --- | --- |
| Donna | 26 (16%) | 31 (19%) | 109 (66%) | 166 (101%) |
| Joseph | 20 (24%) | 22 (26%) | 43 (51%) | 85 (100%) |
| Michael | 3 (6%) | 24 (44%) | 27 (50%) | 54 (100%) |
| William | 5 (5%) | 27 (29%) | 60 (65%) | 92 (99%) |

*Note. Total percentages do not equal 100 due to rounding.*

Whereas Donna's book talk was minimal, her social interactions were many. Of particular significance were her personal correspondences in which she often wrote detailed descriptions of her life that were storylike in nature. In one correspondence, for example, she described her roller-blading accident and invited Kris to "just sit back and relax" (e-mail, 3-31-99) as she recounted skating down a hill, crashing into a mailbox, scraping her chin, and being rushed to the hospital. In other correspondences, Donna shared her rather complex life as a child who alternates weekends living with her biological father. Donna's interview confirmed that she enjoyed writing about her life. She said, "I . . . wrote about my life . . . and about my family and what was happening" (interview, 5-19-99). Mrs. Collins shared that she learned more about Donna by reading her e-mail than she would have otherwise known about the child (interview, 5-25-99). For example, she shared that she would not have realized how complex Donna's living arrangments were had she not read her correspondences about spending alternate weekends with her biological father.

In addition to writing about school, Joseph chose to write about troublesome events in his life. He shared, for example,"my greatgrandfather died" (e-mail, 2-20-99), and "My best friend Sam has just moved. He moved last Friday . . . I miss him already. He moved to Verginya. He dad was trasfered" (e-mail, 2-24-99). Kathryn responded to Joseph's concerns in a caring way.

Michael's social correspondences were somewhat limited and more factual in nature. It appeared that he wrote about topics that were safe for him (i.e., hobbies, favorite food, favorite school subject). On several occasions, however, Michael elaborated on topics of his choice in detail. For example, he wrote, "I had fun trik or treating. I got 337 pieces of canndy" (e-mail, 11-2-98).

Similar to Donna and Joseph, William's social segments were more personal in nature; he also asked Laura a lot of questions about herself. He wrote, for example, "IM doing poorley in Reading. What subject are [you] doing poorley?" (e-mail, 10-22-98); "I'm doing a reporte on the White House. I [is] eny thing like that going on in your class?" (e-mail, 10-29-98); "Did you got [go] trick or treating? My dad said you probley didn't because of your age" (e-mail, 11-4-98). William frequently asked Laura about her boyfriend; he wrote often about his interest in music and drums; he wrote about his sister and talked about his father; and he shared with Laura that his mother did not live with him anymore.

In addition to the personal segments, each fourth grader wrote positively about meeting his/her partner. The greetings and closings were friendly in nature and included such phrases as "love," "your bud," and "your friend."

### The Participants' Perceptions of the Collaboratives

All of the participants expressed positive perceptions about the collaborative nature of the partnership. Donna, for example, shared, "It was like a dream come true getting to know someone that I never met before . . . I felt like good" (interview, 5-19-99). In one reflection, Kris wrote, "I think she really likes writing to me about what she's been up to" (document, 3-18-99). Regarding Donna's self-confidence, Mrs. Collins shared, "I think [it] *definitely, definitely* improved" (interview, 5-25-99).

Joseph shared, "I thought [it] was really cool . . . I'd just tell her a lot of things" (interview, 5-19-99). According to Kathryn, Joseph expressed emotions in his correspondences. Mrs. Collins commented that since Joseph was unsure of himself in the classroom, the individual attention he received enhanced his self-confidence.

Michael was very businesslike in his interviews and focused on the book. Kelley, however, observed, "We got personal . . . [Michael signed his letters] 'your friend' . . . and [when he asked me questions], I'm sure [it made] him feel good to be the teacher of a college student!" (interview, 12-2-98). Mrs. Smith felt that Michael enjoyed the partnership because he perceived the status of working with a college student as a positive experience.

William explained that he and Laura took turns telling each other about themselves. He said, "I liked talking to [Laura]" (interview, 12-15-98); William shared that a favorite part of the collaborative was meeting his partner. Laura reflected that she and William bonded as friends. Mrs. Smith shared, "I think, by far, [William] benefited [the] most because of personal self-esteem, added practice on skills, being able to have a dialogue with someone who was concerned just about him . . . motivating him to read, because he is not motivated to read" (interview, 12-8-98).

There were a variety of perceptions about using e-mail. Donna struggled with process but shared, "I just like typing. It's easier because I hate writing . . . I just like the computer [and] like typing cause it's like on the screen and it's easier" (interview, 5-19-99). Mrs. Collins shared that the quality and quantity of Donna's writing via e-mail was significantly better than her handwritten class assignments. Joseph shared that, "e-mailing is faster because of electricity" (interview, 5-19-99); he said that he would rather e-mail than write. Joseph apologized that his letters were short and added, "I really want to learn how to type faster and be a better typer" (interview, 5-19-99). For Michael, the best part of the project was learning how to e-mail. William shared, "I wish it went all year because it took some of our time and now we have to work . . . now that the e-mail thing's done, now I have to do papers and work" (interview, 12-15-98).

## Conclusions

A synthesis of the findings suggests eight major conclusions that emerged from this study which are discussed below. Table 4 displays the relationship between the conclusions and the research questions and how multiple sources of data (i.e., triangulation) increased the credibility of the study.

**Table 4. Matrix of Research Question and Conclusion**

|  | RESEARCH QUESTION | | | | |
| --- | --- | --- | --- | --- | --- |
| CONCLUSION | NATURE OF LITERATURE SEGMENTS | NATURE OF SOCIAL SEGMENTS | 4TH GRADER PERCEPTION | PRESERVICE PERCEPTIONS | TEACHER PERCEPTIONS |
| Ownership | X | X | X | X | X |
| Literature knowledge | X |  | X | X |  |
| Multiple texts | X | X | X | X | X |
| Self-confidence | X |  | X | X | X |
| Self/other knowledge | X | X | X | X | X |
| Optimal challenge |  | X | X |  | X |
| Curriculum |  | X |  |  | X |
| Adult friend |  | X | X | X | X |

*Note. X indicates the conclusions as they relate to each research question based on the data analysis.*

### E-mail Was a Student-Centered Literacy Event that Fostered Ownership

The e-mail collaborative was social in nature and provided the struggling readers with an environment in which they demonstrated ownership in the process of reading and writing.

The fourth graders made decisions about the pace of reading the book, how they would write about it, and how they would correspond socially. Freedom of choice is a key component that motivates students to persist in an activity (Deci, 1992; Deci & Ryan, 1985). Allowing students to make choices and direct their own literacy experiences gives them ownership and provides a motivating context for developing readers (Morrow & Gambrell, 1998).

### E-mail Became an Alternative Way to Share Knowledge About Literature

Each of the fourth graders conversed on some level about the literature. Computer applications used with at-risk readers are often in the form of games and tasks that serve as electronic worksheets (Pemberton & Zenhausern, 1995). The struggling readers in this study, however, constructed knowledge about literature in a socially engaging context. The preservice teachers scaffolded learning by asking questions, modeling, and elaborating on topics. From a sociocultural perspective, providing students with prompts and feedback in a social context enhances learning (Althauser & Matuga, 1998; Resnick, 1991; Vygotsky, 1978).

### Engagement with Multiple Authentic Texts

In this study, the students engaged in reading and writing authentic text. Authentic text is reading material "representative of the real world" (Harris & Hodges, 1995, p. 15). The fourth graders read literature, reread the books to answer and construct questions about the literature, read e-mail, wrote about their lives, proofread e-mail, and read the computer screen in order to retrieve, save, and send e-mail. The e-mail collaborative provided the struggling readers with multiple opportunities to create their own literacy events as they selected the text they would read or write and made decisions about how they would engage with it. The theory of self-determination (Deci, 1992) suggests that students are motivated when activities tap their personal needs and capabilities.

### Enhanced Self-Confidence

A combination of choice, appropriate challenge, and social positive feedback enhances self-confidence (Bandura, 1989; Schunk & Zimmerman, 1997; Turner, 1997). The classroom teachers and preservice teachers each commented on the fourth graders' positive self-confidence and their ability to succeed in a variety of ways through the collaborative. Struggling readers often have low self-concepts as readers. Reading experiences, such as the e-mail collaborative, that de-emphasize competition and increase involvement and cooperation are like to reduce feelings of failure (Johnston & Allington, 1991).

### Self-Knowledge and Knowledge About Others

The social interactions revealed that the fourth graders constructed self-knowledge and learned about their partners. Social interactions foster self-identity and are an important component of the learning process (Vygotsky, 1978). According to McCombs (1996), a sense of reflective awareness makes it possible "for learners to assess metacognitively the validity and usefulness of their own thoughts, feelings, and actions . . . [This] positively influence[s] goals selected, affect, motivation, and performance in a complex learning situation" (p. 73).

### E-mail as an Optimal Challenging, Motivating Literacy Event

The fourth graders found the process of e-mailing initially challenging, but not so difficult that they were unwilling to attempt the task. Succeeding in challenges that are optimal for one's capability is a key determinant in one's enjoyment of an activity (Deci & Ryan, 1985). Literacy activities that are social, meaningful, and encourage children to persist in tasks that are challenging result in motivating experiences (Turner, 1997).

***Technology Implementation that Tied to the Curriculum***
Effective classroom teachers help students make connections and build new understandings based on prior knowledge and experiences (Zemelman, Daniels, & Hyde, 1998). The teachers selected the literature with the intention that it tied to other areas of the curriculum, particularly social studies. The classroom teachers' perceptions of the collaborative included benefits of integrating the project with other areas of the curriculum. Sociocultural theory suggests that individuals learn in a variety of social contexts (Forman et al., 1993). The fourth graders' social interactions revealed that they chose to write about what they were learning in social studies class; the collaborative provided them with that choice.

***Friendly Relationship with an Adult***
***Who Provided Individual Attention***
The e-mail interactions were unlike typical classroom conversations in which the teacher usually takes the dominant role. The correspondences were friendly in nature and suggested a non-traditional teacher-student relationship; the e-mail collaborative allowed the preservice teachers to facilitate the students' construction of knowledge in a caring, non-threatening, noncompetitive way. The struggling readers chose to write about issues that seemed important to them, and the preservice teachers responded to those issues by providing individual attention. For example, Donna chose to write about issues regarding her confusing life as a child who had alternate living arrangements on the weekends. Joseph chose to write about his grandfather's death and the fact that he missed his best friend who recently moved. The preservice teachers wrote caring messages in response to these issues. Learning environments in which students are given choices and in which they receive individual attention are motivating contexts for literacy learning (Turner, 1997).

## Limitations, Significance, and Implications of the Study

There are several limitations to this study. Only four partnerships were examined; a larger pool of data might reveal different findings. Though case studies can highlight complex issues, unlike large-scale studies they are not meant to guide large-scale programs (Miller & Olson, 1998). This study was not meant to generalize the value of e-mail in a formalistic sense, but rather to observe how it was used in a particular context. Patton (1990) acknowledges this a trade-off "between breadth and depth" (p. 165). Selecting samples for case study analysis is a complex issue. This study is limited in that the cases were selected based on teacher professional judgment regarding the students' low reading ability, reluctance to read, and high motivation for the project.

The significance of this study lies in the need to understand how small groups of learners use digital text and engage in electronic collaborations in literacy and language arts classrooms. Case studies grounded in sound pedagogical theory can provide insight into the nature of learning that occurs during electronic collaborations (Labbo & Reinking, 1999). This multiple-case study suggested how e-mail, used in a particular context, provided four struggling readers with a motivating literacy event that contributed to their development as readers and writers in multiple ways.

Several implications can be drawn from this study. For teachers of low-achieving readers, this study suggests that e-mailing with adults might provide other children with a motivating literacy event that fosters enhanced self-confidence in their abilities, provides them with choices and ownership, and encourages them to take responsibility for their reading. E-mail collaboratives with children might also provide other preservice teachers with a potentially purposeful way to use technology in their own literacy classrooms, as well as provide them with a technological way to work with children in reading during teacher preparation training. Future reading research is recommended that examines e-mail from other literacy perspectives. Literacy experts agree that children need to engage with multiple authentic texts. Authentic texts include books that represent a variety of genres, environmental print, reference materials and textbooks, magazines, newspapers, as well as children's own writing (Vacca, Vacca, & Gove, 2000). More research that examines the nature of e-mail as an alternative, authentic text, as suggested by this study, is recommended.

This multiple-case study provides literacy teachers with a new way to view e-mail collaboratives based on sound pedagogical principles. This research will serve as a powerful reminder that through close observation, teachers and researchers can discover many lessons about the nature of learning that occur for children when technology is implemented in classrooms.

---

# References

Althauser, R., & Matuga, J. M. (1998). On the pedagogy of electronic instruction. In C. J. Bonk & K. S. King (Eds.), *Electronic collaborators: Learner-centered technologies for literacy, apprenticeship, and discourse* (pp. 183-208). Mahwah, NJ: Erlbaum.

Bandura, A. (1986). *Social foundations of thought and action: A social cognitive theory.* Englewood Cliffs, NJ: Prentice-Hall.

Bandura, A. (1989). Human agency in social cognitive theory. *American Psychologist, 44,*1175-1184.

Baugh, I. W., & Baugh, J. G. (1997). Global classrooms—e-mail learning communities. *Learning and Leading with Technology, 25*(3), 38-41.

Baumann, J. F., Hoffman, J. V., Duffy-Hester, A. M., & Ro, J. M. (2000). The first R yesterday and today: U. S. elementary reading instruction practices reported by teachers and administrators. *Reading Research Quarterly, 35*(3), 338-377.

Bonk, C. J., & King, L. S. (Eds.). (1998). *Electronic collaborators: Learner-centered technologies for literacy, apprenticeship, and discourse.* Mahwah, NJ: Erlbaum.

Boone, R., & Higgins, K. (1992). Hypermedia applications for content-area study guides. *Reading & Writing Quarterly, 8,* 379-393.

Bruce, B. C., & Rubin, A. (1993). *Electronic quills: A situated evaluation of using computers for writing in classrooms.* Hillsdale, NJ: Erlbaum.

Chong, S. M. (1998). Models of asynchronous computer conferencing for collaborative learning in large college classes. In C. J. Bonk & K. S. King. (Eds.), *Electronic collaborators: Learner-centered technologies for literacy, apprenticeship, and discourse* (pp. 157-182). Mahwah, NJ: Erlbaum.

Cunningham, J. W., Many, J. E., Carver, R. P., Gunderson, L., & Mosenthal, P. B. (2000). Snippets: How will literacy be defined? *Reading Research Quarterly, 35*(1), 64-71.

Curtiss, P. M., & Curtiss, K. M. (1995). What 2nd graders taught college students and vice versa. *Educational Leadership, 53*(2), 60-63.

Deci, E. L. (1992). The relation of interest to the motivation of behavior: A self-determination theory perspective. In K. A. Renninger, S. Hidi, & A. Krapp (Eds.), *The role of interest in learning and development* (pp.43-70). Hillsdale, NJ: Erlbaum.

Deci, E. L., & Ryan, R. M. (1985). *Intrinsic motivation and self-determination in human behavior.* New York: Plenum.

Ellsworth, J. H. (1995). Using computer-mediated communication in teaching university courses. In Z. L. Berge & M. P. Collins (Eds.), *Computer mediated communication and the online classroom: Vol. 1. Overview and perspectives* (pp. 29-36). Cresskill, NJ: Hampton..

Fey, M. (1994). Transforming the literacy classroom through reader response and computer networking. In C. K. Kinzer & D. J. Leu (Eds.), *Multidimensional aspects of literacy research, theory, and practice.* Forty-third yearbook of the National Reading Conference (pp. 296-305). Chicago, IL: National Reading Conference.

Fey, M. H. (1997). Literate behavior in a cross-age computer-mediated discussion: A question of empowerment. In C. K. Kinzer, K. A. Hinchman, & D. J. Leu (Eds.), *Inquiries in literacy theory and practice.* Forty-sixth yearbook of the National Reading Conference (pp. 507-518). Chicago, IL: National Reading Conference.

Flower, L., & Hayes, J. R. (1983). Uncovering cognitive processes in writing: An introduction to protocol analysis. In P. Mosenthal, L. Tamor, & S. Walmsley, (Eds.), *Research on written language: Principles and methods* (pp. 206-219). New York: Guilford Press.

Forman, E. A., Minick, N., & Stone, C. A. (1993). *Contexts for learning: Sociocultural dynamics in children's development.* New York: Oxford University Press.

Fowler, L. S., & Wheeler, D. D. (1995). Online from the K-12 classroom. In Z. L. Berge & M. P. Collins (Eds.), *Computer mediated communication and the online classroom: Vol. 1. Overview and perspectives* (pp. 83-100). Cresskill, NJ: Hampton.

Garner, R., & Gillingham, M. G. (1996). *Internet communication in six classrooms: Conversations across time, space, and culture.* Mahwah, NJ: Erlbaum.

Glaser, B. G., & Strauss, A. L. (1967). *The discovery of grounded theory.* Chicago: Aldine.

Harris, T. L., & Hodges, R. E. (Eds.). (1995). *The literacy dictionary: The vocabulary of reading and writing.* Newark, DE: International Reading Association.

Harter, S. (1983). Developmental perspectives on the self-system. In E. M. Hetherington (Ed.), *Handbook of child psychology: Socialization, personality, and social development* (Vol. 4; pp. 275-385). New York: John Wiley & Sons.

Higgins, K., & Boone, R. (1990). Hypertext computer study guides and the social studies achievement of students with learning disabilities, remedial students and regular education students. *Journal of Learning Disabilities, 23,* 529-540.

Higgins, K., Boone, R., & Lovitt, T. C. (1996). Hypertext support for remedial students and students with learning disabilities. *Journal of Learning Disabilities, 29,* 02-412.

Honebein, P. C. (1996). Seven goals for the design of constructivist learning environments. In B. G. Wilson (Ed.), *Constructivist learning environments: Case studies in instructional design* (pp. 11-24). Englewood Cliffs, NJ: Educational Technology Publications.

Horney, M. A., & Anderson-Inman, L. (1994). The ElectroText project: Hypertext reading patterns of middle school students. *Journal of Educational Multimedia and Hypermedia, 3*(1), 71-91.

Horney, M. A., & Anderson-Inman, L. (1999). Supported text in electronic reading environments. *Reading & Writing Quarterly: Overcoming Learning Difficulties, 15,* 127-168.

Hunt, K. W. (1965). *Grammatical structures written at three grade levels.* Champaign, IL: National Council of Teachers of English.

Johnston, P., & Allington, R. (1991). Remediation. In R. Barr, M. L. Kamil, P. Mosenthal, & P. D. Pearson (Eds.), *Handbook of reading research: Volume II* (pp. 984-1012). New York: Longman.

Labbo, L. D., & Kuhn, M. (1998). Electronic symbol making: Young children's computer-related emerging concepts about literacy. In D. Reinking, M. C. McKenna, L. D. Labbo, & R. D. Kieffer (Eds.), *Handbook of literacy and technology: Transformations in a post-typographic world* (pp. 79-91). Mahwah, NJ: Erlbaum.

Labbo, L. B., & Reinking, D. (1999). Negotiating the multiple realities of technology in literacy research and instruction. *Reading Research Quarterly, 34*(4), 478-492).

Leu, D. J., Jr. (1996). Sarah's secret: Social aspects of literacy and learning in a digitial information age. *The Reading Teacher, 50*(2), 162-165.

Leu, D. J., Jr., & Kinzer, C. K. (2000). The convergence of literacy instruction with networked technologies for information and communication. *Reading Research Quarterly, 35*(1), 108-127.

Lincoln, Y. S., & Guba, E. G. (1985). *Naturalistic inquiry.* Beverly Hills, CA: Sage.

Manrique, C. G., & Gardiner, H. W. (1995). Computer mediated communications applications in selected psychology and political science courses. In M. Collins, & Z.

L. Berge (Eds.), *Computer mediated communication and the online classroom: Vol. 2. Higher Education* (pp. 123-136). Cresskill, NJ: Hampton.

McCombs, B. L. (1996). Alternative perspectives for motivation: In L. Baker, P. Afflerbach, & D. Reinking (Eds.), *Developing engaged readers in school and home communities* (pp. 67-87). Mahwah, NJ: Erlbaum.

McKenna, M. C., Reinking, D., Labbo, L. D., & Kieffer, R. D. (1999). The electronic transformation of literacy and its implications for the struggling reader. *Reading & Writing Quarterly: Overcoming Learning Disabilities, 15,* 111-126.

McKenna, M. C., & Watkins, J. H. (1995, November). *The effects of computer-mediated books on the development of beginning readers.* Paper presented at the meeting of the National Reading Conference, New Orleans, LA.

McKeon, C. A. (1999). The nature of children's e-mail in one classroom. *The Reading Teacher, 52*(7), 698-706.

McNabb, M. L. (1998). Using electronic books to enhance the reading comprehension of struggling readers. In T. Shanahan & F. V. Rodriguez-Brown (Eds.), *47th Yearbook of the National Reading Conference* (pp. 405-414). Chicago, IL: National Reading Conference.

Miller, L., & Olson, J. (1998). Literacy research oriented toward features of technology and classrooms. In D. Reinking, M. C. McKenna, L. D. Labbo, & R. D. Kieffer (Eds.), *Handbook of Literacy and Technology: Transformations in a post-typographic world* (pp. 343-360). Mahwah, NJ: Erlbaum.

Moore, M. A. (1991). Electronic dialoguing: An avenue to literacy. *The Reading Teacher, 45*(4), 280-286.

Morrow, L. M., & Gambrell, L. B. (1998). How do we motivate children toward independent reading and writing? In S. B. Neuman & K. A. Roskos (Eds.), *Children achieving: Best practices in early literacy* (pp. 144-161). Newark, DE: International Reading Association.

Patton, M. Q. (1990). *Qualitative evaluation and research methods* (2nd ed.). Newbury Park, CA: Sage.

Pemberton, A., & Zenhausern, R. (1995). CMC and the educationally disabled student. In Z. L. Berge & M. P. Collings (Eds.), *Computer mediated communication and the online classroom: Vol. 1. Overview and perspectives* (pp. 69-82). Cresskill, NJ: Hampton.

Rasinski, T., & Padak, N. (2000). *Effective reading strategies: Teaching children who find reading difficult* (2nd ed.). Columbus, OH: Merrill.

Reinking, D., McKenna, M. C., Labbo, L. D., & Kieffer, R. E. (Eds.). (1998). *Handbook of literacy and technology: Transformations in a post-typographic world.* Mahwah, NJ: Erlbaum.

Resnick, L. B. (1991). Shared cognition: Thinking as social practice. In L. B. Resnick, J. M. Levine, & S. D. Teasley (Eds.), *Perspectives on socially shared cognition.* Washington, DC: American Psychological Association.

Rogoff, B. (1990). *Apprenticeship in thinking: Cognitive development in social context.* New York: Oxford University Press.

Schunk, D. H., & Zimmerman, B. J. (1997). Developing self-efficacious readers and writers: The role of social and self-regulatory processes. In J. T. Guthrie & A. Wigfield (Eds.), *Reading engagement: Motivating readers through integrated instruction* (pp. 34-50). Newark, DE: International Reading Association.

Seme, P. J. N. (1997, December). *Student-teachers' experiences using electronic dialogue journal with fifth graders.* Paper presented at the annual meeting of the National Reading Conference, Scottsdale, AZ.

Smith, R. K. (1984). *The war with grandpa*. New York: Bantam Doubleday Dell.

Sobol, D. J. (1961). *The Wright Brothers at Kitty Hawk*. New York: Scholastic.

Stutevant, E. G., & Padak, N. D. (1998). 'der nansy I miss you'—A beginning writer connects and communicates through electronic mail. *The Ohio Reading Teacher, 32*(2), 12-21.

Tao, L., & Reinking, D. (2000). Issues in technology: E-mail and literacy education. *Reading & Writing Quarterly, 16,* 169-174.

Topping, K. J., & McKenna, M. C. (1999). Introduction to electronic literacy – Part 1. *Reading & Writing Quarterly: Overcoming Learning Disabilities, 15,* 107-110.

Turner, J. C. (1997). Starting right: Strategies for engaging young literacy learners. In J. T. Guthrie & A. Wigfield (Eds.), *Reading engagement: Motivating readers through integrated instruction* (pp. 183-204). Newark, DE: International Reading Association.

Vacca, J. L., Vacca, R. T., & Gove, M. K. (2000). *Reading and learning to read* (4th ed.). New York: Longman.

Vygotsky, L. S. (1962). *Thought and language*. Cambridge, MA: MIT Press.

Vygotsky, L. S. (1978). *Mind in society: The development of higher psychological processes*. Cambridge, MA: Harvard University Press.

Worthy, J., Moorman, M., & Turner, M. (1999). What Johnny likes to read is hard to find in school. *Reading Research Quarterly, 34*(1), 12-27.

Yin, R. K. (1994). *Case study research: Design and methods* (2nd ed.). Thousand Oaks, CA: Sage.

Zemelman, S., Daniels, H., & Hyde, A. (1998). *Best practice: New standards for teaching and learning in America's schools* (2nd ed.). Portsmouth, NH: Heinemann.

# THE INFLUENCE OF AUDIENCE AWARENESS IN CHILDREN'S WRITING OF DIFFERENT GENRES: A CASE STUDY OF A SECOND-GRADE CLASS

## Distinguished Finalist
## Doctoral Research Award

### Ruth A. Oswald

The University of Akron

## Abstract

*Conducted in a classroom organized to reflect the teacher-researcher's constructivist philosophy, this yearlong study describes the influence of audience awareness on second-grade students' construction of fiction, nonfiction and hybrid texts. Data were collected in the form of audiotaped conferences, videotaped conversations, and student texts. Using the constant comparative method of qualitative analysis, conceptual groups emerged. This evidence was sorted into categories: humor, nontextual, syntax, semantic, and voice. Comparison of these categories and consideration of current knowledge about writing development resulted in theory grounded in these findings and this context. This theory suggests that an awareness of audience in young writers is a developmental dimension. Audience response served as a scaffolding device for many of these children's transition from egocentric to socialized thought. This transition was not always a linear process, but gradually many of these writers were able to consider the needs of their audiences as they composed texts.*

In today's American schools, with the influence of the constructivist philosophy (Fosnot, 1996) and the arrival of the process approach to writing instruction (Graves, 1983), there is a rediscovery of the importance of audience specifications to writing assignments. The process approach to writing instruction promotes the idea of a community of learners, children working together, listening to each other, and peer editing of written drafts. This approach provides peers as the first audience, rather than the teacher relating as an assessment audience. Is it possible that even young children improve as writers when they focus on specific audiences?

## Purpose of the Study

With the rekindled interest in sense of audience and its importance to the teaching of writing, a great deal of research is being generated on the topic of audience. Most of this research is being conducted with older students and more advanced writers. In addition, research has yet to focus on the effect of audience awareness on children's use of genre as they compose texts. There is a need for descriptive research conducted in real classrooms concerning an audience-awareness approach to writing instruction with primary grade children. This study documented the influence of an awareness of different audiences on second-grade students' construction of texts in different genres and as represented by different tasks.

## The Role of Genres

Littlefair (1991) emphasized the importance of children developing an awareness of the different ways in which texts are written. The classifications of different types of language used for different purposes are referred to as genres (Harris & Hodges, 1995). To simplify the categorization of this variety of genres, educators often refer to fiction and nonfiction as the main genres used to teach reading and writing. Recently a new genre has emerged which Leal (1989) referred to as the "gray genre." It is also called hybrid genre because it combines information and story. It is an effort to introduce children to the nonfiction genre by placing information within the familiar genre of narrative.

Green (1992) pointed out that recounts and narratives are the most commonly used genres in the writing of primary children. However, Littlefair (1991) stressed the importance of many forms of writing to develop full literacy in children. There are more demands than ever on children to write for a variety of reasons. The 1994 (NAEP) items demand the ability to communicate understanding in writing. State proficiency tests require more written responses in all subject areas.

This study documented a group of second-grade children's writing progress as they wrote for different audiences and different purposes in response to fiction, nonfiction, and hybrid genres. The two types of tasks required of these students were generative and reconstructive. The generative task required students to independently construct their text at the conclusion of a thematic study. The reconstructive task required a written recount of past events or retelling of fiction, nonfiction or hybrid trade books.

## Conceptual Framework

The teaching strategies and curricular goals used in this second-grade classroom are reflective of the researcher's constructivist philosophy. Children were given many opportunities to build their own knowledge as they were allowed to make choices about the topic of their texts as well as who might serve as their audience. A process approach to writing instruction was used as children were given time to write and talk about their projects.

The students engaged in both reconstructive and generative writing tasks as they constructed texts in a variety of genres for different audiences. The general research question that guided this study was: What is the influence of audience on the writing of second-grade students? The specific research question was: How does audience awareness influence second-grade students' construction of fiction text, nonfiction text, and hybrid text? The audiences used in this study were peers, kindergarten partners, and parents. While the researcher was mindful of current knowledge about how children develop as writers, an exploratory, inductive approach was used to obtain the information from the perspective of the participants in this classroom. The significance of this study resides in the insights provided by this holistic account of these young writers' development as they engaged in writing that was important to them and then shared it with audiences who valued this importance.

**Figure 1. Framework**

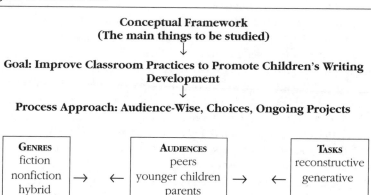

**Conceptual Framework
(The main things to be studied)**
↓
**Goal: Improve Classroom Practices to Promote Children's Writing Development**
↓
**Process Approach: Audience-Wise, Choices, Ongoing Projects**

| **Genres** | **Audiences** | **Tasks** |
|---|---|---|
| fiction | peers | reconstructive |
| nonfiction | younger children | generative |
| hybrid | parents | |

## Methodology

Since research questions guiding this study focused on concepts such as children's cognitive awareness of various audiences as they write and the influence of this cognizance on their texts, a qualitative, case study approach was appropriate. The researcher was the teacher in a second-grade classroom. Baumann, Shockley, and Allen (1996) discussed the importance of the teacher-researcher's unique perspective, the daily presence and intimate relationship between teacher and students and research situation. This insider, or emic, perspective offered insights not available to an outside researcher visiting the classroom.

## Setting

The site for this study was a second-grade classroom in a public elementary school in northeastern Ohio. One group of 21 second graders was targeted for this study. The student population represented very little cultural diversity, since only one child was African American and the remainder of the children were Caucasian. The majority of the school's population was middle to low socioeconomic status.

## Participants

Twenty-one second-grade students were the informants for this study. The researcher was the teacher in this classroom, had her master's degree as a reading specialist and was a doctoral student specializing in elementary education. She had twenty-two years of teaching experience. The majority of these children came from first-grade classrooms that followed a traditional, skills-based, basal approach to writing and reading instruction. They had not been exposed to many of the instructional strategies associated with the process approach to writing instruction.

The children in this second-grade class were between the ages of 7 and 9. According to Piaget's theory of cognitive development, children between the ages of 7 and 9 are moving from the stage of preoperational thought to the stage of concrete operational thought. As explained by Wadsworth (1989), Piaget characterized a preoperational child's behavior and thinking as egocentric, that is, the child cannot take the role of, or see the viewpoint of another. Since many of the characteristics of both of these cognitive stages are evident in the thinking processes of second-grade children, Piaget's theory was relevant to this study. As egocentric thought diminishes, second-grade students may gradually be able to consider the needs of different audiences as they construct text.

## Classroom Context

This classroom exemplified characteristics that were consistent with the teacher's constuctivist viewpoint. Gould (1996) explained the implications of this theory for the instruction of the language arts. He concluded that the language arts are, in fact, highly social arts and cited Graves (1983) as he stressed that social activities integrated into the language arts processes can actually lead to better writing, reading, and spelling. To facilitate this social approach to learning, this second-grade classroom was organized so students could interact.

Siemens (1996) emphasized the importance of teachers believing that any classroom can become a room full of writers. The researcher in this study believes that children can function as authors in a place where they are exposed to quality literature representing a variety of genres, given time and choices and an audience. Newkirk (1989) said it is the "Pygmalion" effect; "When children are treated as writers, they think of themselves as writers and pretend their way into literacy" (p. 3).

Since the research questions guiding this study included the concept of children's ability to respond to different genres and to construct these genres, reading selections included fiction, nonfiction, and hybrid text. The texts were chosen because the researcher used them successfully in the past to elicit responses from students (See Appendix C for a list of these trade books). The researcher used a process, or workshop, approach to teaching writing (Calkins, 1994). There was daily, interactive time for writing, and mini-lessons were used at the beginning of each writing workshop, following the format explained by Calkins (1994). At the conclusion of these sessions, there was a time for sharing texts with an audience.

As these second-grade students refined their writing, the "best" texts based on their evaluations, were published. After the piece of writing had been edited, parent volunteers typed and bound the books. The published texts were then shared with a variety of audiences.

## Data Collection

In an effort to add structure to this study, the researcher organized the research plan into three phases: Phase One, Building a Community of Writers; Phase Two, Ongoing Classroom Activities; and Phase Three, Final Writing Activities and Collection of Data. To gain an understanding of the influence of audience on the writing of these second-grade students, data were collected from a variety of sources throughout the school year including students' texts, oral conferences, and audio as well as videotapes. Because of the teacher as researcher role present in this study, the stance changed periodically from researcher participant to complete participant.

## Data Analysis

Analysis of data in this investigation followed the method of constant comparative analysis outlined by Glaser and Strauss (1967). The goal was to uncover patterns in the data, and this strategy consisted of four stages: 1) in the first stage, incidents were compared, and preliminary categories were developed; 2) in the second stage, "the level of comparison changed from 'incident with incident' to 'incident with properties of the category'" (p. 60); 3) in the third stage, similar categories were combined, and the result was a few highly conceptual categories, hypotheses were generated, and data were checked against the framework of the study; 4) the fourth stage was the actual writing of the theory from the coded data. In this study, the research questions, the research plan, and the three phases of the data collection guided the analysis of data.

During phase one of the study, student texts were collected to gain insights about students' responses to audience cues and their abilities as well as developmental levels as writers. Interviews were conducted to gain information about students' understanding of different genres and to determine if they held some sort of audience in mind as they wrote. The data collected during phase two were in the form of responses captured on audio and video tapes as well as students' texts. The focus was on student responses to different audience cues given prior to writing. The construction of different genres continued to be a secondary focus. Phase three, the final season of this study included the introduction of a new genre, the hybrid genre, and students wrote for an audience of their choice. As students exercised choice of topic and genre, emphasis was on shaping a text for a given audience. A guiding question was: can these second-grade students determine a purpose for their writing with respect to a particular audience?

Participant observation was a common practice during this study because the researcher was living among the informants. Daily memoing provided important descriptions of behaviors to offer insights concerning the perspectives of the informants. Multiple sources of data were used in this study to support a holistic perspective. As the data obtained from one method supported that obtained from other methods, the results became more credible.

## Findings

As the data were collected they were continuously compared throughout this study. There were a number of recurring themes that were then sorted into categories. This evidence emerged in the children's verbal responses during class discussions and interviews as well as in the texts they constructed in the three genres for different audiences. In the discussion of these categories, examples of students' responses and texts are offered to clarify the findings.

### Category #1: Desire to Amuse Audience

Humor was an important part of this classroom context. As the children were introduced to the *Arthur* series by Marc Brown, to the humor of Joanna Cole present in *The Magic School Bus* series and to other fine children's literature, they soon came to enjoy the funny, ordinary traits of the characters and happenings in these texts. In light of this background, it was not surprising that humor was the first evidence of audience awareness in these children's texts. Several students included jokes in their nonfiction texts about crickets that they wrote for the kindergarten audience, such as this example:

**Figure 2. Humor**

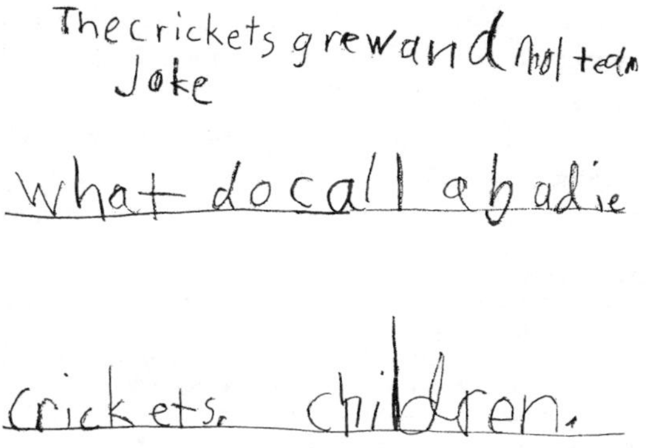

The crickets grew and molten
Joke

What do call a b adie

crickets. children.

Other children liked this idea and began to use jokes in their texts. These second-grade authors were very perceptive, because the kindergarten children responded with giggles. Their peers began to wait for the jokes in texts as they listened, and complained if there was no humor included. This was a recurring theme in their writing throughout the year. Humor was included in all three genres but was more frequent in texts created for the kindergarten and peer audiences.

These children often shared humor with peers as they constructed texts. During phase three while constructing a nonfiction text about a dinosaur, Edward was certainly aware of his audience as he quipped, "Velociraptor ate eggs . . . the kindergarten kids will know about eggs; they probably eat scrambled eggs." He and his classmates chuckled as they resumed their writing. Mem Fox (1993) emphasized the importance of the fun of writing. She pointed out that too often writing is seen as a chore. She also indicated that within the fun of writing there is power. Writers of all ages are empowered when they learn that they can make their point or share their information while also entertaining their audience.

As these young writers shared humor with their audience, they certainly experienced the fun and satisfaction that is part of writing for a purpose. Yes, they often imitated their peers, but through this imitation they learned so much about the process of communication and the power that writing brings to this process. The socialization of this group of learners served as a scaffold to their development as writers, moving many of them to a higher level of competence.

### Category #2: Nontextual Elements

Sipe (1998) in a summary of his investigation of primary children's responses to picture storybook read-alouds, reminded educators to reflect on how nontextual elements of picture books offer rich potential for meaning making. In this study the definition of nontextual elements includes title page, dedication, illustrations, format or organization of text, labels and endpages such as author information. The nontextual elements enhance the main body of the texts in important ways.

When these second-grade writers prepared texts for specific audiences, some of the evidence of audience adaptations appeared in the nontextual parts of the text such as illustrations and dedications. Sometimes texts were

**Figure 3. Comic Strip**

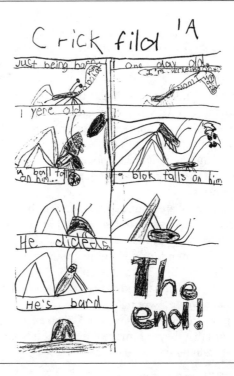

dedicated to the audience or labels were included in illustrations to clarify information for the sake of an audience.

As these children became comfortable with the context of writers' workshop and the basic concepts of process writing, they began to organize their texts in a variety of ways. The use of plain paper supported these young authors' freedom to organize the piece of writing in their own way. Sometimes they organized their text into chapters even including a table of contents. They soon began using title pages, dedications, and a section at the end about the author. These formats often included adaptations for the sake of a specified audience. Edward used a comic strip format for a nonfiction text constructed for the kindergarten audience (see Fig. 3). The information at the top right refers the reader to the table of contents (Cricket File 1 A).

Moline (1995) explained that young writers or students whose strengths are based in visual perception can be excellent communicators when they are allowed the option to write information in a visual form. As these second-grade students prepared texts for specific audiences, some of the evidence of audience adaptations appeared in the nontextual parts of the text. Visual adaptations for an audience were more frequent in nonfiction texts than in fiction or hybrid texts. There are many ways to organize nonfiction texts, and information is often displayed in visuals such as diagrams, charts, labels, and timelines. The fact that these young writers experimented with visual displays is evidence of

**Figure 4: Visual Display**

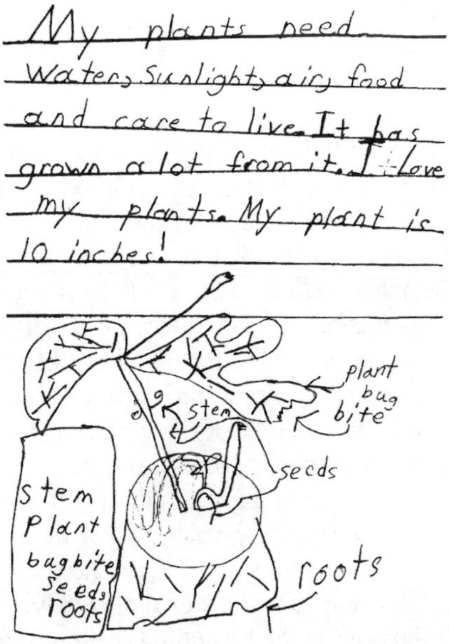

their understanding of the nonfiction genre and their purpose for writing. Figure 4 is an example of a visual display using labels to convey information to the reader. These students made more visual adaptations for the kindergarten audience than they did for either peers or parents. These are examples of comments from students during interviews:

> *Teacher:* What did you do to help your kindergarten audience understand your book?
>
> *Gavin:* I didn't put as many words on a page so they could look at pictures more often.
>
> *Molly:* I put like bigger words so they could see better, and I put more pictures (Fieldnotes, 12/17/98).

Although the development of audience awareness in these students' writing was not always present, it became more consistent as the year progressed. Coming face-to-face with the intended audience supported this development. They needed to meet and interact with the intended audiences. Sometimes these students were disappointed in the kindergarten children's lack of response, although Molly reminded her classmates, "Sometimes little kids are shy" (Fieldnotes, 2/17/99).

These young writers were working hard as they experimented with interesting ways to integrate the language in their texts with illustrations. Not only were they thinking about this integration, but many of them were also considering the needs and interests of their audiences as they made decisions about the format of their texts. It was evident that these thoughtful considerations were moving many of these writers to an improved level of competence as authors.

### Category #3: Syntax

According to Harris and Hodges (1995), syntax is "how sentences are formed and the grammatical rules that govern their formation" (p. 249). During phases one and two of this study some of the children expressed concern about the syntax or grammatical correctness of their texts. In the very beginning this concern was not necessarily related to audience awareness but rather to previous writing instruction. These children did not want to take risks, because they were not accustomed to having choices in their writing or the freedom to take longer than one session to complete a text. As they began to feel comfortable with the context of daily writing workshop there was less concern about the correctness of their writing.

However, as an awareness of audience emerged, some children again expressed concern about syntax, especially when the audience was their parents. During phase two a child shared that when you write for parents you have to take lots of time to make detail and make sure everything is right. One of the mini-lessons at the beginning of writer's workshop had just focused on the importance of detail to good writing. During this same time period another child expressed concern about correctness for parents during an interview about a written retelling he had done for parents:

*Teacher:* When you were writing it, did you think about your parents at all?

*Donnie:* Sort of . . . I just wouldn't stop writing. My hand got so tired. Right here is where I had to stop.

*Teacher:* Why did you work so hard on it?

*Donnie:* I was trying to get an O on it, because I've been getting S's in writing.

*Teacher:* Was that because you were writing for your parents?

*Donnie:* Yes, they want me to get O's. (Fieldnotes, 2/16/99).

Toward the end of phase three when the students were allowed to choose the audience for a writing assignment, one student chose classmates because, "It will be easier to make for friends than for parents" (Fieldnotes, 5/28/99). Several other children agreed that writing for parents was hard, because they want everything to be right.

Toward the end of the study, the children had gained a good understanding of the three genres and were accustomed to writing for a specific audience. One student who was a fluent reader with an advanced vocabulary defended his decision to write for classmates during an interview:

*Gavin:* For classmates it's easiest; you're around them; you know them and the kindergartners, it's like, who are these people? I don't know any of them. And then parents you know them too well, or whatever. It's just classmates, you see more often; they're just there pretty much all day (Fieldnotes, 5/26/99).

These young writers were much more concerned about the syntax or grammatical correctness for the parent audience.

### Category #4: Semantics

Semantics is meaning in language. Harris and Hodges (1995) pointed out that it can be meanings of words, phrases, sentences, discourse, and whole texts. The first incident of a semantic adaptation to benefit the intended audience of a text occurred early in phase two of the study. The incident happened during a class discussion. A child talked about a semantic change to accommodate a kindergarten audience, but the idea shared was never transferred into the actual text. The class was discussing how to adapt a nonfiction text for a kindergarten audience:

*Teacher:* What could you do to help your audience understand your book about crickets?

*Marsha:* I kinda thought about when you say "thorax" explain what it is (Fieldnotes, 12/17/98). Was this evidence of a cognitive stage limitation? She could think and talk about an adaptation for a younger audience, but then failed to follow through and use this idea in the actual text.

As these students chose their own topics to write about and shared their texts with a variety of audiences, they became very aware of the purpose for their writing. This awareness, in turn, led to some of the students matching their topic, or purpose to the intended audience. The following incident supports this speculation:

> *Teacher:* Who was your audience, and how did you change your book for that audience?
>
> *Kristen:* My parents were my audience. I wrote about dogs first, then changed it to cats because we just had to get rid of our dog when we moved. I thought it would make my mom sad if I wrote about dogs (Fieldnotes, 5/20/99).

As this investigation progressed it became clear that the majority of semantic accommodations to texts by these children were made for the parent and peer audiences. Many of the accommodations made for the kindergarten audience were nontextual and humorous in nature. Even though these children were young writers, it was evident that many of them were learning not only to shape the texts they created to suit their own interests, but to also consider the interests of a wider audience as well. Writing is a very social act, and sharing texts with a variety of audiences helps children realize that texts should be understood by other people.

As these children considered their audience, it added purpose and new meaning to their writing. Wells (1986) believed that all people, children as well as adults, are meaning makers as they are involved in speech and writing. When readers and writers try to make sense of texts and share them with others, the meaning making that results is an important part of being human. As these young writers considered the interests and feelings of their audience, it had a positive effect on the semantic quality of the texts they constructed.

### Category #5: Voice

Spandel and Stiggins (1997) defined voice as, "the ability to communicate in a way that is appropriate for the identified, intended audience and that engages and holds the attention of that audience" (p. 213). A prominent feature of audience awareness as it emerged in these young children was the improvement of voice in the texts they created for specified audiences. Voice is an important trait in writing that can be difficult to define, yet is often included in writing assessment instruments. Graves (1985) discussed the importance of helping young writers sound like themselves as they construct texts. As many of these children became aware of their audience, the texts they created expressed genuine interest in the topic and invited the audience to share this engagement. One child shared his feelings in his text as he wrote, "I love to have crickets in my school" (Fieldnotes, 1/21/99). Figure 5 is another example of voice.

As these children became aware of their audience, many of their texts contained dialogue or conversations posed directly to the reader. One child initiated this conversation with the intended audience in his text, "I really like baseball, do you? You do? Great, you might be able to play with me sometime" (Fieldnotes, 2/17/99). It became obvious that they were moving away from egocentric thought as they composed these texts, and a more advanced level of thinking was evident in their writing.

Although the development of audience awareness in these students' writing was not always present, it became more consistent as the year progressed. Coming face to face with the intended audience supported this

**Figure 5. Voice**

I Likecrickets, They are cool, a cricket can Jump more than twenty times the length of its own body. a cricets can Jump. cricets have an tanse.

development. Sometimes these students were disappointed in the kindergarten children's lack of response. The majority of them came to prefer classmates as their audience because of the caring, enthusiastic responses they received from one another.

## Toward A Grounded Theory

This study suggests that children as young as these second graders are capable of making adaptations to texts in a variety of genres to meet the needs of a specific audience. A further speculation suggests that when they do consider their audience as they construct texts, this consideration improves their writing in a variety of ways. Based on the knowledge from these findings and what was known prior to this study, the investigator went beyond this data and speculated about the implications for future writing instruction in primary classrooms.

Calkins (1994) confirmed that writing development in young children is not always a linear process. It should not be assumed that children's writing will develop in any fixed order. Indeed Flower and Hays (1981) reached a similar conclusion about older writers and stressed that writing is a complicated intellectual process. The steps in the writing process are often recursive as writers move back and forth between the stages of planning, translating, and reviewing. Their cognitive process theory indicated that writers make meaning as they construct texts.

The data in this study support the suggestion that an awareness of audience in young writers is a developmental dimension. Just as children's development as writers is not always a linear process, so audience awareness is likewise a recursive process. First young writers can only think and talk about the needs of an audience, and later they are able to include these adaptations in their texts.

There is ample evidence in this study to support this theory that audience awareness is developmental. Children who are in the Piagetian preoperational cognitive stage do not suddenly, one day jump into the concrete cognitive stage. It is a gradual transition, and traces of egocentric thought reappear periodically as the child gradually begins to see things from others' perspective. This is precisely what occurred in regard to evidence of audience awareness in these children's writing. One week a child's writing might contain adaptations for a specific audience, but the next week there might be little or no evidence that they wrote for anyone but themselves. However, as the school year progressed, and the children shared texts with a variety of audiences, evidence of audience awareness became more consistent.

The findings from this study demonstrate the individual differences in children's development as writers including their awareness of audience. In spite of the recursive pattern of this sense of audience and the differences in individual children, the majority of these young writers improved as authors as they shared texts with a variety of audiences. Not only did the feedback from these audiences provide a different perspective for these children, but it also served as a great motivator that helped them work harder on their texts.

## Pedagogical Implications

An important implication resulting from this study is connected to the impact that social and cultural contexts have on children's literacy achievements. As McLane and McNamee (1990) confirmed, reading and writing are so much more than decoding and encoding print. They are ways of communicating meaning with written language. The purposes for reading and writing are closely connected to specific relationships and social and cultural situations and activities. Children's awareness of their purposes for writing and anticipation of the needs of their audience foster their full literacy development. Human relationships in the form of a community of learners in a classroom or feedback from a variety of audiences are so important to the process by which children become literate.

The results of this study support the importance of classroom talk, ongoing dialogue between teacher and student as well as between student and student. Classroom talk should not only be allowed; it should be promoted. First these children talked about audience adaptations to their texts, and then they incorporated them in their writing. Sowers (1979) pointed out that this kind of social interaction of talking about pieces of writing in progress is an example of scaffolding.

This study validates research that asserts the importance of the teacher's role in creating the context for learning. In order for children to become successful authors, teachers must believe their students can become writers. While it is important for educators to consider cognitive stage limitations of young children, it is equally important not to underestimate their capabilities. Creating a climate of mutual respect and trust will make it possible for students to take risks as they learn to construct texts for a variety of audiences.

The furniture and materials in a classroom should be arranged in a way that promotes opportunities for children to interact with classmates as they construct texts. Regular routines should be established. Gould (1996) explained that they need "appropriate boundaries" and "dependable structures" (p. 94). Results of this study also support the importance of classroom libraries that include a variety of genres.

Learning to adjust texts to meet the needs of a wide range of audiences is a vital skill of authorship. Children's sense of audience needs to be nurtured steadily and consistently as they move up through the grades. Audience specifications should be included in writing assignments as soon as children begin to construct texts. Then writers need to meet their audience, share their texts and interact.

Teachers' questions are a very important scaffolding practice to support audience awareness. Posing hypothetical questions proved to be a valuable source of information in the study. These kinds of questions really made the children consider the needs of their audiences.

The process approach to writing instruction supports an awareness of audience on the part of the author. Sometimes this awareness is evident as the writer chooses a topic, sometimes during revision or editing and sometimes not until the writer comes face-to-face with an audience. Maintaining children's voices in their writing is important. When they are given choices, the result is a text with a wonderful quality of the author's unique voice. Granting children the choices of topic, genre and audience allows them to build their own knowledge and make their own meaning as they improve their writing skills. Publishing children's texts not only motivates young authors to write again, but the impressive appearance of a published book also inspires audiences of all ages to be better listeners and more responsive.

Children should learn to construct both generative and reconstructive texts. As much recent research suggests, written retellings are an excellent way to assess students' comprehension (Moss, 1997). They also need to understand the difference between the tasks. A wonderful way to introduce this difference is through the use of children's literature.

An ongoing problem throughout this study occurred when these children were faced with the task of constructing nonfiction and hybrid texts. They often had difficulty organizing the information and putting it in their own words. This finding supported the implication that primary children need some instructional strategies to scaffold their writing of nonfiction and hybrid texts.

As the children in this study became more aware of audience, their writing improved in a variety of ways. Adams (1990) pointed out that emphasis on writing activities is repeatedly shown to result in gains in early reading achievement. Future research could focus on the effect that children's audience awareness in writing has on reading achievement.

# References

Adams, J. J. (1990). *Beginning to read: Thinking and learning about print.* (a summary) Champaign, IL: University of Illinois.

Baumann, J. F., Shockley, B., & Allen, J. (1996). *Methodology in teacher research: Three cases* (Perspectives in Reading Research No. 10). The University of Georgia and University of Maryland: National Reading Research Center.

Calkins, L. (1994). *The art of teaching writing* (Rev. Ed.). Portsmouth, NH: Heinemann Educational Books.

Flower, L., & Hayes, J. R. (1981). A cognitive process theory of writing. *College Composition and Communication, 32* (1), 365-387.

Fosnot, C. T. (Ed.) (1996). *Constructivism: Theory, perspectives, and practice.* New York: Teachers College Press.

Fox, M. (1993). *Radical reflections: Passionate opinions on teaching, learning, and living.* New York: Harcourt Brace & Company.

Glaser, B. G., & Strauss, A. L. (1967). *The discovery of grounded theory: Strategies for qualitative research.* Chicago, IL: Aldine Publishing Company.

Gould, J. S. (1996). A constructivist perspective on teaching and learning in the language arts. In Fosnot, C. T. (Ed.), *Constructivism: Theory, perspectives, and practice.* New York: Teachers College Press.

Graves, D. (1983). *Writing: Teachers and children at work.* Portsmouth, NH: Heinemann Educational Books.

Graves, D. (1985). The reader's audience. In Hansen, J., Newkirk, T., and Graves, D. (Eds.), *Breaking ground: Teachers relate reading and writing in the elementary school.* Portsmouth, NH: Heinemann Educational Books Inc.

Green, P. (1992). *A matter of fact.* Winnipeg, MB Canada: Peguis Publishers.

Harris, T. L., & Hodges, R. E. (Eds.). (1995). *The literacy dictionary.* Newark, DE: International Reading Association.

Leal, D. (1989). Possibilities unlimited: An initial look into the gray genre. *The New Advocate, 6* (1), 61-70.

Littlefair, A. B. (1991). *Reading all types of writing.* Bristol, PA: Open University Press.

Littlefair, A. (1992). Information books in the primary school: The language of action or reflection? In Mayhoe, M. and Parker, S. (Eds.), *Reassessing language and literacy.* Bristol, PA: Open University Press.

McLane, J. B., & McNamee, G. D. (1990). *Early literacy: The developing child.* Cambridge, MA: Harvard University Press.

Moline, S. (1995). *I see what you mean.* York, ME: Stenhouse Publishers.

Moss, B. (1997). A qualitative assessment of first graders' retellings of expository text. *Reading Research and instruction, 37,* 1-14.

National Center For Education Statistics. (1994). *NAEP 1992 Writing Report Card* (Report No. 23-W01). Washington, DC: U. S. Printing Office.

Newkirk, T. (1989). *More than stories.* Portsmouth, NH: Heinemann.

Siemens, L. (1996). "Walking through the time of kids": Going places with poetry. *Language Arts, 73* (April), 234-240.

Sipe, L. R. (1998). IRA Outstanding Dissertation Award for 1998: The construction of literary understanding by first and second graders in response to picture storybook read-alouds, *Reading Research Quarterly, 33,* (4), 376-378.

Sowers, S. (1979). A six-year-old's writing process: The first half of first grade. *Language Arts, 56,* 829-835.

Spandel, V., & Stiggins, R. J. (1997). *Creating writers,* (2nd Ed.). White Plains, NY: Longman Publishers.

Wadsworth, B. J. (1989). *Piaget's theory of cognitive and affective development* (4th ed.). New York: Longman.

Wells, G. (1986). *The meaning makers: Children learning language and using language to learn.* Portsmouth, NH: Heinemann.

## Appendix A. Research Plan

| RESEARCH QUESTION | PURPOSE | ASSUMPTION | PROCEDURE |
|---|---|---|---|
| What is the influence of audience on the writing of second-grade students? | To describe and analyze how awareness of audience affect student's writing | Audience-awareness may influence children's writing. | • Audience cues will be given to students prior to writing.<br>• Students' texts<br>• Oral conferences<br>• Video tapes<br>• Participant observation |
| What is the influence of different audiences on second-grade students' construction of fiction text? | To describe and analyze children's attempts to construct fiction text for different audiences. | The awareness of contrasting audiences may have different effects on children's construction of fiction text as opposed to nonfiction or hybrid. | • Generative and reconstructive tasks<br>• Students' texts<br>• Oral conferences<br>• Video tapes<br>• Participant observation |
| What is the influence of different audiences on second-grade students' construction of nonfiction text? | To describe and analyze children's attempts to construct nonfiction text for different audiences. | The awareness of contrasting audiences may have different effects on children's construction of nonfiction text as opposed to fiction or hybrid. | • Generative and reconstructive tasks<br>• Students' texts<br>• Oral conferences<br>• Video tapes<br>• Participant observation |
| What is the influence of different audiences on second-grade students' construction of hybrid text? | To describe and analyze children's attempts to construct hybrid text for different audiences | The awareness of contrasting audiences may have different effects on children's construction of hybrid text as opposed to fiction or nonfiction. | • Generative and reconstructive tasks<br>• Students' texts<br>• Oral conferences<br>• Video tapes<br>• Participant observation |

## Appendix B. Study Plan

| PHASES | GENRES | TASKS | AUDIENCES | ACTIVITIES |
|---|---|---|---|---|
| Phase One: Building a Community of Writers | Fiction and Nonfiction | Generative and Reconstructive but and emphasis on Reconstructive | Teacher and Peers | Introduce daily writing workshop, audience cues, choice of topics, sharing writing with peers, conferencing with teacher |
| Phase Two: Ongoing classroom activities | Fiction and Nonfiction | Generative and Reconstructive | Teacher, Peers, and Parents | Continue routine of writing workshop, audience cues, generate text in response to thematic units, sharing writing with peers, teacher and parents |
| Phase Three: Final Writing Activities and Collection of Data | Fiction, Nonfiction, and Hybrid | Generative and Reconstructive with an emphasis on Generative | Teacher, Peers, and Parents | Continue writing workshop emphasizing writing in a variety of genres for various audiences |

## Appendix C. Bibliography of Children's Literature

### Fiction

Brett, J. (1981). *Fritz and the beautiful horses*. New York: G. P. Putnam's Sons.

Brett, J. (1987). *Goldilocks and the three bears*. New York: G. P. Putnam's Sons.

Brett, J. (1989). *The mitten*. New York: G. P. Putnam's Sons.

Brett, J. (1990). *The wild Christmas reindeer*. New York: G. P. Putnam's Sons.

Brett, J. (1996). *Comet's nine lives*. New York: G. P. Putnam's Sons.

Brown, M. T. (1990). *Arthur's pet business*. Boston, MA: Little, Brown and Company.

Giff, P. R. (1988). *Ronald Morgan goes to bat*. Ill. Susanna Natti. New York: Viking Kestrel/Penguin Books.

Henkes, K. (1993). *Owen*. New York: Greenwillow Books.

### Hybrid

Cole, J. (1986). *The magic school bus at the waterworks*. Ill. Bruce Degen. New York: Scholastic, Inc.

Cole, J. (1994). *The magic school bus: In the time of the dinosaurs*. Ill. Bruce Degan. New York: Scholastic, Inc.

DePaola, T. (1978). *The popcorn book*. New York: Holiday House.

### Nonfiction

Dorros, A. (1987). *Ant cities*. New York: Harper & Row, Publishers, Inc.

Lauber, P. (1996). *How dinosaurs came to be*. Ill. Douglas Henderson. New York: Simon & Schuster Books for Young Readers.

Maestro, B. (1996). *Coming to America*. Ill. Susannah Ryan. New York: Scholastic Inc.

Patent, D. H. (1996). *Children save the rain forest*. New York: Cobblehill Books/Dutton.

# Using Repeated Reading, Paired Reading, and Demonstration to Improve Reading Fluency

## Stephanie Gerdes

Grand Rapids, MI

## Abstract

*This study evaluates the impact of repeated reading, paired reading, and demonstration on the reading fluency of regular education students. Results suggest that integrating these strategies into the context of the regular education curriculum has a positive effect on students' reading fluency and comprehension. Practical suggestions for integrating these methods into classroom activities are provided.*

## Introduction

There he was again—standing in the book area aimlessly thumbing through the paperbacks, pulling one off the shelf, looking at the cover and pictures, and trading it for another. Five minutes later, he was back at his desk, turning pages too quickly to be reading, shifting in his chair to discover the cause of a slight disturbance, and, finally, slipping out of the room with the bathroom pass. When silent reading time was finished, Dan's book was shut and in his desk before the direction to stop was entirely given. No, Dan was not exactly what one would call an enthusiastic reader.

And why should he be? Reading was a painful, disappointing experience for him. Every word he couldn't read screamed aloud what he was trying desperately to hide. Every sentence he couldn't comprehend forced him to feign interest in something to which he was indifferent. Every book he couldn't complete promoted one image of himself . . . and that image was one of failure.

Unfortunately, Dan is not alone. Too many children are not able to read grade level material fluently. That is, they cannot read with accuracy, smoothness, and expression (Rasinski, 1989). Furthermore, educators rarely make fluency a goal of reading instruction (Allington, 1983; Rasinski, 1989). They view fluency as an outcome of skillfulness rather than as a factor of good reading (Allington,1983; Zutell & Rasinski, 1991). Moreover, reading instruction generally includes reading-related activities intended to improve subskills rather than actual reading practice intended to improve fluency (Allington, 1980; Mathes, Simmons, & Davis, 1992; Nathan & Stanovich, 1991). Subsequently, many readers are not fluent, and many educators ignore the problem.

The purpose of this study was to determine the impact of repeated reading, paired reading, and demonstration on the reading fluency of third graders when these techniques were incorporated into the daily routine of a regular education classroom. The goal was to increase the reading rates of five target students by 30%.

## Why Is Fluency Important?

The ability to read fluently is very important. First, it contributes to the enjoyment of reading, causing students to be enthusiastic readers (Mathes, Simmons, & Davis, 1992). Second, it aids comprehension (Breznitz, 1997; Dahl, 1974; LaBerge & Samuels, 1974; Lovett, 1987; Mathes, Simmons, & Davis, 1992). Third, it makes available to the reader an abundance of material to process, learn from, and appreciate (Chomsky, 1976; Mastropieri, Leinart, & Scruggs, 1999; Mathes, Simmons, & Davis, 1992). Fourth, it positively affects self-concept and permits students to see themselves as readers (Chomsky, 1976; May, 1994). Ultimately, a vast array of job opportunities are available (Greenberg,1996), and much information designed to improve quality of life is accessible.

Dysfluency, or lack of fluency, has several possible causes. It may result from spending too much time reading overly difficult text (Nathan & Stanovich, 1991), failing to use all three cuing systems—semantic, syntactic, and phonetic—to identify unknown words (Allington, 1980), not recognizing phrases (Schreiber, 1980, 1991), lacking reading practice both in and out of the classroom (Allington, 1980; Anderson, Wilson, & Fielding, 1988; Mathes, Simmons, & Davis, 1992), or devoting more time to subskills and reading-related activities than to actual reading (Allington, 1980; Mathes, Simmons, & Davis, 1992; Nathan & Stanovich, 1991).

If students are to become successful readers, educators must avoid these pitfalls. They must instruct children at their own instructional levels. They need to teach them to use all three cuing systems and to group words into phrases. They should implement home reading programs and devote more time to reading in school. In essence, they need to make fluency a goal of reading instruction. The following three interventions help accomplish that goal.

## Interventions for Improving Reading Fluency
### Repeated Reading

The first intervention is repeated reading. The student rereads a short selection until he can easily read it at a predetermined rate (Dahl, 1974; Koskinen & Blum, 1986; Samuels, 1979). Researchers suggest a target rate of 100 words per minute on independent reading level material (Dahl, 1974; Dowhower, 1987). Speed and ease of reading are the goals, while accuracy in word recognition is deemed less important. Therefore, corrections are held to a minimum (Dahl, 1974; LaBerge & Samuels, 1974; Rasinski, 1990; Zutell & Rasinski, 1991). Rereading may also be done with the support of an audio recording or with a partner (Chomsky, 1976; Rasinski, 1990). Chomsky recommends 20 minute sessions daily. When reading with a partner, each student reads a passage three times and evaluates his improvement in rate, expression, and smoothness (Koskinen & Blum, 1986; Rasinski, 1990).

Many studies indicate that repeated reading has several positive effects. It increases reading rate (Chomsky, 1976; Dahl, 1974; Dowhower, 1987; O'Shea, Sindelar, & O'Shea, 1985; Rasinski, 1990; Samuels, 1979; Sindelar, Monda, & O'Shea, 1990) and reduces the number of word recognition errors (Dahl, 1974; Dowhower, 1987; Gonzales & Elijah, 1975; O'Shea, Sindelar, & O'Shea, 1985; Perfetti & Lesgold, 1979; Rasinski, 1990; Samuels, 1979; Sindelar, Monda, & O'Shea, 1990). Repeated reading also appears to improve comprehension (Allington, 1983; Dahl, 1974; LaBerge & Samuels, 1974; Mathes, Simmons, & Davis, 1992; O'Shea, Sindelar, & O'Shea, 1985; Rasinski, 1990; Samuels, 1979; Stayter & Allington, 1991).

There are several possible reasons for the success of repeated reading. It offers direct, immediate feedback (Jensen, 1998) and immerses readers in meaningful text rather than in reading-related activities (Samuels, 1979; Stayter & Allington, 1991). Repeated reading also offers time to develop an awareness of how words are grouped into phrases (Screiber, 1980,1991). Moreover, some readers simply cannot attend to all cuing systems simultaneously, and repeated reading offers the time needed to do so (Schreiber, 1980, 1991). Last, repeated reading allows the reader to master a passage and know the feel of "real" reading (LaBerge & Samuels, 1974).

### Paired Reading

Another method for improving fluency is paired reading. In paired reading, students tutor one another. The pairs may be self-chosen or teacher-selected. In sustained paired reading, students read straight through the text stopping only for assistance or to perform certain tasks, such as "shrinking" a paragraph into ten words or less or engaging in a prediction relay. In paired repeated reading, the first student reads a short passage aloud and analyzes his reading. After reading the same passage two more times, the reader and tutor discuss how the reading improved. Then they reverse roles (Koskinen & Blum, 1986).

Paired reading has continually demonstrated positive results both academically and socially. Academically, students demonstrate improvement in reading rate, comprehension, and word recognition (Koskinen & Blum, 1986; Mathes & Fuchs, 1993; Mathes, Fuchs, Fuchs, Henley, & Sanders, 1994). Socially, students develop empathy for peers and feel supported. Attitudes about themselves, academics, and school greatly improve (Utley, Mortweet, & Greenwood, 1997). Paired reading is also enjoyable (Rasinski, 1990).

There are several possible reasons for the success of paired reading. It increases individual instruction time and gives more immediate feedback (Heibert, 1980; Mathes & Fuchs, 1993; Utley, Mortweet, & Greenwood, 1997). It increases time spent reading meaningful text (Heibert, 1980; Mathes, et al., 1994; Utley, Mortweet, & Greenwood, 1997) and offers readers models of fluent reading. Paired reading promotes a helping and cooperative classroom atmosphere (Heibert, 1980; Mathes, et al., 1994).

### Demonstration

The last method described here is demonstration. Various forms of demonstration occur before, during, and after reading. Demonstration that occurs before reading includes echo reading, in which students echo phrases first read by an adult, and listening passage preview (LPP), in which students read longer passages to which they have been pre-exposed by a fluent reader. Forms of demonstration that take place during reading include "taped books," in which students read with a tape recording either repeatedly or a single time (Carbo, 1978, 1995, 1996; Chomsky, 1976; Rasinski, 1990) and the Neurological Impress Method (NIM). In NIM, a mature reader sits slightly behind and next to the student. He points to the text and gently reads into the students' right ear at a slightly faster rate than the student until the student is able to take over pointing to and reading the text (Heckleman, 1969). A third method is the shared reading experience. The teacher reads aloud and points to the texts of big books, class paragraphs, or large-typed poems as students read with her (Carbo, 1995, 1996; Rasinski, 1988). Another form of listening-while-reading is choral reading. The students and teacher read text simultaneously (Carbo, 1995, 1996; Kelly, 1995). Last, in echo reading the teacher reads a phrase, sentence, or short passage, modelling good phrasing and expression. Students repeat, copying the fluent example (Carbo, 1995, 1996; Henk, Helfeldt, & Platt, 1986; Huey, 1908/1968).

Two implicit forms of demonstration are reading aloud and paired reading. As students hear books read aloud, they develop vocabulary and acquire a sense of phrasing and expression (McCurdy, Cundari, & Lentz, 1990) as well as receive implicit modelling in phrasing and word identification (Greenwood, Granger, Bailey, Carta, Dorsey, Kohler, Nelson, Rotholz, & Schulte, 1987).

Demonstration in all these forms appears to have positive effects. Studies suggest that it increases reading rate and decreases word recognition errors (Conte & Humphreys, 1989; Daly & Martens, 1994; Rasinski, 1990; Smith, 1979). It also contributes to an enjoyment of reading and increases students' self-concept. During NIM, students receive individual attention, making them feel valuable. Last, shared reading and reading aloud builds a strong sense of classroom community.

There are several possibilities why demonstration is effective. First, it offers a fluent model, which is far more helpful to dysfluent readers than listening to slow, laborious reading of their peers (Kelly, 1995; Schrieber, 1980; Smith, 1979). Second, NIM and taped books maximize time reading meaningful text (Allington, 1980, 1983; Anderson, 1981; Chomsky, 1976; Kelly, 1995; Rasinski, 1990; Smith, 1979). Third, with the exception of NIM, demonstration allows teachers to impact many students at once. Choral and echo reading can be enjoyable, whole-class activities requiring no individual attention yet helping the students who need it, and LPP demonstrates fluent reading to everyone (Carbo, 1995, 1996). Taped books allows the teacher to impact many students simultaneously and gives dysfluent readers fluent modeling without the teacher being present (Rasinski, 1990).

Unfortunately, repeated reading, paired reading, and demonstration are absent in much reading instruction despite studies indicating that they positively affect reading fluency (Chomsky, 1976; Dahl, 1974; Delquadri, Greenwood, Whorton, Carta, & Hall, 1986; Dowhower, 1987; Koskinen & Blum, 1986; O'Shea, Sindelar, & O'Shea, 1985; Rasinski, 1990). The following study was conducted to determine the effects of repeated reading, paired reading, and demonstration when they were used in the context of a regular education classroom.

## Research
### Subjects

Five third graders—four boys and one girl—participated in this four-week study. All were nine years old and had average intelligence, poor comprehension, and slow reading rates. One boy was diagnosed with a reading disability. None had significant attentional or behavioral problems.

### Setting

This study was conducted in a public elementary school in a Midwestern middle class suburb. Most interventions were incorporated into the regular education instruction of all twenty-two third graders. However, the teacher-researcher also worked individually with the subjects while the rest of the class was engaged in sustained silent reading. She met with the subjects at her desk, at their desks, and in the carpeted hallway just outside the classroom.

## Materials

Various texts were used. They included teacher-selected literature such as *Little House in the Big Woods*, by L. I. Wilder and *The Boxcar Children*, by Gertrude Warner, as well as various student-selected chapter books. They also included Addison-Wesley science texts, students' journal writing, poetry, and tape-recorded picture books.

## Procedures

Three procedures were used to establish baseline data. First, the five subjects read three 100-word passages. These rates were averaged to determine each child's baseline rate, noted in words per minute (wpm). Next, the students took the reading comprehension section of the Houghton-Mifflin (1989) reading test to determine their baseline comprehension. Last, the remainder of the class read a single 100-word passage to determine their reading rates, used to create reading pairs. The fastest reader was matched with the middle reader, the next fastest with the student just below the middle, and so on. This ensured that no partnership had two weak readers. Care was taken that partners would feel comfortable together. To expedite this process, students read into a tape recorder, allowing the teacher-researcher to listen to their reading samples after school. In counting 100-word passages, every six letters and/or spaces represented a single word. For a sample of teacher notes, see Appendix A.

During the next four weeks, four whole-class and two one-on-one interventions were incorporated into the daily routine. The first whole-class intervention was using repeated reading during journal time. Four times a week, students journaled for eight minutes. Then they were told to "read over what you wrote so you are ready to read to your partner." After doing so, they took turns reading to someone nearby. Next, volunteers read to the class.

A second whole-class intervention was reading poetry for ten minutes three times a week. When new poetry was handed out, students silently read their copies as soon as they received them, thus preparing to successfully read aloud. New and familiar poetry was then read in partners or as a class.

A third classwide intervention was using paired reading four times a week for 15-20 minutes. In assigned or self-selected pairs, students either read in a sustained manner or repeatedly. When reading in a sustained manner, students took turns acting as tutor and tutee as they played "Prediction Relay" or "Paragraph Shrinking." To support peer tutoring, the teacher-researcher taught mini-lessons on using all three cuing systems to identify unknown words (i.e. using phonics, syntax, and meaning). When reading repeatedly, students evaluated themselves after one reading and again after practice. Appendix B contains a self-evaluation form for duplication.

The last whole-class intervention was demonstrating fluent reading. This was done in a variety of ways, one of which was using listener-passage-preview. In LPP, the teacher-researcher read the beginning of a chapter aloud while students silently followed in their texts. They later reread the chapter from the beginning. She also wrote sentences on the board and lead discussions about how phrases were "chunked" together. She used echo and choral reading, directing students to note her phrasing, intonation, and expression. These demonstrations took place at the beginning of reading time for approximately five minutes.

While the above procedures were used classwide, some strategies were used with the five subjects individually. Cory, Erin, Nate, and Wade used repeated reading. During the daily 30 minutes of sustained silent reading, in which the class was quietly reading at self-chosen places about the room, the teacher-researcher met with two to three subjects individually each day for approximately 10 minutes each. They repeatedly read a paragraph or two or sometimes as much as a page from their self-chosen chapter books while the teacher-researcher recorded how long it took them to read it and what errors were made. Students were asked, "Do you think you could read that passage more quickly?" Although at first surprised by their progress, they soon eagerly expected it (see Appendix C for teacher notes). Another way repeated reading was used was by having students to read as far as they could in one minute and then rereading from the beginning, attempting to read farther than the first time. This was repeated as long as progress was made and interest was held. The teacher-researcher tallied each word read correctly and noted word recognition errors so students could see their improvement. It should be stressed that each tally did not represent a word in the same way the six letters and/or spaces represented a word when figuring wpm. These tallies were solely used to motivate students and not to measure correct wpm. (For a sample of teacher notes, see Appendix D).

During the study Dan announced that his family would be moving. Because of this and his particularly poor reading ability, Dan used the taped books method. This offered him constant modeling and allowed him to master his own picture books. He read with recordings of his picture books twice a day in twenty minute sessions. This was more than the single daily sessions Chomsky (1976) recommends, but it seemed imperative to increase his practice time. His reading rates and word recognition errors before and after practice were recorded. Errors included mispronunciations, substitutions, omissions, insertions, and refusals. They did not include self-corrections and minor (1-2 second) hesitations. Dan's pre-and post-intervention rates and comprehension scores were not compiled.

At the end of the four week study, the teacher-researcher again averaged three reading samples from Cory, Erin, Nate, and Wade. The passages were from the same texts used to obtain baseline data. Also, she readministered the Houghton-Mifflin (1989) comprehension test.

To summarize, the reading rates and comprehension levels of the subjects were determined before and after the four week intervention. Whole-class strategies included using repeated reading in conjunction with journals and poetry, using paired reading, and using teacher demonstration, including explicit teaching of phrasing, listener-passage-preview, and echo and choral reading. At the end of four weeks, pre-and post-intervention reading rates and comprehension levels were compared. Dan alone used the taped books method.

### Results
Table 1 contains a comparison of the mean pre-and post-intervention reading rates of Cory, Erin, Nate, and Wade. Their gain ranged from 8 to 22 wpm, or 16-42%. Their average gain was 17 wpm, or 30%.

**Table 1. Mean Pre-and Post-Intervention Reading Rates of the Subjects Measured in Words Per Minute (WPM).**

| | PRE AND POST-INTERVENTION READING RATES | | | |
| | PRE-INTERVENTION | POST-INTERVENTION | GAIN IN WPM | %GAIN |
|---|---|---|---|---|
| Cory | 53 | 75 | 22 | 42% |
| Erin | 51 | 64 | 13 | 26% |
| Nate | 49 | 57 | 8 | 16% |
| Wade | 54 | 73 | 19 | 35% |

Thus, the desired 30% increase in reading rate was met by two students, with another coming close. Nate, however, demonstrated less improvement.
The pre and post-comprehension scores indicated improvement, as well. See Table 2.

**Table 2. Pre and Post-Intervention Comprehension Scores as Indicated by the Houghton-Mifflin Reading Test, 1989.**

| | PERCENTAGE OF COMPREHENSION QUESTIONS ANSWERED CORRECTLY | | | |
| | *Test Level* | *Pre-Intervention* | *Post-Intervention* | *Gain* |
|---|---|---|---|---|
| Cory | 3rd grade | 100% | 100% | 0% |
| | 4th grade | 67% | 83% | 16% |
| Erin | 3rd grade | 67% | 83% | 18% |
| | 4th grade | 33% | 17% | -16% |
| Nate | 3rd grade | 50% | 67% | 17% |
| | 4th grade | 50% | 50% | 0% |
| Wade | 3rd grade | 67% | 100% | 33% |
| | 4th grade | 83% | 100% | 17% |

Dan showed gains using the taped books method. See Table 3 for rate changes after three 20-minute taped books sessions with each book.

**Table 3— Changes of One Student in Rate and Word Recognition Errors Before and After Three Taped Books Sessions**

| | | Before Taped Books Sessions | After Three 20-Minute Taped Books Sessions |
|---|---|---|---|
| Picture book #1 | speed # of errors | 5:00 minutes 20 | 2:18 minutes 0 |
| Picture Book #2 | speed # of errors | 6:00 minutes 38 | 2:50 minutes 0 |
| Picture Book #3 | speed # of errors | 9:15 minutes 24 | 7:15 minutes 0 |

Moreover, Dan's post-intervention fluency was impeccable for Picture Books #1 and #2. The stress, phrase lengthening, and intonation were highly expressive. He would have benefited from more time on Picture Book #3 to develop this same level of fluency, but even with just three readings, he made no word recognition errors.

## Discussion

The major findings of this study suggest that the combination of repeated reading, paired reading, and demonstration had a positive effect on reading fluency, that taped books alone had a positive effect on reading fluency, and that instruction in reading fluency had a positive effect on comprehension. These findings are consistent with previous research in repeated reading (Dahl, 1974; Dowhower, 1987; Samuels, 1979), paired reading (Delquadri, et. al., 1986; Greenwood, et al., 1987; Koskinen & Blum, 1986), and demonstration (Daly & Martens, 1994). They are also consistent with research in taped books (Chomsky, 1976; Rasinski, 1990) and support theories on the usefulness of demonstration (Carbo, 1995, 1996). Last, they are consistent with research in the effects of fluency on comprehension (Dowhower, 1987; O'Shea, Sindelar, & O'Shea, 1985).

Student and teacher reaction to these methods was highly positive. The children eagerly read their journal entries to friends and then again to the class. In fact, on two occasions when the teacher-researcher forgot to direct the students to silently read their entries, the students quickly reminded her.

In addition, when asked if the repetition was helpful, students answered very positively. They also enjoyed the poetry, happily chanting favorite poems across the room. When reading in pairs, partners eagerly took up their books and found corners in which to nestle. They were attentive and enjoyed tutoring one another. These methods also developed positive self-concepts. It was obvious that Dan, in particular, enjoyed a new confidence, as indicated by the broad smile on his face, the quickness of his step, and the proud poise of this head. Moreover, wearing headphones as he read with the taped books allowed him to immerse himself in reading. The students who read repeatedly with the teacher were pleased to learn how much faster they could read after practice and were eager to try again. The teacher-researcher found that she had a better knowledge of individual student performance as a result of daily, anecdotal information and from ranking the entire class based on their reading rates. Furthermore, she became convinced that, just as musicians and athletes practice before performing, so should readers practice before reading to others.

### Implications for Classroom Instruction

From this study come several implications for classroom instruction. First, teachers must offer more opportunities to reread text. Options include rereading poetry, listening to taped books, and reading with individual students during silent sustained reading. Second, teachers must increase the amount of time students read meaningful text. One way is to set up a system of classwide paired reading. Pairs may be assigned or self-chosen. If they are self-chosen, teachers should note if anyone is being left out. If so, then perhaps she should assign them. Third, teachers must make demonstration of fluent reading an integral part of instruction. This can be done explicitly by identifying phrases within sentences written on a board or by modeling when reading with a student. It can also be done implicitly by making reading aloud a priority. Setting up a listening station containing books on tape and using listening passage preview during daily lessons are other ways of incorporating demonstration into a reading program. For further suggestions on using repeated reading, paired reading, and demonstration, see Appendix E, Appendix F, and Appendix G.

Because this study was conducted in the teacher-researcher's own third grade classroom, the results may not be generalized to all classrooms. However, this study does exhibit how teachers might provide additional support in regular education settings. The multi-element design recognizes that reading is a very complex function and refrains from using any one strategy in isolation. Furthermore, these interventions were enjoyable, motivating, and good instructional practice. For example, practicing reading journal entries before reading aloud is similar to practicing music before performing. Reading in pairs is *sharing* literature—not merely reading an assignment. And identifying proper phrasing is good pedagogy when working with poor readers.

A few words of caution are necessary for anyone replicating portions of this study. First, when recording books and passages, one must read slowly enough that students can actually read aloud with the tape. If the recording is too fast and students resort to listening only, their reading may not improve. Second, students' interest in an intervention should be monitored. If they become bored with repetition, for example, the length or frequency of the sessions should be decreased. Last, when assigning pairs for paired reading, care should be taken that everyone is matched with someone with whom they will feel comfortable. Paired reading could be a miserable experience for someone poorly matched. If these cautions are carefully heeded, these interventions have the potential to offer a rewarding experience.

## Conclusion

This study suggests that when repeated reading, paired reading, and demonstration are used in a regular education classroom they have a positive effect on reading fluency, contribute to a positive classroom atmosphere, and foster healthy self-concepts.

One image in particular confirms the importance of instruction in fluency. Dan had been reading aloud to the teacher-researcher in the back of the classroom when she quietly slipped away to monitor the students as they lined up for gym class. As the last student left the room, she looked back. There was Dan, alone at the table, intently finishing the book he had been reading aloud. The world was forgotten, and the book was everything. At that moment he was no longer the easily-distracted reader, perusing the bookshelves to avoid genuine reading, quickly shutting a book and stuffing it into his desk at the earliest opportunity, known to all as the "nonreader." Instead, he was the successful student, delighting in the sound of his own voice moving smoothly and swiftly over the words, relishing the ease with which he was accomplishing his task, beginning to claim a new identify. Yes, indeed . . . fluency must have a central place in reading instruction.

# References

Allington, R. L. (1980). Poor readers don't get to read much in reading groups. *Language Arts,* 57(8), 872-876.

Allington, R. L. (1983). Fluency: The neglected reading goal. *The Reading Teacher,* 36, 556-561.

Anderson, B. (1981). The missing ingredient: Fluent oral reading. *Elementary School Journal, 81(3),* 173-177.

Anderson R. C., Wilson, P. T., & Fielding, L. G. (1988). Growth in reading and how children spend their time outside of school. *Reading Research Quarterly, 23,* 285-303.

Breznitz, Z. (1997). Reading rate acceleration: Developmental aspects. *The Journal of Genetic Psychology, 158,* 427-441.

Carbo, M. (1978). Teaching reading with talking books. *The Reading Teacher, 32,* 267-273.

Carbo, M. (1995). Continuum of modeling reading methods. *Teaching PreK-8, 26,* 85.

Carbo, M. (1996). Selecting the "right" reading method. *Teaching PreK-8, 27,* 84.

Chomsky, C. (1976). After decoding: What? *Language Arts, 53,* 288-296.

Clark, C.H. (1995) Teaching students about reading: A fluency example. *Reading Horizons, 35(3),* 250-266.

Conte, R., & Humphreys, R. (1989). Repeated reading: Using audio-taped material enhances oral reading in children with reading difficulties. *Journal of Communication Disorders, 22,* 65-79.

Dahl, P. R. (1974). An experimental program for teaching high speed word recognition and comprehension skills. (Final report of Project No. 3-1154). Washington, DC: National Institute of Education, Office of Research. (ERIC Document Reproduction Service No. ED 099 812).

Daly, E.J., & Martens, B. K. (1994). A comparison of three interventions for increasing oral reading performance: Application of the instructional hierarchy. *Journal of Applied Behavior Analysis, 27,* 459-469.

Delquadri, J., Greenwood, C. R., Whorton, D., Carta, J. J., & Hall, R. V. (1986). Classwide peer tutoring. *Exceptional Children, 52(6),* 535-542.

Dowhower, S. L. (1987). The effects of repeated reading on second grade transitional readers' fluency and comprehension. *Reading Research Quarterly, 22(4),* 389-406.

Dowhower, S. L. (1991). Speaking of prosody: Fluency's unattended bedfellow. *Theory into Practice, 30(3),* 165-175.

Durham, J. (1997). On time and poetry. *The Reading Teacher, 51 (1),* 76-79.

Gonzales, P. C., & Elijah, D. V. (1975). Rereading: Effect on error patterns and performance levels on the IRI. *The Reading Teacher, 28,* 647-652.

Greenberg, E. R. (1996). One-third of applicants lack job skills. *HR Focus, 73,* 24.

Greenwood, C. R., Granger, D., Bailey, V., Carta, J. J., Dorsey, D., Kohler, F. W., Nelson, C., Rotholz, D., & Schulte, D. (1987). Field replication of classwide peer tutoring. *Journal of Applied Behavior Analysis, 20(2),* 151-160.

Heckleman, R. A. (1969). A neurological impress method. *Academic Therapy, 4,* 277-282.

Hiebert, E. H. (1980). Peers as reading teachers. *Language Arts* 57(8), 877-881.

Henk, W. A., Helfeldt, J. S., & Platt, J. M. (1986). Developing reading fluency in learning disabled students. *Teaching Exceptional Children, 18,* 202-206.

Huey, E. (1908/1968). *The psychology and pedagogy of reading,* Cambridge, MA: Massachusetts Institute of Technology Press.

Jensen, E. (1998). *Teaching with the brain in mind.* Alexandria, VA: Association for Supervision and Curriculum Development.

Kelly, P. R. (1995). Round robin reading: Considering alternative instructional practices that make more sense. *Reading Horizons, 36(2)*, 99-115.

Koskinen, P. S., & Blum, I. H. (1986). Paired repeated reading: A classroom strategy for developing fluent reading. *The Reading Teacher, 40*, 70-75.

LaBerge, D., & Samuels, S. J. (1974). Toward a theory of automatic information processing in reading. *Cognitive Psychology, 6*, 293-323.

Lovett, M. W. (1987). A developmental approach to reading disability: Accuracy and speed criteria of normal and deficient reading skill. *Child Development, 58*, 234-260.

Martinez, M., Roser, N.L., & Strecker, S. (1998). I never thought I could be a star: A readers theatre ticket to fluency. *The Reading Teacher, 52(4)*, 326-334.

Mastropieri, M. A., Leinart, A., & Scruggs, T. E. (1999). Strategies to increase reading fluency. *Intervention in School and Clinic, 34(5)*, 278-283.

Mathes, P. G., Fuchs, D., Fuchs, L. S., Henley, A. M., & Sanders, A. (1994). Increasing strategic reading practice with Peabody classwide peer tutoring. *Learning Disabilities Research & Practice, 9(1)*, 44-48.

Mathes, P. G., & Fuchs, L. S. (1993). Peer-mediated reading instruction in special education resource rooms. *Research & Practice, 8(4)*, 233-243.

Mathes, P. G., Simmons, D. C., & Davis, B. I. (1992). Assisted reading techniques for developing reading fluency. *Reading Research and Instruction, 31(4)*, 70-77.

May, F. (1994). *Reading as communication.* Upper Saddle River, NJ: Prentice-Hall, Inc.

McCurdy, B., Cundari, L., & Lentz, F. E. (1990). Enhancing instructional efficiency: An examination of time delay and the opportunity to observe instruction. *Education and Treatment of Children, 13(3)*, 226-238.

Nathan, R. G., & Stanovich, K. E. (1991). The causes and consequences of differences in reading fluency. *Theory Into Practice, 30(3)*, 176-184.

O'Shea, L. J., Sindelar, P. T., & O'Shea, D. J. (1985). The effects of repeated readings and attentional cues on reading fluency and comprehension. *Journal of Reading Behavior, 17(2)*, 129-142.

Perfect, K. A. (1999). Rhyme and reason: Poetry for the heart and head. *The Reading Teacher, 52(7)*, 728-737.

Perfetti, C. A. & Lesgold, A. M. (1979). Coding and comprehension in skilled reading and implications for reading instruction. In L. B. Resnick & P. A. Weaver (Eds.), *Theory and practice of early reading* (pp. 57-84). Hillsdale, NJ: Erlbaum.

Rasinski, T. V. (1988). Making repeated readings a functional part of classroom reading instruction. *Reading Horizons, 28*, 250-254.

Rasinski, T. V. (1989). Fluency for everyone: Incorporating fluency instruction in the classroom. *The Reading Teacher, 42*, 690-693.

Rasinski, T. V. (1990). Effects of repeated reading and listening-while-reading on reading fluency. *Journal of Educational Research, 83(3)*, 147-150.

Samuels, S. J. (1979). The method of repeated readings. *The Reading Teacher, 32*, 403-408.

Schreiber, P. A. (1980). On the acquisition of reading fluency. *The Reaching Teacher, 12(3)*, 177-186.

Schreiber, P. A. (1991). Understanding prosody's role in reading acquisition. *Theory Into Practice, 30(3)*, 158-164.

Sindelar, P. T., Monda, L. E., & O'Shea, L. J. (1990). Effects of repeated readings on instructional- and mastery-level readers. *Journal of Educational Research, 83(4)*, 220-226.

Smith, D. D. (1979). The improvement of children's oral reading through the use of teacher modeling. *Journal of Learning Disabilities, 12(3)*, 39-42.

Stayter, F. Z., & Allington, R. L. (1991). Fluency and the understanding of texts. *Theory Into Practice, 30(3)*, 143-148.

Utley, C. A., Mortweet, S. L., & Greenwood, C. R. (1997). Peer-mediated instruction and interventions. *Focus on Exceptional Children, 29*, 1-23.

Zutell, J., & Rasinski, T. V. (1991). Training teachers to attend to their students' oral reading fluency. *Theory Into Practice, 30(3)*, 211-217.

## Books Read by Participants

Sobel, D. J. (1963). *Encyclopedia Brown, Boy Detective*. New York: Bantam Books.
Warner, G. C. (1942). *The Boxcar Children*. Niles, IL: Albert Whitman & Company.
Wilder, L. I. (1932). *Little House in the Big Woods*. New York: HarperCollins Books.

## Appendix A. Sample of Teacher Notes From a 100 Word Passage

|  | miscues | Speed | wpm |
|---|---|---|---|
| Student #1 | ✓✓✓✓✓ | 1:40 = | 74 wpm |
| Student #2 | ✓✓ | 1:20 = | 92 wpm |

Formula for figuring wpm

$$\frac{100 - \#\,of\ miscues}{student's\ time\ in\ sec.} \times \frac{60\,sec}{1\ min.} = \underline{\qquad}\ wpm$$

## Appendix B. Student Self-Evaluation Form for Duplication

My name_____  My peer's name _____

Date _____

### Read the passage once.

Describe your reading. Use words like choppy, smooth, fast, slow, full of expression, lacks expression, ran sentences together, etc.

_____

_____

### Now read the same passage again until your reading gets better.

Discuss with your partner how your reading improved. Use words like faster, smoother, better expression, paused at periods, didn't run sentences together, less-choppy, etc.

_____

_____

**Appendix C. Sample of Teacher Notes
During the Rereading of a Short Passage**

Title, p.4, paragraph 2

3/10

(1st time)
won't –
||| wonderful ||||||| figured /   finger
|||||||| teasing ||||| thoughtful |   testing ⊘   (30 sec)

(2nd time)
wouldn't
||| wonderful |||||||| figured /   finger/sc
|||||||| / ||| ||| thoughtful |   though –   (27 sec)

(3rd time)
||| | |||||||| | / though-ful/sc
|||||||||| |||||| thoughtful   (25 sec)

(4th time)
||| ||||||||||| /
|||||||||||||||||| |   (21 sec)
very fluent!

KEY:  tallies = words read correctly
words = miscues
sc = self-correction
⊘ = omitted word

## Appendix D. Sample of Teacher Notes During a One Minute Reading

Title, p. 13

3/9   ||||| ||| ||||| || ||| |||| ||| sq-/squad

(1st reading)   biggest ||||| ||||  ex-/sc English   channel ||||| inky

|||||  ?/couldn't  |||| ||||| || /   ≈ 55 words

(2nd reading)   mid-/midnight ||||| |||| ||| ||| ||| |||||

||||||| || channel ||||| in-?/inky |||||

|||||| || ||/ bud-/buddies || |||||||| |||   ≈ 71 words

(3rd reading)   |   ||||||||||||| ||| ||| |||| |||

||||||| ||| ||| ||||||| could/sc couldn't ||)

|||||| ||| bud-/buddies ||||| ||||||||||
in-/Infantry |||||||||||   ≈ 85 words

KEY:  tallies = words read correctly
words = miscues
sc = self-correct
∅ = omitted word

## Appendix E. Classroom Applications of Repeated Reading

### Recorded Books
Older students record short books for younger students. Before recording, students practice to attain fluency (Conte & Humphreys, 1989; Rasinski, 1988).

### Cross-age Tutoring
Older low-level readers read easier books with younger students. This allows older students to read materials at their independent reading level without embarrassment. Moreover, as they assist younger readers, they become more aware of reading cues that they themselves must watch more closely (Rasinski, 1988).

### Board Games
Students play games that require reading short texts. For example, in Monopoly, players read aloud task cards (Rasinski, 1988).

### Readers' Theatre and Plays
Students rehearse and then perform for an audience. This is practical, meaningful, and fun (Clark, 1995; Kelly, 1995; Martinez, Roser, & Strecker, 1998; Rasinski, 1989).

### Storytelling
Children practice reading a story until they can retell it to an audience in their own words (Rasinski, 1988).

### Shared Book Experience
Groups of students read chorally and repeatedly from a common text. It may be from a big book, on chart paper, or on an overhead. When a common text is shared, enthusiasm spreads, heightening interest in the topic and in reading (Rasinski, 1988).

### Songs
Children sing songs pertaining to the curriculum, seasons, or holidays. They generally enjoy singing their favorites again and again (Rasinski, 1988).

### Poetry
Durham (1997), Perfect (1999), and Rasinski (1988) all state that poetry begs to be repeated, thus giving children the practice they need to become fluent. Individual pages of poetry may be passed out, read silently first as students are receiving their copies, then read together, and kept in student folders for subsequent rereadings. Students may also memorize poetry and perform it for peers, other classes, or parents at a "Poetry and Drama" night.

## Echo Reading

The teacher reads a portion of text, modeling fluent reading. Students then echo the text, copying the fluent intonation, stress, and expression (Anderson, 1981; Carbo, 1995, 1996; Kelly, 1995).

## Silent Passage Preview (SPP)

Students silently read a passage to themselves before reading aloud with a partner or to the class. Materials for SPP include journal entries, reports, notes going home to parents, directions, science texts, and chapters in novels. This is beneficial to student performance as well as to self-concept (Dahl, 1974; Rasinski, 1990).

## Individual Repeated Reading

Working individually with the teacher, students read a 50-200 word portion of text while the teacher records errors and speed. The same text is repeated, with the teacher again recording errors and speed. This continues several times until either the desired level of fluency or a plateau is reached. The student is made aware of his progress after each reading. This activity is generally motivating for children, as they can easily track their progress and are encouraged by their success (Rasinski, 1988; Samuels, 1979).

## Classwide Repeated Reading

Students and their partners take turns reading and listening. While one reads a passage aloud several times, the other reads silently with him. Together they analyze the reader's strengths and weaknesses. After the first reader has achieved the desired level of fluency, students reverse roles (Koskinen & Blum, 1986). This strategy can be used with basal or literature-based reading programs.

## Listening-While-Reading/Recorded Books/Taped Books

Known by several names, this activity uses a tape recorder, head set, and book. Students repeatedly read aloud with a fluent recording of a picture book. They practice the same book daily until the desired level of fluency is reached. It is helpful for students to keep a log of these sessions, keeping track of the number of times they practice each book and describing their reading. Once they are fluent, students delight in celebrating their success by reading aloud to another adult in the school or at home. It is important that students actually read aloud and not simply listen, and sessions should last no longer than twenty minutes. More difficult books are gradually introduced (Carbo, 1978; Chomsky, 1976; Conte & Humphreys, 1989).

## Appendix F. Classroom Applications of Paired Reading

**Paired Reading During Reading Instruction**

Students read in teacher-or self-chosen pairs. The teacher moves from student to student taking notes on reading performance. This impresses upon the students the value of the activity, resulting in on-task behavior and enabling him to obtain the information needed to make further instructional decisions. Because partners act as models for one another, it is imperative that dyads do not have two weak readers. Using this strategy is not advisable for LD classrooms. Follow-up activities should be explained prior to reading, as pairs will finish reading at different times (Delquadri, et al., 1986; Greenwood et al., 1987; Hiebert, 1980; Koskinen & Blum, 1986).

**Paired Reading Across the Curriculum**

Students read short passages in mathematics, science, and social studies texts with a partner. If desirable, a competent reader may later read the same text aloud to the whole class (Delquadri, et al., 1986; Greenwood, et al., 1987; Hiebert, 1980; Koskinen & Blum, 1986).

**Paired Reading of Directions**

Students read directions to assignments and put them into their own words with a partner before someone is called upon to read them aloud.

**Peabody Classwide Paired Reading**

In pairs, students complete certain tasks while they read. One task is "paragraph shrinking," in which the reader retells the paragraph in 10 words or less. The other task is a prediction relay, in which partners take turns making predictions and checking them (Koskinen & Blum, 1986).

## Appendix G. Classroom Applications of Demonstration

The following strategies are listed in order from High Teacher Involvement/Low Student Independence to Low Teacher Involvement/High Student Independence. While some methods should obviously be implemented as good general practices, others should be implemented based on the needs of individual students. Students ought be placed in the most independent situation possible (Carbo, 1995, 1996).

### Reading Aloud

Fiction, non-fiction, biographies, poetry, rhymes, and a variety of other genre are read aloud to the class. When selecting materials, it is important to keep in mind that students' listening vocabularies are greater than their reading vocabulary and that listening leads to further acquisition of word knowledge (Carbo, 1995, 1996). Therefore, it is beneficial to choose books slightly above students' reading level.

### Shared Reading

Big books, paragraphs composed by students, or poems on an overhead or chart paper are read together as a class. Students read aloud with the teacher as she points to the words. It is important that everyone read from the same text and that it be an enjoyable and relaxing experience (Carbo, 1995, 1996).

### Explicit Teaching of Phrasing

A sentence or two is written where all students can view it, and the teacher leads a discussion about "chunking" words into phrases, stressing individual words, and using proper voice intonation. Volunteers take turns reading the sentence aloud to the class in an attempt to read it fluently. This activity should have a playful air and be fast-paced (Schrieber 1980, 1991).

### Neurological Impress Method (NIM)

A mature reader and student read simultaneously. The mature reader sits slightly behind and on the right side of the student. He points to the text and gently reads into the students' right ear at a slightly faster rate than the student until the student is able to take over pointing to and reading the text (Heckleman, 1969). Parent or high school volunteers can be trained to use this method.

### Echo Reading

When reading a poem, science book, literature, or other text, the teacher reads a short passage, modeling good phrasing and expression. Students echo, copying the phrasing and expression (Carbo, 1995, 1996; Kelly, 1995).

## Choral Reading

Students and teacher read text simultaneously with no repetition. Unlike echo reading, no prior modeling is given. This can be done with poems, literature, and reading materials across the curriculum (Carbo, 1995, 1996; Kelly, 1995).

## Recorded Books

Students read aloud with a recording of chapter books, classroom theme books, or picture books. Books pertaining to classroom themes can be recorded and placed in a listening station through which students rotate during science or social studies activities. In this activity, students receive the support of a fluent reader but do not reread any text. It is important that the recording be slow enough for the reader to read aloud with it (Carbo, 1978).

## Listener Passage Preview (LPP)

After directing students to note his expression and phrasing, the teacher reads aloud the first few paragraphs of a text while students follow along in their own books. Later, in partners or individually, students read the same text *from the beginning*, rereading what was previewed and continuing as far as directed (Rasinski, 1990).

## Listening-While-Reading/Recorded Books/Taped Books

Known by several names, this method uses a tape recorder, head set, and book. Students repeatedly read aloud with a fluent recording of a picture book. They practice the same book daily until the desired level of fluency is reached. It is helpful for students to keep a log of these sessions, keeping track of the number of times they practice each book and describing their reading. Once they are fluent, students delight in celebrating their success by reading aloud to another adult in the school or at home. It is important that students actually read aloud and not simply listen, and sessions should last no longer than twenty minutes. More difficult books are gradually introduced (Carbo, 1978; Chomsky, 1976; Conte & Humphreys, 1989).

## Paired Reading

Students read with partners. The teacher moves from student to student taking notes on reading performance. This impresses upon the students the value of the activity, which results in better on-task behavior while enabling the teacher to obtain information needed to make further instructional decisions. Because pairs will finish reading at different times, follow-up activities must be explained prior to reading. Partners act as models for one another, making it imperative that partnerships do not have two weak readers. Using this strategy is not advisable for LD classrooms (Delquadri, et al., 1986; Greenwood et al., 1987; Hiebert, 1980; Koskinen & Blum, 1986).

**Peabody Classwide Paired Reading**

In pairs, students complete certain tasks while they read. One task is "paragraph shrinking," in which the reader retells the paragraph in ten words or less. The other task is a prediction relay, in which partners take turns making predictions and checking them. The stronger reader is demonstrating more fluent reading for the weaker reader (Koskinen & Blum, 1986).

# ELEMENTARY
# VOICES

# CHILDREN'S AESTHETIC AND ETHNIC INVOLVEMENT IN RESPONSE TO MULTICULTURAL PICTURE BOOKS

**Rebecca P. Harlin**

Barry University

**Lisbeth Dixon-Krauss**

Florida International University

## Abstract

*This purpose of this study was to categorize young children's verbal responses to eight multiethnic storybooks, especially their comments related to story elements, aesthetic involvement, personal life experiences, and ethnicity. The sample included 293 children from kindergarten through third grade enrolled in public elementary schools and was comprised of 69% Hispanic, 15% African-American and Caribbean, 14% Caucasian, and 2% Asian. Children were assigned to small groups of 4-7 members for read-aloud sessions. Data were collected from audiotaped responses to three discussion prompts. Results showed that most children made comments about the character, plot, and setting of the books. Children's comments about all eight books were mostly positive. The majority of the children connected the books to their own lives by identifying relevant people, personal events, and places. Few ethnic-focused responses for all three discussion questions were found.*

With each census, it is evident that the United States population becomes increasingly diverse due to immigration from Latin America, the Pacific Rim, and the Caribbean. In response to these changing demographics, schools have incorporated multicultural books into the curriculum. School librarians have purchased collections of Hispanic, Asian, African-American, and Native American children's literature to reflect the cultures, languages, and values of various ethnic groups. Many schools use multicultural literature as one means of developing culturally literate and sensitive citizens (Gersten, 1995). Educators claimed that reading multicultural literature encourages children to reaffirm the values of their own culture and come to appreciate those of others (Creany et al, 1993; Rasinski & Padak, 1990).

To compete successfully in the global marketplace, American schools must produce students who are not only bilingual and biliterate, but also culturally aware (Yokota, 1993). Through multicultural literature, children develop awareness of the uniqueness of each culture as well as the similarities in beliefs and values across cultures. Furthermore, it is especially important that Caucasian children in monoethnic classrooms are exposed to other cultures to avoid the perception that most of the world's significant or important people are white (Abbott & Grose, 1998; Macphee, 1997). Research studies of how multicultural literature was used in elementary classrooms addressed questions related to three aspects: a) development of children's awareness and sensitivity to other cultures and languages, b) the effectiveness of the books in building minority children's self-concepts or enhancing their cultural self-esteem, and c) comparisons of children's responses to the same book across ethnic groups.

How can ethnic folktales, realistic fiction, and non-fiction books introduce children to other cultures and languages? Several recent studies included mostly Caucasian children along with smaller percentages of Asian, African-American, or Hispanic children (Abbott & Grose, 1998; Rosberg, 1995; Walker-Dalhouse, 1992). Teacher-guided discussions, children's spontaneous comments, children's written responses, and pictures of significant events provided the data sources in these studies. One study aimed to increase children's sensitivity to social issues (Macphee, 1997) while others examined the relationships between children's ethnic backgrounds and their critical thinking about character's actions (Commeyras & Guy, 1995; Walker-Dalhouse, 1992). The results showed children experienced greater interest in the books' culture and language (Abbott & Grose, 1998; Rosberg, 1995), made better connections to their own culture, and increased participation in discussions across time (Macphee, 1997; Walker-Dalhouse, 1992). Realistic fiction seemed to be more effective than ethnic folktales in developing young children's appreciation and empathy for characters and in making connections to their own lives (Macphee, 1997).

What happens when Asian or African-American children respond to literature from their own cultures? Studies examining the link between children's ethnicity and their responses to multicultural literature found several connections. Both Asian and African-American children not only comprehended the stories fully, but also drew personal relevance to the characters and showed greater involvement during the reading (Diller, 1999; Liaw, 1995; Smith, 1995). In addition, Smith (1995) found that the fifth graders' writing reflected the styles, language, and themes of the African-American literature they had read. Subsequently, the fifth graders selected more African-American books for their recreational reading. For the Chinese first graders, Liaw (1995) found that the book's illustrations determined whether or not the children liked the book.

All studies found a range of children's responses to each book, not one common response.

How do children from varying ethnic backgrounds respond to the same book? In studies of multiethnic classrooms, researchers collected data through individual interviews and written responses. When the results for both primary (Altieri, 1993; Towell et al, 1997) and intermediate children (Altieri, 1996) were compared, children's ethnicity did not significantly affect the level of response. Young children identified with characters in stories based on plots, main character's personality, and similarities to the main character's interest. For these children, a good story transcended ethnicity—the culture of the main character was secondary to an interesting, realistic plot. (Altieri, 1993; Towell et al, 1997). No differences in children's ability to make inferences, level of engagement, aesthetic involvement, or character judgement were found across ethnic groups. For older children (fifth and seventh graders) however, ethnicity did affect the child's ability to place self into the character's shoes (Altieri, 1996). Caucasian children identified less often with characters in African-American stories than for those in Hispanic or white books.

## Purpose of the Study

Previous research found that reading aloud contributes to a child's concept of story (Nistler, 1989) and when children read culturally familiar text, their comprehension increased (Droop & Verhoeven, 1998). Children were likely to draw personal relevance from these stories when the protagonists were close to the children's age (Liaw, 1995). Along with their increased interest and engagement with these texts, children were more likely to state high quality aesthetic responses (Altieri, 1993). Since smaller numbers of Hispanic and African-American children were included in the multiethnic samples of previous research (Altieri, 1993; 1996; Rosberg, 1995; Towell et al 1997), this study was designed to increase the representation of these groups.

The present study is designed to connect Vygotsky's theory on concept development (Vygotsky, 1986) to literacy learning by examining how children's everyday, spontaneous concepts are restructured into scientific, "schooled" concepts through literacy activities with children's literature (Dixon-Krauss, 1996). These literacy activities, in the form of discussion groups, allow children to acquire academic "schooled" knowledge by building on a foundation of personal experience. The manner in which the discussions are conducted affects the on-going social interaction of the groups, which in turn affects how the children's thinking develops. Previous studies described the limitations of teachers and researchers conducting discussions that were too adult-focused and interfered with children's reasoning (Abbott & Grose, 1998; Commeyras & Guy, 1995; Wollman-Bonilla & Werchadlo, 1995). Studies intending to encourage children's personal responses to literature demonstrated the advantages of using prompts rather than a prescribed series of discussion questions (Bleich, 1978; Kelly, 1990).

In the study reported here, open-ended questions were used to tap children's self-reflections and identify what they see in the stories, not what an adult directs them to see. Multicultural realistic fiction, representing Hispanic/ Latino and African-American/ Caribbean populations of South Florida, was read to the children prior to their literature discussion. These books with realistic characters of Hispanic/Latino and African-American/Caribbean ethnicity were selected to tap students' everyday spontaneous concepts related to their own ethnic backgrounds. The books were also selected because their main characters were close in age to the children in the research sample. The study's purpose was to categorize young children's responses to multiethnic storybooks by analyzing their comments related to story elements, aesthetic involvement, personal life experiences, and those related to ethnicity. The following questions were addressed:

1. How does reading culturally familiar text aloud to children affect their story comprehension?
2. What types of affective responses do culturally familiar texts elicit?
3. What types of personal experiences do children connect to culturally familiar texts?
4. Do culturally familiar texts elicit ethnic-related responses?

# Method
## Subjects

The sample included 293 primary grade children including 21 kindergarten, 85 first grade, 96 second grade, and 91 third grade public elementary school students. Many children were recent immigrants or first generation American citizens from Central and South America, Cuba, Haiti, the Bahamas, and Jamaica within the ethnic distribution of 69% Hispanic, 15% African-American and Caribbean, 14% Caucasian, and 2% Asian. Children were assigned to small groups of four to seven members for read-aloud sessions. Twenty-eight of the groups were ethnically heterogeneous and twenty-five of the groups were homogeneous. Group membership remained constant across all read-aloud sessions.

## Procedures

Preservice teachers in their field schools conducted small group read-aloud sessions each week for eight weeks. The preservice teachers were juniors enrolled in a primary literacy methods course. Preservice teachers received explicit instruction in adult-child storybook reading practices including book handling, reading with expression, and responsive engagement.

The preservice teachers received further support by analyzing adult child videotapes of storybook reading and through instructor modeling. The preservice teachers read a total of eight multicultural books to the children, presenting one story with discussion session per week. Hispanic/Latino and African American/ Caribbean realistic fiction picture books were read in an alternating weekly sequence. Previous studies found that realistic fiction genre tended to engage young children better than ethnic folktales (Altieri, 1993; 1996; Rosberg, 1995; Towell et al, 1997). Books read were also sequenced from least to most difficult based on story complexity and book length, ranging from 20 pages to 40 pages (See Appendix A for books listed in the sequence they were read to the children).

Each read-aloud session was audiotaped. The preservice teachers introduced each book with a brief discussion of the cover picture and title. The following three discussion question prompts were introduced prior to the reading and discussed after reading: (a) Question 1, What did you notice in the story? (b) Question 2, How did the story make you feel? and (c) Question 3, What does the story remind you of in your own life? These prompts were designed to encourage children's thinking and personal responses to books (Bleich, 1978; Kelly & Farnan, 1989; Kelly, 1990). Children commented freely during the reading, but these comments were not solicited or transcribed. After the book was read, each child responded orally to discussion question 1. The preservice teachers called on children in a random sequence to ensure an individual personal response from every child in the group. This continued for discussion question 2 and then for question 3.

## Results

The audiotaped responses for the read-aloud sessions were transcribed, sorted to identify categories, and then analyzed using descriptive statistics. The two researchers independently read and categorized each child's responses to the three questions. Consensus for categorizing responses was reached through discussion. Responses for Question 1 were sorted into story element categories of author style, plot, problem, characters, setting, and book format categories. Examples of responses for each category are shown in Figure 1.

Responses in the story element categories identified for Question 1 were reported in percentages in Table 1. For all children grades K-3, the highest percentage of students noticed the characters (mean =39%), followed by both the plot and setting (21%), and then the problem (13%). These results are consistent with previous findings that reading realistic fiction aloud was effective in developing young children's appreciation and empathy for characters (Macphee, 1997; Nistler, 1989).

Examination of the story element responses by grade level showed an

**Figure 1. Question 1 Response Categories**

| Category | Examples |
|---|---|
| Author Style | "The author gave a lot of detail about their journey"<br>—*How Many Days to America?*<br>"The title matched the story because he took a trip."<br>—*The Trip* |
| Plot | "That when the baby grows, the tree also grows."<br>—*Pablo's Tree*<br>"The man noticed that he really missed his grandmother and he still thinks about her."—*Bigmama's* |
| Characters | "The baby was cute when he came home."—*Pablo's Tree*<br>"The girls were different." *Margaret and Margarita* |
| Setting | "That they were in a big garden." *Isla*<br>"It was Halloween."—*The Trip* |
| Book Format | "The pictures looked like paintings."—*Aunt Flossie's Hats*<br>"The pictures were small." *Margaret and Margarita* |

increase toward noticing the plot plus the problem, from 25% in kindergarten to 45% in third grade. There was a substantial increase in plot focus from kindergarten to first grade (12% to 29%) and from second to third grade (17% to 27%). These results coincide with previous research findings that by first grade most children have demonstrated knowledge of setting, character, and plot (Droop & Verhoeven, 1998; Nistler, 1989). Furthermore, the results show that the children's concepts of story continued to develop and expand with age when culturally familiar texts were read.

**Table 1. Percent of Story Element Responses for Question 1**

| Story Element | K | 1 | 2 | 3 | Mean (K-3) |
|---|---|---|---|---|---|
| Character | 47 | 34 | 40 | 35 | 39 |
| Plot | 12 | 29 | 17 | 27 | 21 |
| Problem | 13 | 11 | 11 | 18 | 13 |
| Setting | 24 | 20 | 24 | 17 | 21 |
| Author Style | 4 | 5 | 7 | 3 | 5 |
| Book Format | – | 1 | 1 | – | 1 |

*Note. Question 1: What did you notice in the story?*

## Table 2. Percent of Story Affect Responses for Question 2

| STORY AFFECT | K | 1 | 2 | 3 | MEAN (K-3) |
|---|---|---|---|---|---|
| Positive | 76 | 73 | 63 | 73 | 71 |
| Negative | 9 | 15 | 16 | 14 | 13 |
| Aroused | 15 | 11 | 19 | 9 | 14 |
| Disengaged | – | 1 | 2 | 3 | 2 |

*Note. Question 2: How did the story make you feel?*

The affective categories identified for Question 2 responses included positive, negative, aroused, and disengaged. The categories were identified to reflect polar opposites of emotions and their connotations as follows: a) positive (happy) vs. negative (sad), and b) aroused (emotionally involved) vs. disengaged (emotionally uninvolved). Examples of these positive responses included, "I was happy because I know what 'C'est la vie' means." (*Tap-Tap*). Examples of negative responses are "Lonely, because he had no one to play with."(*The Trip); "*It made me feel sad when they said her grandfather died because my grandfather died last year." (*Isla*). "I was curious to see how many people could fit on the bus." (*Tap-Tap*) is an example of an aroused comment. Disengaged responses resembled this example, "It doesn't make me feel anything." (*Bigmama's*)

In the affective responses to Question 2 for all children grades K-3, most of the students made positive comments (71%) about the story (see Table 2). Only 13% of the comments were negative, 14% aroused, and 3% disengaged. The positive responses remained consistent across all grade levels from Kindergarten through third, 76%, 73%, 63%, 73%, respectively, indicating that the children seemed to enjoy the culturally familiar realistic fiction stories.

## Table 3. Percent of Personal Experience Responses for Question 3

| STORY AFFECT | K | 1 | 2 | 3 | MEAN (K-3) |
|---|---|---|---|---|---|
| People | 22 | 66 | 43 | 53 | 46 |
| Places | 19 | 2 | 11 | 9 | 10 |
| Events | 41 | 26 | 39 | 31 | 34 |
| Objects | 11 | 5 | 5 | 1 | 6 |
| Activities | 8 | 1 | 1 | 5 | 4 |

*Note. Question 3: What does the story remind you of in your own life?*

Responses for Question 3 were grouped into personal life experience categories labeled people, places, events, objects, and activities. When asked to relate the stories to their own lives, 46% of the children (K-3) identified people they knew, 34% described personal events and 10% identified places they had lived or visited (see Table 3). The highest percentage of students in first (66%), second (43%), and third (53%) grades related the stories to people, while the highest percentage of kindergarten responses (41%) related the story to events. An example of the personal experience responses in the people category included "The lady reminded me of my grandma 'cause she was old', too" (*Aunt Flossie's Hats*). "When I got my parrot, it was laying on the ground having babies" (*Isla*). is representative of the events responses. Again, these results highlight the effectiveness of culturally familiar realistic fiction in developing young children's ability to identify with characters and make connections to their own lives (Altieri, 1993; Macphee, 1997; Towell et al, 1997).

**Table 4. Percent of Ethnic Related Responses**

| Grade Level | Question 1 | Question 2 | Question 3 | Mean % |
|:---:|:---:|:---:|:---:|:---:|
| K | 2 | 0 | 9 | 4 |
| 1 | 5 | 2 | 11 | 6 |
| 2 | 8 | 4 | 1 | 4 |
| 3 | 9 | 5 | 15 | 10 |
| Mean % | 6 | 3 | 9 | |

All responses to the three questions were analyzed to determine the percent of ethnic-related responses at each grade level. Ethnic-focused responses included any references made to a language other than English (Spanish, Haitian, etc.), a country or geographic location other than the United States, or a specific nationality of the story characters or the children themselves. Examples of ethnic-related responses were, "Those people are black like me!" As shown in Table 4, the percent of ethnic related responses for all grade levels was low, ranging from 0 to 15%. The most ethnic-related responses for all grade levels occurred for Question 3 when children were prompted to relate the stories to their own lives (mean =9%). This small percentage of ethnic-related responses could be expected due to the diversity of this sample of children and the frequency of their encounters with members of multiethnic groups in their daily lives. Another interesting trend was that the oldest students, third graders, had the largest percentage of ethnic related responses for all three questions (9%, 5%, and 15%). These findings are consistent with previous studies where the culture of the characters was secondary to an interesting, realistic plot (Altieri, 1993; Towell et al, 1997)

One of the books, *Margaret and Margarita,* was written half in English and half in Spanish. This book did receive the most notice in the students' responses pertaining to ethnicity, but they still mentioned the language less than half of the time. Raul's comment, "Special to be Puerto Rican and to know the language" reflected a positive response to the book's language. In contrast Michael, a Haitian boy, had a negative response, "Stupid because I don't understand Spanish." When children remarked on the book's language, their responses were more like Eric's, an African-American, "One girl speaks Spanish and one girl speaks English."

## Implications of the Study

Since this study included larger numbers of Hispanic and African-American subjects than previous research, the findings expand the understanding of children's responses to multiethnic books by increasing the representation of these groups. Furthermore, the results demonstrate the effectiveness of using prompts rather than a series of discussion questions as a means of encouraging children's thinking and personal responses to literature. The open-ended questions used in this study did enable children to self-reflect and to identify what they saw in each book without adult's explicit direction. These findings add to the body of work on reading aloud to children as a means of developing their story concepts and increasing comprehension by reading culturally familiar text.

Analysis of the number and types of primary children's responses to the three open-ended questions reaffirms the common sense interpretation that young children identify with the characters and their actions in realistic fiction. When children were prompted by Question 1 to reflect on what they noticed in the stories, most of the responses were in the category of characters, followed by plot and problem. These results were consistent with findings in previous studies of children's responses to multiethnic literature (Altieri, 1993, 1996; Towell, et al., 1997). The majority of the responses in the people and events categories for Question 3 further support the use of multicultural realistic fiction for developing young children's appreciation and empathy for characters, and helping young children build connections between the stories and their own lives (Macphee, 1997).

The low number of ethnic related responses to all three question prompts (10% or less) raises some interesting questions on the effectiveness of using multicultural literature to enhance children's cultural awareness and sensitivity. Is it possible that children in this study were exposed to ethnically diverse groups of people in their schools, so they simply did not notice the ethnicity of the characters in the stories? Or could these children already possess high levels of cultural awareness? Perhaps these children may, in light of their environment, expect to meet characters of various ethnicities in the books they read. If multicultural books elicit children's sensitivity and ethnic aware-ness, how do the age of the children, and the level of diversity they already experience in their classroom settings affect this?

Previous researchers have been unable to identify specifically at what age or developmental level ethnicity in children's literature begins to make a difference in reader response (Towell et al, 1997). In the study reported here, ethnic-related responses began to increase at third grade level for books read and discussed. Further investigation of the interactions of children's ethnicity to their cultural sensitivity and awareness needs to be clarified. Future studies should investigate the effects of multiple readings and discussions of the same book on the intensity of children's responses.

Within this study's sample, half of the small groups were ethnically homogeneous, while half were heterogeneous. Both were representative of the ethnic composition of their classroom and school populations. A major-ity of these students were from countries or islands represented in the sto-ries. Many had heard stories or recently visited their native countries. It would seem that these children would mention more of the places in response to Question 3 and give more geographic responses related to ethnicity. These results were not found. Thus, a second avenue for further study is the role of group membership and the context of multiethnic literature discussion.

In summary, this study found reader-response prompts used with multiethnic storybooks effective in fostering higher order thinking in primary grade students beyond concrete literal retelling. These prompts afford young children opportunities to connect their prior knowledge to texts and to se-lect their relevant personal experiences for comparison. Over time, consis-tent use of small group discussions and reader-response prompts should enable young readers to explore various text interpretations, instead of seeking the one "correct" meaning.

---

# References

Abbott, S., & Grose, C. (1998). "I know English so many, Mrs. Abbott": Recipro-cal discoveries in a linguistically diverse classroom. *Language Arts, 75* (3), 175-184.

Altieri, J. L. (1993). African-American stories and literary responses: Does a child's ethnicity affect the focus of a response? *Reading Horizons, 33* (3), 236-244.

Altieri, J. L. (1996). Children's written responses to multicultural texts: A look at aesthetic involvement and the focuses of aesthetically complex responses. *Reading Research and Instruction, 35* (3), 237-248.

Commeyras, M., & Guy, J. (1995). Parole officers and the king's guards: Challenges in understanding children's thinking about stories. *Language Arts, 72(7)*, 512-516.

Creany, A. D., Couch, R. A., & Caropreso, E. J. (1993). Representation of culture in children's picture books. Paper presented at the Annual Conference of the International Visual Literacy Association, Rochester, NY. (ERIC Document Reproduction Service No. ED 370 570)

Diller, D. (1999). Opening the dialogue: Using culture as a tool in teaching young African American children. *The Reading Teacher, 52* (8), 820-828.

Dixon-Krauss, L. (1996). *Vygotsky in the classroom.* White Plains, NY: Longman.

Droop, M., & Verhoeven, L. (1998). Background knowledge, linguistic complexity, and second-language reading comprehension. *Journal of Literacy Research, 30* (2) 253-271.

Gersten, K. (1995). Multicultural education. Literacy report No.22. DeKalb, IL: Northern Illinois University. (ERIC Document Reproduction Service No. ED 386 709)

Kelly, P. R., & Farnan, N. (1989). Effects of a reader response approach on students' ways of thinking about text. Paper presented at the National Reading Conference, Austin, TX. (ERIC Document Reproduction Service No. ED 315 742)

Kelly, P. R. (1990) Guiding young students' response to literature. *The Reading Teacher, 43(7),* 464-470.

Liaw, M. (1995). Looking in the mirror: Chinese children's responses to Chinese children's books. *Reading Horizons, 35(3),* 185-198.

Macphee, J. S. (1997). "That's not fair!": A white teacher reports on white first graders' responses to multicultural literature. *Language Arts, 74* (1), 33-40.

Narahara, M. M. (1998). Gender stereotypes in children's picture books. Long Beach, CA: University of California. (ERIC Document Reproduction Service No. ED 419 248)

Nistler, R. J. (1987). Reading aloud as a contributor to a child's concept of story. Paper presented at the Annual Meeting of the National Council of Teachers of English, Los Angeles, CA. (ERIC Document Reproduction Service No. ED 291 071)

Rasinski, T. V., & Padak, N. (1990). Multicultural learning through children's literature. *Language Arts, 67,* 576-580.

Rosberg, M. (1995). Exploring language through multicultural literature. (ERIC Document Reproduction Service No. ED 389 175)

Smagorinsky, P. (1992). Towards a civic education in a multicultural society: Ethical problems in teaching literature. *English Education,* 24 (4), 212-228.

Smith, E. B. (1995). Anchored in our literature: Students responding to African American literature. *Language Arts, 72 (8),* 571-574.

Towell, J. H., Schulz, A., & Demetrulias, D.M. (1997). Does ethnicity really matter in literature for young children? Tulock, CA: California State University- Stanislaus. (ERIC Document Reproduction Service No. ED 412 571)

Vygotsky, L. S. (1986). *Thought and language* (A. Kozulin, trans.) Cambridge, MA: MIT Press.

Walker-Dalhouse, D. (1992). Using African-American literature to increase understanding. *The Reading Teacher, 45(6),* 416-422.

Wollman-Bonilla, J. E., & Werchadlo, B. (1995). Literature response journals in a first-grade classroom. *Language Arts, 72 (8),* 562-570.

Yokota, J. (1993). Issues in selecting multicultural children's literature. *Language Arts, 70* (3), 156-167.

## Appendix. Multiethnic Books Sequenced in the Order Read to the Children

Keats, E. J. (1978). *The Trip*. New York: Mulberry Books. (Hispanic/ Latino)

Crews, D. (1991). *Bigmama's*. New York: Greenwillow Books. (African-American)

Reiser, L. (1996). *Margaret and Margarita*. New York: Mulberry Books. (Hispanic/Latino)

Williams, K. L. (1994). *Tap Tap*. New York: Clarion Books. (African-American/ Caribbean)

Mora, P. 1994). *Pablo's Tree*. New York: Simon & Schuster Books for Young Readers. (Hispanic/ Latino)

Bunting, E. (1988). *How Many Days to America?* New York: Clarion Books. (African-American/Caribbean)

Dorros, A. (1995). *Isla*. New York: Puffin Books. (Hispanic/ Latino)

Howard, E. F. (1991). *Aunt Flossie's Hats (And Crab Cakes Later)*. New York: Clarion Books. (African-American)

# THE INSTANT PHONOGRAMS: PHONOGRAMS WORTH TEACHING

**Timothy Rasinski**
**Barbara O'Connor**

Kent State University

## Abstract

*Recent research has identified onsets and rimes (phonograms) as key phonemic units for decoding instruction. The present study identifies those rimes that may have the greatest instructional and reading utility—rimes that can be used to decode the high frequency words students encounter in their reading. We have termed these rimes the Instant Phonograms.*

Onsets and rimes have become very popular in reading instruction over the past few years. They refer to key parts of the syllable—onsets referring to any consonants that precede the sounded vowel in a syllable and rimes referring to the sounded vowel and any following letters within the syllable. In the word *take*, for example, *t* is the onset and *ake* is the rime. In the word *cap*, *c* is the onset and *ap* is the rime. And in the word *stripe*, *str* is the onset and *ipe* is the rime. Not all syllables need onsets (e.g., the word *ink*), but all syllables in English must have a vowel and therefore must also have a rime.

Recent research into word decoding has identified onsets and rimes as particularly useful units for instruction. For example, Adams notes ". . . they provide a means of introducing and exercising many printed words with relative efficiency and this . . . is in marked contrast to the slowness with which words can be developed through individual letter-sound correspondences" (1990, p. 324). Moreover, Johnston (1999) adds that word family instruction using letter chunking is more efficient than synthetic phonics approaches that expect readers to decode words in a letter-by-letter fashion. Through the years reading teachers have recognized the utility of teaching phonics using onsets and rimes, but have tended to have other names for rimes—word families, vowel clusters, and phonograms. According to researchers in word decoding, the use of word families helps readers remember sight words, decode unfamiliar words, and spell words accurately and efficiently (Ehri & Robbins, 1992; Goswami & Bryant, 1992; Johnston, 1999). Adams (1990) and Wylie and Durrell (1970) argue that the pronunciation of vowels is more stable and consistent within word families than across word families, thus making the teaching and learning of word families a valuable part of early decoding instruction.

Teacher educators, recognizing the importance of onsets and rimes in a phonics program, also advocate their inclusion in word study programs. As Vacca, Vacca, and Gove note,

> Phonics instruction needs to include the teaching of onsets and rimes. Instead of teaching phonics rules, teach children to use onsets and rimes . . . As children grow in their ability to identify words, it is easier and quicker for them to identify words when rimes and other letter patterns are taught than when they attempt to sound out all of the individual letters and blend them (2000, p. 163).

Although the utility of onsets and rimes as valuable units of instruction is widely accepted among word recognition scholars and reading teacher educators, the order in which they should be taught as well as the nature of instruction in the rimes has not been firmly established. The research reported in this paper makes a contribution toward the answer to the first question—in just what order should rimes or phongrams be taught?

Francine Johnston (1999) recognized the value of teaching rimes, and suggests a general developmental order in which they should be presented to children. Johnston suggests beginning with one short vowel word family at a time (consonant-vowel-consonant pattern), followed by comparing and contrasting word families that contain the same short vowel sound. Next, word families with other short vowel sounds and words that include consonant blends and digraphs should be added. This should be followed by studying vowel patterns across rimes, such as single short vowel words in CVC, CVCC, and CCVC patterns, compared to the same patterns using other short vowels. Then, word families containing the short and long sounds of the same vowel should be introduced and followed by word families with mixed long vowel sounds. According to Johnston, such a progression follows the documented development of children's spelling knowledge.

In response to Johnston's suggestions, Rasinski (2000) suggests that other principles may guide teachers in the order in which rimes are presented to students. Teachers may look to the students themselves for guidance in rimes that may be most manifest in students' minds. In particular, Rasinski suggests that students' first names may provide some proximal tangibility for students' interest and awareness of rimes. Names such as *Jim, Tom, Mike, Jane,* and *Jen,* especially if there are students who have those names in the classroom, may be some of the first rimes to teach to children.

Edward Fry (1998) weighs in on the debate over the order of rime instruction by suggesting that those rimes that produce the largest number of one syllable words may be the rimes that should be taught to students as they give students the opportunity to spell and decode the largest number of single syllable words. Fry identifies 37 rimes that will result, by adding an onset, in 654 one-syllable words.

Although Fry's list of phonograms is impressive, the words produced by the addition of an onset may not be among those commonly used and decoded by students in the primary grades. Moreover, Fry's list of common rimes does not take into account the multi-syllabic words that can be decoded. Other rimes, not on Fry's list, could actually be more useful in decoding longer words of more than one syllable, the very words that often cause students' the greatest difficulty in decoding.

Given the various possibilities and limitations for determining useful rimes to teach children, we decided to take an approach that combined Fry's quest for common rimes with his earlier list of high frequency words. We reasoned

## Table 1. Most Common Phonograms Based on the First 100 Instant Words

| PHONOGRAM | NUMBER OF OCCURRENCES IN FIRST 100 INSTANT WORDS |
|---|---|
| an[1] | 6 |
| o[2] | 5 |
| e[3] | 4 |
| er | 4 |
| is | 4 |
| ay | 3 |
| o[4] | 3 |
| ow[5] | 3 |
| as | 2 |
| at | 2 |
| all | 2 |
| en | 2 |
| in | 2 |
| ould | 2 |
| out | 2 |
| y[6] | 2 |
| TOTAL    16 | 48 |

[1]also include *ant*     [3]as in *he*     [5]as in *how*
[2]as in *do*     [4]as in *go*     [6]as in *my*

## Table 2. Most Common Phonograms Based on the 300 Instant Words

| PHONOGRAM | NUMBER OF OCCURRENCES IN FIRST 100 INSTANT WORDS |
|---|---|
| er | 19 |
| an +[1] | 17 |
| e[2] | 14 |
| y[3] | 11 |
| en + | 10 |
| in + | 10 |
| or + | 8 |
| al + | 7 |
| ay | 7 |
| is + | 6 |
| o[4] | 6 |
| a[5] | 5 |
| igh + | 5 |
| o[6] | 5 |
| ow[7] | 5 |
| el + | 4 |
| et | 4 |
| it | 4 |
| on + | 4 |
| ow[8] + | 4 |
| y[9] | 4 |
| ame | 3 |
| ear[10] | 3 |
| il + | 3 |
| ook[11] | 3 |
| ound | 3 |
| ould | 3 |
| out | 3 |
| un | 3 |
| us + | 3 |
| TOTAL    30 | 186 |

[1]addition signs (+) refers to following consonants that may be part of the rime (e.g. *and* and *ant*)
[2]as in *he*
[3]as in *carry*
[4]as in *go*
[5]schwa sounds as the first syllable in *around*
[6]as in *do*
[7]as in *low*
[8]as in *how* and *down*
[9]as in *my*
[10]as in *hear*
[11]as in *book*

that some of the most useful words for students to learn are the high frequency words that they regularly encounter in their reading. In 1980, Fry reported on 300 "Instant Words" that, according to his analysis of Carroll, Davies, and Richman's (1971) frequency count of five million running words, comprise approximately two-thirds of all the words that children encounter in their elementary school reading. If these words are worth learning early because of their high frequency nature, perhaps the most frequent rimes embedded within those words are the rimes that are most worth teaching students early in their school careers.

With this in mind, then, we made an analysis of the 300 words in Fry's list of "Instant Words." From each word on the list we abstracted the embedded rime(s). We tallied the rimes for the first 100 words that represent 50% of the words students encounter in their reading (Fry, 1980) and for the full corpus of 300 "Instant Words." Our findings are reported in Tables 1 and 2.

Fry (1980) reported that the first 100 of his Instant Words make up about 50% of all elementary school reading. According to our analysis, knowledge of just 16 rimes or phonograms can be used to decode nearly half of the first 100 Instant Words. Moreover, well over half (186) of the 300 words have embedded in them 30 phonograms. Thus, over half of the 300 most common words found in English writing can be decoded with knowledge of just 30 specific phonograms. We call these phonograms or rimes the Instant Phonograms.

## Discussion

The list of 30 common phonograms identified in Table 2, then, would appear to be good candidates for early instruction. Students' knowledge of just those 30 phonograms, easily taught in three to four months, would provide students with the knowledge to help them decode and spell a very significant percentage (between 20-30%) of the total number of words they will encounter in their reading during elementary school.

Plenty of contextual reading will provide students with good practice in identifying these key phonograms because of their high frequency nature. However, given their high utility, we recommend that more direct instructional efforts complement students' contextual reading. Word building activities, word sorts, word collecting, word walls, drawing students' attention to various features in key words, and word games are just some of the ways that teachers can provide direct and intensive instruction in recognizing and using the Instant Phonograms.

The Instant Phonograms can also be used diagnostically. Given their high utility value in reading and spelling, teachers should expect students to have mastery of the Instant Phonograms as early as possible in their school careers, certainly by the end of the second grade. For students who are experiencing difficulty in the decoding portion of reading, teachers can devise and administer a brief test made up of single and multiple syllable words containing the Instant Phonograms. Phonograms embedded in those words not easily and accurately recognized by students should become candidates for remedial instruction.

Although knowledge of phonograms or rimes is certainly important for student success in reading, questions regarding the identification of which phonograms to teach early in a student's school career and how those phonograms are best taught remain to be answered. The results of this study provide teachers and teacher educators with more valuable knowledge for making informed and productive instructional decisions in response to that first question.

---

# References

Adams, M. J. (1990). *Beginning to read.* Cambridge, MA: MIT Press.

Carroll, J. B., Davies, P., & Richman, B. (1971). *The American Heritage Word Frequency Book.* Boston: Houghton Mifflin.

Ehri, L. C., & Robbins, C. (1992). Beginners need some decoding skill to read words by analogy. *Reading Research Quarterly, 34,* 284-289.

Fry, E. (1980). The new instant word list. *The Reading Teacher, 34,* 284-289.

Fry, E. (1998). The most common phonograms. *The Reading Teacher, 51,* 620-622.

Goswami, U., & Bryant, P. (1992). Rhyme, analogy, and children's reading. In P. Gough, L. C. Ehri, & Trieman (Eds.), *Reading Acquisition* (pp. 49-63). Hillsdale, NJ: Erlbaum.

Invernizzi, M., Abouzeid, M., & Gill, J. T. (1994). Using students' invented spellings as a guide for spelling instruction that emphasizes word study. *Elementary School Journal, 95,* 155-167.

Johnston, F. R. (1999). The timing and teaching of word families. *The Reading Teacher, 53,* 64-75.

Rasinski, T. (2000). Balancing word family instruction. *The Reading Teacher, 54,* 126.

Vacca, J. L., Vacca, R. T., & Gove, M. K. (2000). *Reading and learning to read* (4th ed.). New York: Addison Wesley Longman, Inc.

Wylie, R. E., & Durrell, D. D. (1970). Teaching vowels through phonograms. *Elementary School Journal, 47,* 696-703.

# Tuesdays with Nora

## C. Richele O'Connor

Wright State University

## Abstract

*This manuscript describes how an elementary school principal (pseud-onym Nora), was the impetus for changes in course scheduling and program delivery for a university's post-baccalaureate, field-based teacher education program. With Nora's help, the instructor designed a course that served as a pre-field literacy methods class for university students and set up a tutoring program. The highlights of this course are presented as well as comments and reactions from the university students as they responded to the tutoring ses-sions. This change in program delivery serves as an example of how teacher education changes can occur when public school personnel, such as Nora, collaborate with university faculty.*

In creating effective university and public school partnerships, the success of such endeavors weighs heavily upon the creation of "powerfully pro-ductive symbioses" (Goodlad, 1994, p. 103). When Nora, the principal of Lincoln Elementary School, asked for help from the university, I leapt at the opportunity. Feeling that the time was ripe for forging a symbiotic relation-ship, I grasped for what I hoped would become a contextually-rich, field-based experience for my literacy methods students. Since my university and Nora's school, Lincoln Elementary, had been partners for several years, the groundwork had been laid for a field-based experience. Thus, I saw my role as guiding our preservice teachers toward reaching a goal that would please both Nora and myself. Together, we would all become partners as the result of a tutorial program that would benefit both the fourth graders and my university students.

The need for creating such partnerships has been well documented (National Commission on Teaching & America's Future, 1996). Since 1958, when representatives from both the public schools and higher education gathered at Bowling Green State University for a national conference, the cry for cooperation among the various stakeholders has been heard (Patterson,

Michelli, & Pacheco, 1999). John Goodlad (1984) has maintained, since the early 1980s, that formal partnerships are necessary for promoting and advancing collaborative initiatives for change. If both parties are going to enjoy a symbiotic relationship, or simultaneous renewal, the collaboration must be authentic. That is, involved parties must spend time in each other's culture. As stated by Patterson, Michelli, and Pacheco, colleagues of John Goodlad's who have studied innovations in school-university partnerships, "Strong partnerships are built on equity and trust, often leading to a blurring of boundaries and a sharing of power" (1999, p. 67).

While much has been written about forming effective school-university partnerships, two major goals of such partnerships are quite clear: improved student achievement and improved teacher preparation programs (Goodlad, 1994). Fortunately, Nora and I had previously familiarized ourselves with the body of research on partnerships and the work of John Goodlad as participants in the Institute for Educational Inquiry's Leadership Program (Goodlad, 1999). Therefore, we both felt strongly that, while a partnership had existed for several years, there was a great deal of room for improvement.

The purpose of this paper is to explain how Nora's request for assistance led to changes in my university's teacher education program. First, I will describe how Lincoln Elementary School and one fourth-grade classroom became the impetus for change. Secondly, I will explain the changes in program delivery. This will be followed by a brief description of the responses to the changes. Next, I will explicate how a second fourth-grade classroom became another setting for field-based learning. Lastly, my conclusions will serve as reflections about the value of forming relationships with partner schools. All names used in this paper are pseudonyms.

## Lincoln Elementary

Lincoln Elementary School served a primarily low socioeconomic population in an urban school district. The student population was seventy-percent African American. A majority of these students were transported by bus. Over the last several years, test data indicated an increase in the number of students requiring remediation in reading, listening, and expressive language skills.

Intervention strategies included a review of the literature, ongoing staff development for the staff, implementation of a school-wide Title I program, after-school tutoring for students in grades four and six, and an ongoing collaboration with university faculty and school faculty on effectively utilizing best practices that would have a positive impact on student achievement in reading. However, Nora maintained that much more needed to be done; she alone was the guiding force for bringing forth the impetus for change that serves as the focus of this paper.

During a steering committee meeting in the fall of 1999, attended by both school district administrators and university faculty, Nora expressed her concern that her students would fail miserably, again, in their statewide proficiency test performance. Seizing the opportunity to be helpful, I suggested that as the instructor of the ED 607: Literacy II class, I could hold class at Nora's school, Lincoln Elementary, where my 22 post-baccalaureate, preservice teacher education students could serve as tutors. Because one of the 22 students, Ms. Donnelly, was a long-term substitute teacher at Lincoln, we decided that her fourth-grade students would be the recipients of our tutelage.

The second issue raised by Nora was that the preservice teachers, post-baccalaureate teacher certification candidates who enrolled in a 15-month, field-based program, did not receive any training in literacy methods prior to their placement in the school as a year-long intern. She felt that if they could receive instruction prior to the fall placement, students and teachers alike at Lincoln Elementary would be better served. For this problem, the solution was simply to rearrange the timing of our course offerings.

## The Solutions: Changes in Program Offerings and Program Delivery

To address Nora's first concern, that she wanted students to be better prepared before they started the field component of the program at her school, ED 606: Literacy was offered in the summer. In the past, this course was part of the university students' fall course schedules. Equally important to the timing, of course, was the content. The study questions for the final exam, in which the class achieved a mean score of 88.45%, provide the leitmotif for the summer course's focus and activities. Therefore, a listing of the essay exam questions and a brief discussion follows.

The first two exam questions dealt with effective planning and delivery of instruction: a) Given any objective that you might see on your school's course of study, how would you use the Language Experience Approach to meet this objective? b) Given any objective that you might see on your school's course of study, how would you use the mini-lesson format demonstrated in this class to meet this objective?

The mini-lesson format illustrates the key points of Vygotsky's (1978) Zone of Proximal Development (ZPD) by including shared readings, think alouds, and guided and independent practices. Students appear to embrace the simplicity of nine simple words I've found useful for explaining ZPD: I do it, we do it, you do it.

The third question asked, "What are the ten ways teachers can make reading aloud magical?" Students were also required to tape themselves reading aloud a book of their choice to another person, preferably a child. They were instructed to incorporate ten areas; eight of the ten areas are based on Lamme's (1976) study of the factors that contribute to the quality of a reading performance. To reinforce the importance of activating prior knowledge and guiding students toward purposeful reading, I added two more factors to Lamme's list: background and purpose. Students were also required to exchange their read-aloud tapes with another intern who then provided an evaluation using the ten-step criteria.

The fourth question on the exam queried, "What are the three ways readers create meaning with text?" Based on the synthesis of research on comprehension compiled by Harp and Brewer (1996), this is a critical question that I highlight in every literacy class I instruct. The desirable response to this query involves a detailed explanation of methods for activating prior knowledge, teaching students to self-monitor, and allowing and encouraging students to respond, in a variety of ways, to text.

The fifth exam item was an interrelated, three-part question: "What do you say to a child whose errors indicate s/he is not reading for meaning? Similarly, what do you say to the child whose errors indicate s/he needs to pay closer attention to visual cues? Lastly, what is an example of an error a child makes to indicate s/he is not attending to structural cues?" This three-part question was offered in reference to a previous role-playing activity in which students practiced conducting guided reading sessions. Marie Clay (1993) served as the source for the three cues referred to in this question. Quite often, I admonish my students for relying on the ubiquitous "sound it out" prompt. Instead, we practice guiding students to inductively relate to onsets and rimes.

To represent the sixth exam item, students were given a "paper child" to respond to, complete with data from a standardized test, running records, an informal reading inventory, and observational data. Since they were also required to complete a mini-case study for this class, they had prior experience discerning a child's strengths and weaknesses. Not yet reading specialists, they were expected to make at least some attempt at listing recommendations for helping this child.

Lastly, two questions that related to prominent literacy theorists, Brian Cambourne (see Brown & Cambourne, 1987) and Ken Goodman (1989), were offered. Past observations have shown that students readily comprehend these theories. Students have communicated that they are in agreement with these theories and have been able bridge the gap of understanding how these theories are implemented in the classroom. I start each quarter by examining such theorists and by positing my own theory, which I call "The Five Habits of Highly Effective Reading Teachers" (O'Connor, 1999).

In response to the other problem raised by Nora, my Literacy II class was welcomed into Ms. Donnelly's fourth-grade class at Lincoln to provide tutoring. The goal for the tutoring sessions was to facilitate two child-centered, child-directed types of activities: Reciprocal Teaching (Palinscar & Brown, 1985) and Book Talks (Raphael & McMahon, 1994). I chose to focus on these two strategies for two main reasons. First, I felt that both of these strategies would benefit the fourth graders and the preservice teachers by showing them the importance for becoming engaged before the reading act commences, during the reading act, and after reading. I previously instructed my preservice students that these are the three keys for facilitating comprehension. Secondly, both of these strategies are consistent with the types of activities that theorists advocate for in a student-centered classroom.

I also met with the Lincoln students to demonstrate the use of Cambourne and Brown's (1987) teaching strategy, Read and Retell. I explained to my students that providing the fourth graders with retelling practice would enable them to more effectively summarize. Summarization is one of the four steps in Reciprocal Teaching (Palinscar & Brown, 1985). My university students met with Lincoln students on six different occasions. At the first meeting, they provided the students with a book mark that explicated the four steps. For the following sessions, the preservice teachers modeled the Reciprocal Teaching (RT) steps and conducted Book Talks. For the last two sessions, Ms. Donnelly grouped the fourth-graders into heterogeneous groups of four students. By the last session, the fourth graders assumed responsibility for conducting the Book Talks and RT sessions. Ms. Donnelly continued to utilize Read and Retell, Reciprocal Teaching, and Book Talks throughout the rest of the school year.

## A Fourth-Grader and Preservice Teachers Respond

Evidence of how both the university students and the Lincoln students responded to this project is offered first in the form of a letter written by a fourth-grade student and then journal entries penned by university interns.

Keisha wrote:

> When you brought your class to Ms. Donnelly 's class you helped me with my reading. You taught me a lot about reading. I always think reading is stupid but when you came in to teach us about reading I made a different grade in reading. I was the student of the month because I came up with my reading. I just want to say thank you.
> Love, Keisha

University students maintained a reflective journal throughout the experience and wrote about the urban setting and about literacy. One university student revealed:

> Urban children are often disruly [sic] and have below average academic skills. That was my preconception of urban children . . . To my welcome surprise, the students at Lincoln were well behaved, cleanly dressed in school uniforms, and eager to learn.

After our tutoring sessions, we would debrief and reflect on the successes and failures of both the university and elementary students. Another student wrote about one of these debriefing sessions in her journal:

> I got to thinking about our debriefing . . . I thought that our questions and line of thought is [sic] pretty deep. I am glad that we are thinking about how what we are learning in class will apply to the real world. It seems that in class we hear all these ideal strategies and sometimes don't stop to think about how this theory fits in realistically.

At another debriefing session, students concluded that within the context of classrooms characterized by students with varying abilities, interests, and needs, the only truly effective way to teach literacy is to individualize instruction as much as humanly possible. I felt exhilarated because this realization was one they had arrived at on their own; I had not yet addressed the notion of grouping and tracking issues in literacy classes. The lesson I learned was that while I can espouse the position of researchers and theorists that individualized instruction is necessary, showing them is much more valuable than telling them. Because of this experience, the preservice teachers discovered and unraveled some key issues regarding literacy.

In terms of reading pedagogy, I discovered notations in students' journals where they discussed the fourth graders' abilities to self-correct and "make sense" out of what they were reading. Some students also discussed the challenges of finding books to match students' interests and helping students who normally just "couldn't cut it" fit into the literacy community through their participation in Book Talks. This helped to validate that my students were truly concerned with learning to plan for instruction that engages all students.

## Ms. Short Welcomes Us

During the fall of 2000, I instructed the group that was the first cohort to participate in a literacy methods class as part of their summer schedule. However, rather than being offered at Lincoln Elementary as I had expected, I learned that I would be teaching Literacy II at another partner school. I enlisted the help of another fourth-grade teacher, whom I will call Ms. Short, to adopt another fourth-grade class. Ms. Short, a veteran teacher, conducted informal assessments on a regular basis and was able to provide the preservice tutors with data regarding the fourth grade students. I purposefully withheld this information until the tutoring sessions were over. I divulged this information only after my students had reached their own conclusions about the fourth graders.

This time, our efforts focused solely on teaching the steps of Reciprocal Teaching (RT) to the elementary students (Palinscar & Brown, 1985). The materials used were expository and narrative passages from the students' textbooks. After working with the fourth-graders for four consecutive weeks, we decided that the university students would write a progress report for Ms. Short. The only instructions I provided were to predict the reading level of the child and to comment on the progress made during the weeks of practicing RT, focusing on strengths and weaknesses. Excerpts from letters written to the fourth-grade teacher revealed, as was the case with the other university students who had tutored Ms. Donnelly's class, that the preservice teachers were learning to think in a variety of ways about helping young readers.

A sampling of parts of letters follows to demonstrate the understanding gained by the preservice teachers. For example, Don, a preservice teacher, wrote:

> Mike seems to read too quickly, causing him to not comprehend as much as he should. He does a very good job of self-correcting as he reads. Although he didn't engage in reciprocal teaching at the last session, he does know and understand the steps of reciprocal teaching.

Kelli and Jane, who worked as a dyad with Keisha, judged her ability to be average. They wrote of the surprise they encountered at the last session with Keisha:

> At first we didn't feel she was understanding the process of reciprocal teaching. When it was her turn to teach us, she jumped right into asking us to predict and then summarize. She even asked us if there was anything we didn't understand. So after these few short weeks, we realized that she did actually learn reciprocal teaching. We would guess her reading level to be average because she read fluently and struggled with big vocabulary words.

Beth and Kandi, tutoring Deidre, were able to note improvements and comment on the affective benefits of the tutoring sessions. They wrote:

> Deidre seemed to naturally think about most of the reciprocal teaching steps. She was able to make these thoughts more cohesive and verbalize better. Her questioning improved. Since Deidre is so quiet, this program really helped her come out of her shell. She liked the idea of becoming the teacher. She tried to stump us with her questions.

Cole explained the successes experienced while tutoring Mark:

> Mark did an absolutely wonderful job acquiring the four strategies to comprehend text. When it was Mark's turn to play the role of teacher, he constantly told me to stop and summarize and asked me to predict each time there was a new heading.

Chuck reported how he learned that motivation was an important factor in helping a child enjoy a successful reading experience:

> While reading the assigned text, Marshall sometimes seemed to slightly struggle picking out the important information. Today, we finished the

assigned text early and he showed me his book about sharks. Amazing! He had already read about most shark species and retained practically everything. When he reads what he is interested in, he is sharp as a tack!

Marty wrote about the importance of prior knowledge as he explained his discoveries about Jennifer:

Her greatest strength would probably be the way she brings in and relates her world to the text. She would almost relate until the point was exhausted. She sometimes changes words as she reads but they usually make sense. When it did not make sense, she was an excellent self-corrector. She is a very good reader and would probably need to be challenged more while reading.

As was the case with my students reflections regarding their tutorial experiences in Ms. Donnelly's fourth grade class, I was pleased with how the preservice teachers were able to comment on the fourth graders' reading progress.

## Conclusions: We've Only Just Begun

At the outset, the two main goals of this partnership venture were to positively impact student achievement and to improve the preparation of my preservice teachers. These two goals represent the symbiosis for which we were striving.

The results of the state-mandated standardized tests taken by the fourth grade students are unknown as of this writing. However, if the preservice teachers had not intervened, the students would not have been exposed to new strategies for reading. A study involving a more in-depth investigation is needed. Allowing for a longer duration of tutorial sessions and monitoring student achievement so that pretest and posttest gains could be compared.

As an instructor of literacy methods in higher education, I am always seeking the answer to the question that relates to the second goal: How well am I preparing my preservice teachers to teach reading and writing? For now, I can only point to the preservice teachers' responses for evidence that they benefited from participating in the tutorial sessions. But with my guiding question in mind, I plan to correspond with the preservice teachers who worked with Ms. Short's fourth graders. My intentions are to follow these preservice teachers into their first year of teaching, designing a qualitative study that will help me glean data that will improve my teaching and future field-based, tutorial experiences. For example, I plan to examine their reflections as first-year teachers and try to determine if any connections have been made as a result of their participation in the tutorial experience.

As I reflect on the lessons learned from this experience, I believe progress has been made since Nora voiced her plea for help. The symbiotic relationships with Nora, Lincoln Elementary, and Ms. Short continue to evolve. Recently, Lincoln became one of three schools to serve as a site for an Urban Literacy Institute, a heavily financed project headed by my university. In coordination with university faculty and a project director, the goal of the Urban Literacy Institute is for teachers to explore and determine ways that urban children can improve their reading skills. Ms. Short, on the other hand, has become a more active participant in our partnership efforts and intends to become a participant at the Institute for Educational Inquiry, a sign of her commitment to improving school-university partnerships. Without the benefits of forging such relationships with principals like Nora, teachers like Ms. Donnelly and Ms. Short, and the children in the fourth grade classrooms, I truly believe I would be a less informed and less capable instructor of literacy methods.

We have to think of developing school-university partnerships as evolutionary entities whose evolution "can best be visualized as a series of overlapping events rather than a linear path," (Clark & Smith, 1999, p. 200) comprised of five stages. The first stage, aptly named "Getting Organized," describes a partnership that is just beginning to describe its mission and responsibilities. At the other end, "Mature Partnerships" can boast of a theme of "productivity, resulting in high achievement and pride in successes" (Clark & Smith, p. 201). I perceive that the examples presented in this paper describe a partnership that is somewhere in the middle. In comparing our partnerships to Clark and Smith's stages, I believe we are at a point where all partners are concerned with the same goals. Over the last year, we have held several planning sessions, brainstorming a variety of ways to document that our partner schools are enjoying higher rates of success as a result of our preservice teachers' involvement in their schools. It would be extremely gratifying if, in the next few years, we could produce data that show higher K – 12 student achievement and accolades for our teacher education products.

In closing, this example of partners working together to improve literacy instruction is a prime example of simultaneous renewal (Goodlad, 1999). Indeed, I feel renewed from working with fourth grade children and from listening to the voices of my own university students as they learned about teaching literacy. While it hasn't been a perfect symbiosis, I do believe that strides have been made toward achieving higher student achievement and better prepared preservice teachers. While this symbiotic relationship is best described as dawning, I believe that we are on the verge of a new day where we can boast of success for all.

# References

Brown, H., & Cambourne, B. (1987). *Read and retell: A strategy for the whole language/natural learning classroom.* Portsmouth, NH: Heinemann.

Clark, R., & Smith, W. (1999). Partnerships, centers, and schools. In K. Sirotnik & R. Soder (Eds.), *The beat of a different drummer: Essays on educational reform in honor of John I. Goodlad,* 197–216. New York, NY: Peter Lang.

Clay, M. (1993). *An observation of early literacy achievement.* Portsmouth, NH: Heinemann.

Goodlad, J. (1984). *A place called school: Prospects for the future.* New York, NY: McGraw Hill.

Goodlad, J. (1994). *Educational renewal: Better teachers, better schools.* San Francisco: CA: Jossey-Bass.

Goodlad, J. (1999). Flow, eros, and ethos in educational renewal. *Phi Delta Kappan. 80* (8), 571-578.

Goodman, K. (1989). Whole language research: Foundations and development. *Elementary School Journal,* 90, 207-221.

Harp, B., & Brewer, J. (1996). *Reading and writing: Teaching for the connections.* Fort Worth, TX: Harcourt Brace.

Lamme, L. (1976). Reading aloud to young children. *Language Arts, 53,* 886-888.

National Commission on Teaching and America's Future. (1996). *What matters most: Teaching for America's future.* Woodbridge, VA: NCTAF. (ERIC Document Reproduction Service No. ED 395 931)

O'Connor, C. R. (1999). Five habits of highly effective reading teachers. *The Ohio Reading Teacher, 33*(1), 36-41.

Palinscar, A., & Brown, A. (1985). Reciprocal teaching: A means to a meaningful end. In Osborn, J., Wilson, P. T., & Anderson, R.C. (Eds.), *Reading education : Foundations for a literate America.* Lexington, MA: Heath.

Patterson, R., Michelli, N., & Pacheco, A. (1999). *Centers of pedagogy: New structures for educational renewal.* San Francisco, CA: Jossey-Bass.

Raphael, T. E., & McMahon, S. I. (1994). Book club: An alternative framework for reading instruction. *The Reading Teacher, 48*(1), 54-61.

Vysotsky, L. (1978). *Mind in society.* Cambridge, MA: Harvard University.

# MAKING AND WRITING WORDS IN A SECOND GRADE CLASSROOM

**Ruth Oswald**
University of Akron

**Timothy Rasinski**
Kent State University

## Abstract

*This study examined the effects of Making and Writing Words, a varia-tion of Cunningham and Cunningham's Making Words word study activity, on second grade students' word learning. Making and Writing Words (MWW) was implemented daily with a group of second grade students over a ten week period. Results indicated that students who received the MWW treatment made significant gains in decoding ability over a similar group of students receiv-ing a more traditional phonics program.*

Recent large scale reviews of research related to essential components of effective literacy instruction (Snow, Burns, & Griffin, 1998; National Read-ing Panel, 2000) have identified phonics or word decoding as one of those key components. According to these studies, research has demonstrated that phonics or decoding instruction leads to success acquisition of literacy in students. Snow, Burns, and Griffin (1998) specifically identified Making Words as one instructional method in phonics and decoding that held great prom-ise for student learning.

Making Words is an innovative word study and word play activity de-veloped by Pat and Jim Cunningham (1992) in which students make (or spell) a series of words from a list of letters supplied by the instructor. Rather than allowing the students to work on their own in brainstorming and making words from the given list of letters, the teacher guides students in making words using structural, semantic, syntactic, and other clues in the process. Beginning with short words students work their way to longer words until the last word is one that uses the entire list of given letters. Using this constructivist and scaffolded word-building activity, students learn about struc-tural and other characteristics of words so that word recognition improves.

An alternative method for Making Words was developed by the second author and described in an article entitled Making and Writing Words (Rasinski, 1999). In Making and Writing Words (MWW), students use a blank form to write words instead of manipulating letter cards or tiles to make words. In all other respects the activity is essentially the same as Cunningham and Cunningham's Making Words. For students who have some degree of fluency in writing, the Making and Writing Words provides an attractive alternative to or variation of the original activity for teachers.

Making Words is an important part of the word-study portion of a multimethod, multilevel reading instruction program for elementary students that has come to be called the Four Blocks (Cunningham, Hall, & Defee, 1991; 1998). Research on the Four Blocks curriculum framework has demonstrated significant improvements in students' acquisition of literacy in the primary grades (Cunningham, Hall, & Defee, 1991; 1998).

The efficacy of the general Four Blocks framework has been demonstrated in a variety of ways. Moreover, in their review of phonics instruction programs, Stahl, Duffy-Hester, and Stahl (1998) categorize Making Words as a spelling-based contemporary phonics approach and claim that it seems to be effective as part of an overall approach to teaching reading (p. 347). Nevertheless, they note that the effects of individual elements and methods of the Four Blocks, including Making Words, have not been empirically demonstrated. Moreover, we know of no study that has compared Making Words with other approaches to the teaching of phonics and decoding. The present study, then, was an attempt to determine the effects of the Making and Writing Words variant in second grade students' development of word knowledge. The following research question was used to guide this present study:

What are the effects of the Making and Writing Words method of decoding instruction on second grade students' decoding performance?

## Procedures and Results

Ruth Oswald, the first author, was a second grade teacher in the Orrville, Ohio Public Schools at the time of this study, and interested in innovative applications of instructional methodologies. After having read Rasinski's (1999) article on Making and Writing Words in the fall, 1999, she contacted him in December, 1999 about the possibility of trying it out in her own classroom over a restricted period of time in order to determine the effects of the application on her students' word learning. Oswald and Rasinski agreed to collaborate on the study.

Oswald conducted the Making and Writing Words instruction daily in her classroom for ten weeks from January through March, 2000. Approximately 15 to 20 minutes per day were spent on the activity. The MWW lesson cycle took three days to implement. Typically, the first day consisted of the teacher using the overhead projection to guide the students through the process of writing a set of words from a given set of letters. The children followed the example of the teacher as she either pronounced the words or gave clues, and they wrote the words in the appropriate boxes on their MWW form. Then, using scissors, they cut out each boxed word on the sheet in order to make individual word cards. Since they would be working with these same words for two more days, they stored the words in envelopes.

On the second day of the instructional routine students removed the words from their envelopes and sorted them into categories based on prompts from the teacher. The categories focused students' attention on various structural and semantic properties of the words. On the third day, students chose three words from their envelopes and wrote sentences containing these words. This three-day format was repeated throughout the ten-week study on a continuous cycle. In other words, if the third day happened to be on Wednesday, a new lesson cycle began on Thursday and ended the following Monday.

The Making and Writing Words instruction did not replace the spelling program that had been used in the district for some time. Oswald continued to teach spelling but during a different time period. However, the MWW instruction did replace the basal approach to phonics instruction that she had used prior to this study.

Meanwhile, a comparison group of students made up of second grade students in the same school received traditional, basal reading instruction as well as the traditional spelling program. In addition, a commercially available analytic phonics program was followed in this classroom in which words were analyzed to learn phonic rules and generalizations. Direct instruction in words and phonic generalizations was followed by students completing workbook pages that were part of the program. This approach to phonics instruction had been widely used in the district for several years, and the comparison group teacher made no changes to this approach to reading instruction.

A MWW lesson begins with the identification of vowels and consonants to be used in the lesson. In the empty boxes underneath, students will write words made from the letter set. The teacher pronounces or gives clues to the words that the students write in the boxes. The final word, written in box 15, is always the challenge word that is made up of all the letters in the lesson. Students are given no clues at first. Figure 1 is a child's written response to a typical lesson.

After all the words have been written, the teacher guides the students to apply what they learned to a transfer portion of the lesson, where they discover new words that follow or are based on some of the same patterns or principles used in the first fifteen. These transfer words can use the full range

## Figure 1. A second grade student's response to a Making and Writing Words lesson

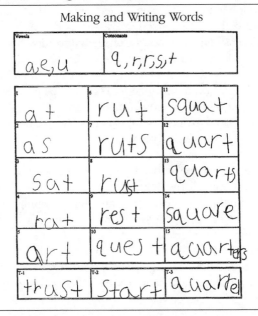

Making and Writing Words

of letters and sounds found in English. In the case of the example in Figure 1, the teacher asked the students to try to write the word, *trust,* in box T-1, then talk about the information they used from part one to figure out the correct spelling. Similarly, *start* and *quarrel* were written by the students based on the patterns they had explored in the initial part of the lesson.

For word sorting, which occurred on the second day of the instructional routine, students organized their word cards into categories provided by the teacher. Here are some of the sorts the teacher posed for the sample in Figure 1:

- Sort 1: Words that belong to the *at* family and words that don't
- Sort 2: Words that contain the *qu* blend and words that don't
- Sort 3: Words that are nouns, words that are verbs and other words
- Sort 4: Words that have words within them and words that don't

On the third day, students are allowed to choose three words from their bank of word cards and write a sentence for each word. This makes the lesson multilevel as students can choose words that fit their level of competence, comfort, and background. By stipulating types of sentences to be constructed, another goal of language arts instruction was achieved.

To plan each MWW lesson, the instructor began with the final, challenge

word. This choice was based on its number and type of vowels and consonants, letter-sound patterns, students' interests, and curriculum tie-ins. The
challenge word in Figure 1, *quarters,* for example, was chosen to draw students' attention to the *qu* letter-sound pattern; additionally, the class was
learning about coins in math. Once the challenge word was chosen, a list of
shorter words, made up of letters from the challenge word, was generated
by the teacher. The words for the lesson were selected from this list in order
to include words that could be sorted into targeted patterns and to emphasize short words and longer words in order to make the lesson multilevel.
Words were also chosen to draw attention to those words that could be made
with the same letters in different places within the word in order to remind
children that when spelling words, the order of the letters is crucial. Finally,
words that were part of the students' listening vocabularies were also selected for inclusion in the MWW lesson.

Given the immediacy of developing and implementing such a study as
well as the pilot nature of the study, a limited number of students (nine)
were selected from Oswald's class as focal students for the study. Based upon
her observations and knowledge of the students over the first four months
of the school year and the previous school record, three students were identified by Oswald,  as high achieving readers, three as average readers, and
three as struggling readers. A veteran, partner teacher, also at the second
grade level at the same school, agreed to serve as the control or comparison
classroom. Students were generally assigned at the beginning of the school
year to one of the two teachers on a random basis. Nine students were identified from this control classroom using the same criteria as that mentioned
previously. It should be recognized that, although limiting the number of
participants in the study to nine aided the researchers in administering pre
and post-test measures in a timely fashion, it is a significant limitation to the
interpretation and generalizability of the results.

The nine focal students from each classroom were pretested and
posttested on two measures of word recognition—the Names Test—Revised
(Cunningham, 1990; Duffelmeyer, 1994) and word lists from the Slosson Oral
Reading Test (1990). The Names Test is a word recognition test of 70 words
that represent some of the most common phonics elements taught in elementary schools. The Slosson Oral Reading Test consists of a set of graded word
lists, each 20 words in length. On the Slosson Test, students were asked to
read word lists that generally corresponded to their general reading ability.
All focal students read, or attempted to read, all the words on the Names
Test. Pretest and posttest performances are summarized on Tables 1 and 2.
Given the small number of students in the sample, we did not feel that statistical tests of significance were appropriate. However, a quick perusal of
the gains made by students in word recognition demonstrates a significant

**Table 1. Gains Scores on Names Test***

|  | N | MEAN PRETEST | MEAN POSTTEST | MEAN GAIN |
|---|---|---|---|---|
| Experimental | 9 | 36.9 | 53.0 | 16.1 |
| Control | 8 | 35.1 | 39.0 | 3.9 |
| Experimental High Achievers | 3 | 54.3 | 61.3 | 7.0 |
| Control High Achievers | 2 | 60.5 | 65.0 | 4.5 |
| Experimental Average Achievers | 3 | 34.7 | 56.7 | 22.0 |
| Control Average Achievers | 3 | 34.3 | 34.0 | - .3 |
| Experimental Low Achievers | 3 | 21.7 | 41.0 | 19.3 |
| Control Low Achievers | 3 | 19.0 | 26.7 | 7.7 |

*\* Total number of items (words) on the Names test is 70.*

**Table 2. Gains Scores on Slosson Oral Reading Test***

|  | N | LISTS READ (GRADE LEVEL) | MEAN GAIN PER WORD LIST |
|---|---|---|---|
| Experimental | 9 |  | 3.8 |
| Control | 8 |  | 1.3 |
| Experimental High Achievers | 3 | 3, 4, 5 | 3.9 |
| Control High Achievers | 2 | 3, 4, 5 | 1.3 |
| Experimental Average Achievers | 3 | 2, 3, 4 | 3.8 |
| Control Average Achievers | 3 | 2, 3, 4 | - .1 |
| Experimental Low Achievers | 3 | 2, 3 | 3.7 |
| Control Low Achievers | 3 | 2, 3 | 1.7 |

*\* Each word list per grade level contains 20 words.*

(not statistically tested) and substantive advantage for the students receiving the Making and Writing Words instruction. Moreover, the greatest gains were made by those students who were identified average or below average readers—the very students who are in most need of effective instruction.

All students in both classrooms were also pretested and posttested on the Test of Written Spelling (Larsen & Hammill, 1994). No substantive differences between the MWW classroom and the control classroom in spelling were detected over the course of the study.

The teacher in the role of researcher in this study observed many benefits for her learners as a result of the MWW instruction. The activity was hands-on, engaging, and everyone was actively involved in the process of making and writing words. The children transferred information from the lessons to other activities throughout the day. Some students saw little words in big words. During spelling tests, children often blurted out words they saw in given spelling words. One child transferred the meaning of "vain" from a MWW discussion to describe a character in a story being read aloud by the teacher.

The following excerpts typify the kind of talk that went on in a MWW discussion:

Student 1: "toe"—"When two vowels go walking, the first one does the talking."
Student 2: "toe"—"If you spell it t-o-w, it means to pull something."
Student 3: "ore"—"If it's a boat oar you spell it o-u-r...no...o-a-r."
(Fieldnotes, 2/21/00).

With each lesson the children not only gained added exposure to words, but they also analyzed the words from different perspectives. This exposure led to greater control over and knowledge about how words are constructed and what they mean. The more the MWW strategy was used, the more eager the children became to invent the words before clues were offered. Very soon the more advanced readers were successful at guessing the "challenge" words.

## Discussion

We need to prelude the discussion by again noting the limitations of this particular research. The sample sizes were very small and the experimental treatment was implemented by one of the co-researchers. Certainly, the manifestation of the Hawthorne effect was possible in this study. Nevertheless, the students were nearly of the same achievement at the beginning of the study and both groups of students were receiving word recognition instruction of some type during the course of the study for approximately the same amount of time. Moreover, the implementation of the Making and Writing

Words method is rather straightforward. The fact that the study was conducted in regular classrooms under normal classroom conditions adds to the face validity of the method and study.

The improvement in word recognition on the part of experimental treatment students was quite striking and remarkable. In only ten weeks of treatment, the students in the Making and Writing Words classroom made four times the gain in word recognition on the Names Test than the students in the comparison classroom and the gain for students who were identified as average and low achievers was even more pronounced. On the Slosson Oral Reading Test, the experimental group had nearly three times the gain over the control group, with students at all three achievement levels more than doubling the gain scores of the control group. Students who were in the Making and Writing activities treatment group substantially accelerated their word recognition learning over the control group.

This study provides some initial empirical evidence that Making and Writing Words, and the method upon which it is based—Making Words, do appear to have potential as a powerful decoding instruction activity for elementary grade students, especially for those students in most need of additional instructional assistance. Anecdotal reports from teachers across the country have indicated that Making Words and Making and Writing Words are powerful instructional activities for developing skill and mastery in word recognition. This study tends to support those reports.

Clearly more studies are required at different grade levels, with greater numbers of students at various achievement levels, by various teachers, using Making Words as well as Making and Writing Words, over different periods of time. In addition, more research needs to examine why the intervention had no comparatively positive effect on students' spelling achievement. Perhaps the length of the intervention was not sufficient to allow students to gain the more in-depth word learning that is required in spelling. Nevertheless, this study adds positively to the anecdotal reports that describe Making and Writing Words as effective instruction for decoding and word recognition.

In addition to the report on student learning, Making and Writing Words is fairly simple to implement and appears to be well liked by students. The teacher in this study soon realized the benefits of her students writing the words rather than managing all the individual letters. More time could be spent on word study. Within one instructional format, there are many possibilities for discovering how our alphabetic system works, the most common spelling patterns and predictable variations. These students immediately became involved in the activity and were very enthusiastic.

As these children became more aware of how words are made, making and writing words empowered them. They soon wanted to invent their own words and sort categories during instruction. The levels of literacy achievement seemed to disappear as all the children participated in the activity and felt successful. The students at a lower reading level learned common letter patterns and their sounds; the more difficult words challenged students at higher literacy levels.

In summary, this study suggests that Making and Writing Words can lead to some extraordinary gains in student word recognition development if used in a regular and sustained manner in the classroom. If word recognition is a goal of the reading program, Making and Writing words may be one effective instructional tool that is at teachers' disposal for improving student literacy learning.

---

## References

Cunningham, P. M. (1990). The Names Test: A quick assessment of decoding ability. *The Reading Teacher, 44,* 124-129.

Cunningham, P. M., & Cunningham, J. W. (1992). Making Words: Enhancing the invented spelling-decoding connection. *The Reading Teacher, 46,* 106-115.

Cunningham, P. M., Hall, D. P., & Defee, M. (1991). Non-ability grouped, multilevel instruction: A year in a first grade classroom. *The Reading Teacher, 45,* 106-115.

Cunningham, P. M., Hall, D. P., & Defee, M. (1998). Nonability-grouped, multilevel instruction: Eight years later. *The Reading Teacher, 51,* 652-664.

Duffelmeyer, F. A. (1994). Further validation and enhancement of the Names Test. *The Reading Teacher, 48,* 118-128.

Larsen, S. C., & Hammill, D. D. (1994). *Test of written spelling* (third edition). Austin, TX: Pro-Ed Publishing.

National Reading Panel. (2000). *Report of the National Reading Panel: Teaching children to read.* Washington, DC: US Department of Health and Human Services.

Rasinski, T. V. (1999). Making and writing words. *Reading Online* (an electronic journal available at *http:///www.readingonline.org/articles/words.rasinski.html).*

Slosson, R. L. (1990). *Slosson oral reading test—revised.* East Aurora, NY: Slosson Educational Publications and Los Angeles: Western Psychological Services.

Snow, C. E., Burns, S. M., & Griffin, P. (Eds.). (1998). *Preventing reading difficulties in young children.* Washington, DC: National Academy Press.

Stahl, S. A., Duffy-Hester, A. M., & Stahl, K. A. L. (1998). Everything you wanted to know about phonics (but were afraid to ask). *Reading Research Quarterly, 33,* 338-355.

# COLLABORATIVE VOICES

# Exploring the Evolution of Public School Teachers' Perceptions of University/Public School Partnerships: The Quest for Collaborative Preparation of Literacy Teachers

**Mary Beth Sampson**
**Martha Foote**
**Leeann Moore**

Texas A&M University-Commerce

**Charlene Fleener**

Old Dominion University

## Abstract

*This study explores the evolving viewpoints of public school mentor (co-operating) teachers in a professional development center. This inquiry focused on the perceptions of mentors in "founding" centers and "new" centers concerning the "status" of the collaborative partnership, and their role(s) in the professional development center. Specific areas examined included public school mentors' perceptions of the goals of the collaborative, their roles, support needed and received, benefits, and difficulties/problems.*

Research has indicated that students in literacy methods courses emphasizing university-based requirements often have difficulty utilizing the "mastered" knowledge when planning and implementing instruction in their own classrooms (Alvermann, Dillon, & O'Brien, 1990; Wendler, Samuels, &

Moore, 1989). Therefore, the call for improved preservice teacher education for reading educators has focused attention on programs that intertwine public school and university experiences.

Professional development schools attempt to merge colleges and universities with public elementary and secondary schools. The goal of this field-based movement is the creation of a new collaborative institution that combines the best current theory and research with the most effective practice in a public school setting (Dixson & Ishler, 1992). Goodlad (1991) identified the use of clinical or "teaching" schools which incorporated university and public school collaboration to enhance the learning of school children and pre-service teachers as a critical component for the redesign of teacher education. The challenge has been issued to focus attention on public schools and universities as they form partnerships (Holmes Group, 1990) in order "to bring practicing teachers and administrators together with university faculty in partnerships that improve teaching and learning on the part of their respective students" (Holmes Group, 1984, p. 56).

In 1984, Goodlad issued a call to form university/public school partnerships and research the process by stating: "In short, the joining of school (and school district) and universities in commonly purposive and mutually beneficial linkages is a virtually untried and therefore, unstudied phenomenon" (p. 12). While the literature on school reform lacks extensive examination of teacher education programs that involve university and public school collaboration (Scharer, Freeman, Lehman, & Allen, 1993; Shapiro, 1994), there is evidence that partnerships in professional development schools do not often provide equal voice and responsibility for all participants (Dixson & Ishler, 1992; Roemer, 1991; Sarason, 1982). However, the learning environment for preservice teachers can be enhanced when the views of all partners are solicited—and valued (Darling-Hammond, 1995; Foote, Walker, & Zeek, 1997; Lieberman, 2000).

Therefore, it is crucial for literacy researchers to examine partnerships between universities and public schools and explore the viewpoints of the public school teachers. In this paper, the authors share the results of an exploration of the viewpoints of two groups of public school mentor (cooperating) teachers in a professional development center. One group involved mentors from the public schools whose faculty and administrators were the initial collaborators in the university/public school partnership that designed and implemented the professional development center. These "initial/founding centers" began implementation of the program during the fall of 1992 and spring of 1993. In contrast, the "new centers" joined the partnership in the fall of 1996 and spring of 1997.

The program was designed so that students' work in the schools spanned an entire academic year at the end of their undergraduate program. Each week the first semester pre-service teachers (interns) spent two days in the public school and one day in an integrated seminar. The second semester, prospective teachers (residents) were in the public school five days per week with the exception of nine day-long integrated seminars interspersed throughout the semester.

In addition, all preservice elementary teachers were required to take a minimum of three reading/literacy courses in their professional sequence. Customarily, approximately 50% of the students chose reading as an area of emphasis within their program. These students were required to take six reading/literacy courses. Therefore, the university reading faculty and the public school mentors saw the formation of the professional development center as a unique opportunity to interweave literacy theory and practice. During the initial planning and implementation of the professional development center the public school and university partners decided that the majority of reading coursework would be field based. Preservice teachers whose emphasis was reading would take four of their six reading courses during the year they were in the professional development center. If the preservice teachers' area of emphasis was another content area such as math, social studies, etc., they would take two of their three reading courses within the context of the professional development center. Therefore, public school mentors and university faculty collaboratively designed integrated seminars that intertwined literacy theory and strategies with the various content areas such as math, science and social studies.

The focus of this inquiry was to examine and compare the perceptions of mentors in "initial/founding" centers and the "new" centers concerning the collaborative partnership and their role(s) in the professional development center. Specific areas examined included mentors' perceptions of the goals of the collaborative; their own roles; support they needed and received; benefits; and difficulties/problems.

## Method
### Participants
The research was conducted within a professional development school partnership at a southwestern state university. The partnership strives to follow a model of organic collaboration in which university and public school partners mutually redefine their roles and responsibilities. Data for this study were collected from mentors in two of the initial/founding centers and two of the new centers during the fall of 1998 and spring of 1999. The two initial/founding centers were involved in the grant writing and year-long planning process. Both initial/founding centers and new centers were comprised of one suburban district and one rural district.

Program implementation for the initial/founding districts occurred in fall 1992 in the urban district with 11 interns, 22 mentors, and 1 liaison (university faculty member) on 3 campuses. The rural district in that center continued the planning process and was involved in program development throughout fall 1992 and spring 1993. Their program implementation occurred in fall 1993 with 9 preservice teachers assuming intern placements with 18 mentors and 1 liaison on 2 campuses. The new center began in the fall of 1996 in the rural district with 16 interns on 5 campuses with 30 mentors and 2 liaisons. The new center added a suburban district in the spring of 1997 with 21 interns on 4 campuses with 25 mentors and 4 liaisons.

### Data Sources and Analysis

Data sources included an open-ended questionnaire (Appendix A) and a guided conversational interview (Appendix B). The open-ended questionnaires were administered to thirty-four mentor teachers from initial/founding centers and twenty-eight from new centers. Responses from the questionnaires were analyzed by the researchers with qualitative approaches that employed the constant comparative method of descriptive analysis (Glaser & Strauss, 1967; Strauss & Corbin, 1990). Overarching themes were identified and modified as the analysis proceeded (Bogdan & Biklen, 1992). As these themes emerged from the data, three members of the research team compared the themes and through discussion and joint recursive analysis reached consensus regarding themes (Glaser & Strauss, 1967; Glaser, 1992).

The researchers extended invitations to all of the mentors in the four districts to participate in the interviews within the context of focus groups. Fourteen mentors/key informants from initial/founding centers and eighteen from new centers volunteered to participate in the interviews. The interviews were recorded and transcribed.

Three of the researchers utilized the constant comparative method of descriptive analysis (Glaser & Strauss, 1967) to analyze the interview transcripts and the questionnaires in order to determine categories of responses within the broad themes. The concurrent analysis of the data sets in order to generate coding categories was guided by the questions derived from the themes that emerged from the initial questionnaires (Bodgan & Biklen, 1992). As the categories emerged from the data, domains, which were consistent across data sources, were examined, verified and corroborated by the research team across multiple data sources until consensus was reached concerning themes and categories.

### Findings

Six major themes emerged from the data analysis. The reporting of results will define the themes by sharing the categories that emerged within each theme. Representative examples and quotes gleaned from the data are also included within each theme.

## Results/Discussion

### Theme #1: Mentor's View of Major Goals of the Professional Development Center

Mentors in both the initial/founding and new centers noted improvement of preservice teacher education, professional development of inservice teachers, collaboration between the university and public school and opportunities for "hands-on" learning in the real world as major goals. However, differences emerged within the categories between the initial/founding centers and the new centers. While both referred to professional development of inservice teachers in the context of staff development opportunities, mentors in the initial/founding centers expanded the concept of professional development by writing statements such as, "The interns and residents bring new ideas to the mentor's classroom," and "Working with interns, residents, and the university keeps veterans abreast of current developments in education." Both initial/founding and new centers cited goals of positively impacting preservice teacher education and enhancing professional development of inservice teachers; however, only the initial/founding centers noted the overall improvement of the quality of teaching—referring to both preservice and inservice teachers.

While responses from mentors in the new centers were limited to the above four categories, initial/founding centers noted additional goals. Mentors from the initial/founding centers expressed the view that reducing attrition was valued. Comments included: "The major goal is to train preservice teachers in such a manner that they will stay in the profession—and be successful," and "This program prepares teachers so they won't experience burnout —and at the same time provides mentor burn-out insurance!" The impact of working in teams was also evident in the initial/founding centers as mentors referred to guiding and developing new teachers by developing strong mentoring relationships as a goal.

### Theme #2: Mentor's View of own Role and How Role Impacts/Influences/Supports the Program

Once again, categories emerged that were consistent in both the initial/ founding and new centers. These categories reflected a focus on the intern/ resident. For example, mentors discussed their roles in supporting and facilitating the interns and residents, engaging in formative and summative evaluation, modeling the role of an effective teacher and providing "real world experiences." A mentor in an initial/founding center stated, "I can't 'teach' someone the individual complexities of children in my classroom, but I can model and provide feedback to her [the intern] as she learns to think on her feet." Comments from new centers continued this focus as mentors stated, "I act as a role model for my resident by giving her a first hand look at all the duties and responsibilities a teacher has," and "I evaluate and offer feedback . . . I am willing to provide constructive feedback and guidance in relation to teaching." Three additional categories were present in the comments of mentors at the new centers: sharing resources, making suggestions for teaching a concept, and helping the intern/resident experience success. These categories maintained an emphasis on the intern/resident.

Within the overall theme, the focus seemed broader in categories that were unique to the initial/founding centers. These included teaming (with the university, other mentors and intern/resident), communicating, maintaining a positive attitude, sharing all aspects of the classroom, and allowing experimentation/ innovation. One mentor noted it was her responsibility to be an "active team member—with the entire team—my intern, my liaison, the other mentor" and "share in the decision making." Another mentor stated:

> "It's my role to be part of the solution. When we started, I would ask 'what should I do about this?' and my liaison would say 'What do you think you should do?' I finally realized my role as a team member involved collaborative problem solving—not just waiting for someone else to provide an answer!"

Another mentor noted, "It's more that just letting her do what I know will work, I have to let her try new ways . . . and that means sharing my kids."

### Theme #3: Mentor's View of Ways Others Have Provided Help/Support for Mentoring Role

There was no overlap of categories between the views of mentors in the initial/founding and new centers regarding this theme. The majority of the concepts from the new centers seemed to refer to aspects of the university liaison providing information (letting me know what is going on, receiving packets and handouts from university, mentor orientation from the university, liaison meeting each month). Comments included "When I have questions, I can get in touch with my liaison" and "The monthly meetings help a lot—they let me know what is going on." Mentors from new centers also noted some interactive aspects of assistance such as support from others on their team and sharing ideas and duties with intern/resident.

However, all of the categories from the initial/founding centers alluded to interactive activities (e.g., team teaching opportunities, shared decision making, bond between public school and university, flexible/supportive liaison, supportive administrators, and new ideas from interns/residents). Comments from mentors in the initial/founding centers reflected a collaborative nature. For example, one mentor noted, "The interns and residents seem eager to help in any way possible...the university liaisons are available . . . Other mentors offer ideas." Others said, "The liaison discusses . . . and helps teachers with every aspect of learning" and "Our interns and residents bring *so* much from the university to help our teaching . . . I can also see the bond being made between the public school and university."

### Theme #4: Mentor's View of Help/Assistance/Support Needed from Others for Mentoring Role

Diverse views also emerged from this theme. The categories that were unique to the new centers addressed the availability of the liaison, communication/information on expectations and goals, and the provision of a day off. The liaison's responsibilities included weekly visits. However, throughout the evolution of the professional development center, new centers often encountered needs that required more frequent interactions. The "day off" referred to a "perk" that mentors had obtained in all of the initial/founding districts through negotiation with administrators. If the building administrator, mentor and resident were in agreement concerning the day and the resident's ability to assume instructional responsibilities for the classroom—and if the resident's other mentor agreed to assume responsibility for the resident that day, the mentor teacher could take a "personal" day. The mentor would not be required to pay for a substitute or be required to use any professional or personal leave time. Even though the university did not have any input in this policy, mentors in new centers often assumed this was university policy rather than a district decision.

In contrast, the responses of the initial/founding centers emphasized several areas. The categories were: no additional assistance/support needed, better communication, uniform university assignments for interns/residents, seminars relate more to classroom experience, provide more information about seminar topics, find other ways to obtain substitutes, and get paperwork straight. Initially, it appeared that communication was a consistent category in both initial/founding centers and new centers; however, the emphasis seemed to be different. Many comments addressing communication from the initial/founding centers focused on issues dealing with the seminar schedule and instruction. For example, mentors commented: "Provide more information about seminar topics so I will be able to extend the info in my classroom," "Let us know the time line for seminars before the semester starts—this helps everyone get the most out of the semester" and "Provide a list of literacy strategies that are being implemented so we can model them." Their comments supported the interdependent concept of partnership by alluding to the belief that the experiences in their public school classrooms should extend and support the instruction preservice teachers were receiving in seminar. However, mentors in new centers tended to have a different communication focus with comments such as "Keep us posted on expectation and goals," and "Let me know what I am supposed to be doing."

Interestingly, some of the comments in the initial/founding centers referred to situations that were an evolution of practices and procedures based on mentor feedback. For example, as the years progressed, revision of forms occurred in order to lessen the paperwork. As a result, experienced mentors sometimes pulled a form from their files, completed it and found that it was no longer in use. During the initial implementation of the program, interns received weekly specific, uniform assignments (i.e. "implement a K-W-L during the next week in your classroom"). Mentor feedback indicated that this practice did not mesh with the "ebb and flow" of individual classrooms. Consequently, this practice had evolved to generic assignments that allowed for the diversity of the content and schedules of the various classrooms (i.e. during the semester document implementation of literacy strategies). In addition, during the initial implementation of the program mentor training sessions were provided via grant funds. In order to facilitate mentors' attendance, administrators were encouraged to utilize interns and residents as "subs" for mentors when they attended staff development. This was in accordance with House Bill 339, an act relating to the legal status, authority, and responsibility of a student teacher that was enacted by the Texas Legislature (Section 1, Subchapter Z, Chapter 13 Texas Education code, as amended by adding Section 13.906) that established a policy stating that a student teacher "may not be required to serve as a substitute teacher." However, the code elaborated that if the student teacher assumed responsibility for the class when the teacher was engaged in "an approved activity relating to student teaching" this was not considered to be substitute teaching. In some instances, however, administrators in the initial/founding centers had "stretched" this policy to extend to other situations.

### Theme #5: Mentor's View of Major Benefits
### Resulting from Program Participation

Both new and initial/founding centers viewed access to new ideas/new research, lower student-teacher ratios and learning from each other as major benefits. Comments included:

> "More educators in the room to help children. They bring new ideas into the class." (initial/founding center)

> "My students now have *two teachers or more.* They can experience more one-on-one help. And, interns and residents continuously bring new ideas into the classroom." (initial/founding center)

"Elementary classrooms that have the benefit of preservice teachers have the teacher student ratio cut drastically. They are also on the cutting edge of new strategy implementation because of the desire of the preservice teacher to practice what they are learning in seminars in a real classroom." (initial/founding center)

"Having an extra 'pair of hands' in the classroom makes a big difference. I am able to reach more children." (new center)

"I am learning new ideas from my intern; she has used reading strategies I didn't know." (new center)

Although teaming was a category in all centers, the new centers emphasized the concept of teaming with interns/residents. The initial/founding centers had an expanded view that included not only the interns/residents but also other mentors and the liaison(s). However, mentors in the new centers discussed the benefit of experiencing more contact with other teachers such as the opportunity to go to other classrooms to watch peers teach. They also addressed attributes of the interns/residents as benefits by noting their enthusiasm, creativity/innovativeness and their presence providing "more opportunity to discuss ideas." In addition, mentors in new centers considered the "extra pair of hands" a benefit by providing an opportunity to "catch up on work."

Mentors in the initial/founding centers recognized intrinsic benefits for themselves such as increased reflection/self awareness, pride, and support. These ideas were reflected in comments such as "The major benefit to me is a feeling of pride" and "Keeps me on my toes—helps me feel I'm teaching on two levels (children and adults)—fulfilling." In addition, initial/founding mentors noted better teacher training as a benefit for both their students and their profession. As one mentor noted, "The better the teachers are in my school, the better I am."

### Theme #6: Mentor's View of Major Difficulties/Problems of Program Participation.

Mentors in both established and new centers identified time and paperwork as difficulties/problems. Interestedly, mentors in the initial/founding centers often linked time and communication together in their responses with statements such as, "TIME!!! Not enough time to conference, brainstorm and plan with interns/residents," and "Finding time to thoroughly communicate with intern/resident (explain decisions, comment on student, give feedback, etc.) during the day." Mentors in the newer centers often mentioned time in the context of the interns "not being there enough" or "not knowing exactly when they would be in the school." In addition, they wrote about concerns with "not knowing what is expected."

The categories of communication, need for strong liaisons, and evaluating/critiquing adults were evident only in the initial founding centers. Mentors in the initial/founding centers expressed the view that if liaison(s) were not "strong" problems were to be expected. One mentor wrote, "*Strong* liaisons are essential. You know what they say about a weak link in a chain."

In contrast, the responses from the new centers focused on the problems/difficulties in giving interns/residents control of the class, differences in styles and expectations, knowing what is expected of the mentor, and the intern schedule. One new center mentor noted, "It's just hard to give the intern or resident the reins. I know I'm ultimately responsible for the success of the children." Mentors in new centers stated difficulty in knowing what their roles were. The comment "I just need to know exactly what I am expected to do . . . what I need to do . . . and when" was indicative of this concern. In addition, mentors of new centers questioned the interns' schedule of Monday, Wednesday, and Friday, which consisted of two days in the public school and one in seminar. Comments included, "They never get to see two consecutive days until they are residents," and "They would learn more if they were in the school more." Concerns about the intern schedule did not surface from the initial/founding centers—even from first-year mentors. Perhaps the fact that their schools had been involved in determining the framework for the intern schedule provided validation for the alternating days.

## Conclusions/Implications

On first perusal, many categories were consistent across the initial/founding centers and the new centers. However, on closer examination, differences became more apparent. These differences seemed indicative of different types of collaboration.

In an examination of partnerships, Whitford, Schlecty, and Shelor (1987) identified three types of collaboration: cooperative, symbiotic, and organic. A foundational premise of a successful university/public school partnership is that over time, it progresses beyond cooperation and symbiosis (Goodlad, 1988) to embrace an organic collaborative model (Dixson & Ishler, 1992; Schlecty & Whitford, 1988). In cooperation, the relationship is a short-term collaboration in which information is shared or a service is provided one partner to the other; whereas, the key feature of symbiotic collaboration is reciprocity—"We'll do this workshop for you, if you supervise student teachers for us." A symbiotic collaboration may extend over a period of time, but usually does not lead to a change within partners. In organic collaboration, partners are equally vested in the goals and issues of the collaborative relationship and the process ultimately changes both (Dixson & Ishler, 1992). This indicates that organic collaboration is a goal worthy of pursuing for maximum learning environments for preservice literacy educators.

It was evident that mentors from the "founding" centers demonstrated characteristics of organic collaboration in some of their responses. New centers focused on the innovative ideas and the added support in the classroom. While these remained important, mentors in the initial/founding centers also discussed the feeling of pride involved in impacting the profession—and their pride in the program.

Additional categories that emerged from the initial/founding centers seemed to reflect feelings of joint ownership of the program with the university. Rather than expecting someone from the university to "fix" a problem, they seemed to view problems as an "opportunity for collaboration" with joint rights and responsibilities. The responses from the mentors from the initial/founding centers indicated an expanded concept of whom they were "learning" from and "teaming" with. In addition, "shared decision making," "self reflection/assessment" and "being stretched and challenged" were concepts that focused on individual professional growth that intertwined through the responses of the mentors from the initial/founding centers. This was a consistent theme, even though none of the current mentors in the initial/founding centers had been involved in the initial planning and implementation. However, through teaming configurations, campus meetings, and the normal interactions of a school culture all of the new members had weekly contact with mentors who had participated in the design and implementation of the program. This may have impacted the pride, ownership and interest that were evident in responses from mentors regardless of their length of time in the program. In addition, perhaps the culture of a school that has been an integral partner in the design and implementation of a collaborative program supports all mentors to assume responsibility for the evolution and success of the endeavor.

Many questions arise from this study. While similarities did exist, differences in the level of collaboration were apparent between the initial/founding centers and the new centers. Were the differences merely a result of length of time in the partnership? Or, are different levels of collaboration a result of one set of partners implementing a program that was designed by an earlier group, rather than having the opportunity to collaboratively design and implement a new entity? Is having "answers to questions" concerning a process/question/concern an asset—or a liability—to collaboration? Is "organic collaboration" a "stage" you reach and then retain? While some categories of comments demonstrated "organic collaboration," other categories demonstrated the continual need for monitoring the "status of the collaborative." It is evident that the "status of collaboration" cannot be neglected. Categories such as "communication", "strong liaisons," "time," "paperwork," and statements such as "keep us informed," and "know timeline before they begin," send loud and clear messages that collaboration, regardless of the "stage," requires constant care and ongoing research.

After an examination of the research focusing on the preparation of literacy educators, Anders, Hoffman, and Duffy (2000) concluded that teacher education research had long been neglected. They stated:

> We must commit our energies to studying our programs, our courses, our teachers and our expectations and requirements. In short, it means consenting to be the subject of study ourselves. It will take courage and creativity. Now is the time to start (p. 734).

Partners in a professional development center must recognize this need for continual study of the collaborative process. As one liaison stated, "We must do all we can to keep our finger on the pulse of the feedback from all partners—otherwise, we will begin to implement a program—and stop collaborating."

---

# References

Alvermann, D. E., O'Brien, D. B., & Dillon, D. R. (1990). What teachers do when they say they're having discussions of content area reading assignments: A qualitative analysis. *Reading Research Quarterly, 25,* 4, 296-322.

Anders, P. L., Hoffman, J. V., & Duffy, G. G. (2000). Teaching teachers to teach reading: Paradigm shifts, persistent problems, and challenges. In M. L. Kamil, P. B. Mosenthal, P. D. Pearson, & R. Barr (Eds.), *Handbook of reading research (Vol. III)* (pp. 719-742). Mahwah, NJ: Lawrence Erlbaum.

Bogdan, R. C., & Biklen, S. K. (1992). *Qualitative research for education: An introduction to theory and methods.* Boston: Allyn & Bacon.

Darling-Hammond, L., & McLaughlin. M. W. (1995). Policies that support professional development in an era of reform. *Phi Delta Kappan 76* (8), 597-604.

Dixson, P. N. & Ishler, R. E. (1992). Professional development schools. Stages in collaboration. *Journal of Teacher Education, 43,* 28-34.

Foote, M., Walker, C., & Zeek, C. (1997, February). Leadership development through mentoring: Professional development with—not for—mentor teachers. Paper presented at the annual meeting of the American Association for Teacher Education. Phoenix, AZ.

Glaser, B. G. (1992). *Basics of grounded theory analysis.* Mill Valley, CA: Sociology Press.

Glaser, B. G., & Strauss, A. L. (1967). *The discovery of grounded theory.* Chicago: Aldine Publishing Company.

Goodlad, J. I. (1984). *A place called school.* New York: McGraw Hill.

Goodlad, J. I. (1991). Why we need a complete redesign of teacher education. *Educational Leadership 48*(4), 4-10.

Holmes Group. (1984). *Tomorrow's teachers: A report of the Holmes Group.* East Lansing, MI: Holmes Group, Inc.

Holmes Group. (1990). *Tomorrow's schools: Principles for the design of professional development schools.* East Lansing, MI: Holmes Group, Inc.

Lieberman, A. (2000). Networks as learning communities: Shaping the future of teacher development. *Journal of Teacher Education, 51,* 221-227.

Roemer, M. (1991). What we talk about when we talk about school reform. *Harvard Educational Review,* 61, 434-448.

Sarason, S. (1982). *The culture of the school and the problem of change* (2nd ed.). Boston: Allyn & Bacon.

Shapiro, J. (1994). Moving toward change: One school's experience. In E. G. Sturtevant & W. M. Linek (Eds.) *Pathways for literacy: Learners teach and teachers learn* (pp. 85-96). Pittsburg, KS: College Reading Association.

Scharer, P. L., Freeman, E. B., Lehman, B. A., & Allen, V. G. (1993). Literacy and literature in elementary classrooms: Teachers beliefs and practices. In D. J. Leu & C. K. Kinzer (Eds.) *Examining central issues in literacy research, theory, and practice* (pp. 359-366). Chicago: National Reading Conference.

Schlechty, P. C., & Whitford, B. L. (1988). Shared problems and shared vision: Organic collaboration. In Sirotnik, K. A. & J. I. Goodlad (Eds.), *School-university partnerships in actions: Concepts, cases, and concerns* (pp. 191-204). New York: Teachers College Press.

Shapiro, J. (1994). Moving toward change: One school's experience. In E. G. Sturtevant & W. M. Linek (Eds.), *Pathways for literacy: Learners teach and teachers learn* (pp. 85-96). Pittsburg, KS: College Reading Association.

Strauss, A. L., & Corbin, J. (1990). *Basics of qualitative research: Grounded theory procedures and techniques.* Newbury Park, CA: Sage.

Wendler, D., Samuels, S. J., & Moore, V. K. (1989). Comprehension instruction of award-winning teachers, teachers with master's degrees, and other teachers. *Reading Research Quarterly, 24*(4), 382-401.

Whitford, B. L., Schlechty, P. C., & Schelor, L. G. (1987). Sustaining action research through collaboration: Inquiries for intervention. *Peabody Journal of Education, 64,* 151-169.

## Appendix A. Mentor Questionnaire: Collaboration Among Partners in the Professional Development Center

As a mentor teacher, your perspectives about collaboration within our professional development center are needed as part of our program evaluation and refinement. Please reflect on the following questions in terms of your own individual experience. Write your thoughts and feelings concerning the following questions.

1. Define collaboration.

2. Have we achieved a collaborative community? (Are we where we want to be in terms of collaborative practices?) Why or Why not?

3. What are the factors positively influencing collaboration within our professional development center partnership?

4. What are the factors hindering collaboration within our professional development center partnership?

## Appendix B. Guided Interview

Your feedback is essential for the continued refinement of our professional development center to best meet your needs and the needs of your students. Please reflect on the following questions in terms of your own individual experience.

1. What do you see as the major goals of the professional development center?

2. In your role, how do you impact/influence/support the program?

3. In what ways have others in the program helped you in performing your role?

4. In what ways should others in the program help you in performing your role?

5. What are the major benefits for you and/or your students in participating in the professional development center?

6. What are the major difficulties or problems in participating in the professional development center?

# Literacy Teacher-Researchers Unite: Factors that Motivate in a Professional Development Setting

**Mary E. Styslinger**
The University of South Carolina

## Abstract

*Teacher research has been heralded as a means of professional development. Especially in the areas of language and literacy, teachers have been actively studying their own and students' experiences. This study is the product of a university teacher reflecting on her own teaching in a professional development setting. Three questions emerged naturally from teacher-researcher meetings. Data were collected from initial, midpoint, and concluding surveys. All meetings with the fluctuating number of participants were recorded and interviews were conducted with nine participants. A cross-analysis of findings over time led to the consideration of those factors influencing and motivating participants conducting research. Overall literacy-teacher-researcher-participants benefited from opportunities for collaboration, experiences with talk, and provision of resources.*

---

> The more you learn,
> the more you want to learn.
> The more you know,
> you don't know.
> (Third Grade Teacher-Researcher-Participant)

## Background

A process specified by many and miscellaneous names (e.g. naturalistic research, classroom inquiry, and action research), teacher research embraces the highly reflexive process of questioning, of **not** knowing, of seeking. Questions typically emerge from the problems of practice; analysis is predominantly interpretive, and findings are intended for application within the context in which they were developed. It is "systematic, intentional inquiry by teachers about their own school and classroom work" (Cochran-Smith & Lytle, 1993, pp. 23-24). A derivative of action research, Hollingsworth et al. (1994) defined and differentiated teacher research:

> Teacher research from a *curriculum improvement* stance seeks to improve practice in social settings by trying out curricular ideas as both a means of increasing knowledge of the situation and improving it. Teacher research from the standpoint of *professional critique* intends to learn about and improve the structures and social conditions of practice. The focus of teachers as researchers relative to *societal reform* is on how schools are shaped in society and what epistemological views are important for their transformation. (p.85)

The effects of teacher research are especially great for participants. Their teaching and perceptions of themselves as writers and teachers are transformed in important ways (Goswami & Stillman, 1987). Elliott (1985), McCutcheon (1981), Noffke and Zeichner (1987), and Sheard (1981) found heightened self-esteem and increased feelings of self-worth and confidence as a result of involvement with teacher research. The work of Fishman and McCarthy (1993) provided evidence that teacher research is effective in promoting teacher empowerment and development. Teacher-researchers become rich resources who can provide the profession with information it simply doesn't have. They become critical, responsive readers and users of current research who study writing and learning and report findings without spending large sums of money or drawing on community resources in new and unexpected ways (Goswami & Stillman, 1987). But the benefits of participation in teacher research are not limited to teachers. Those who actively research their own practice offer opportunities for their students to become similarly engaged (Johnston, 1990; Schwartz, 1988). Researching teachers help to nurture researching students (Branscombe, Goswami, & Schwartz, 1992).

For the above reasons and many more which go unmentioned, teacher research has been heralded as a means of professional development (Erickson, 1986; Goswami & Stillman, 1987). Especially in the areas of language and literacy, teachers have been active, studying their own and students' experiences (Cochran-Smith & Lytle, 1993). Elementary and secondary teachers alike have provided a majority of teacher research, the products of their efforts have increased, and their attitudes toward the process seem positive. In a national survey of literacy professionals sponsored by the National Reading Research Center, DeGroff and Commeyras (1998) reported that nearly half of their respondents were interested or very interested in becoming teacher researchers. More than half also agreed or strongly agreed that their thinking had been influenced by reading and hearing teachers talk about their research or by supporting colleagues engaged in teacher research. Page (1994) documented eight teacher-researchers' affirmations of participating in the process. Bennett (1994), in examining teachers' feelings towards educational research and perceptions of themselves as researchers, found that their attitudes toward research improved dramatically as a result of completing action research projects.

While educators have praised the teacher research process, little consideration has been paid to that which affects participant attitudes. Specifically, what factors influence the attitudes of teachers when conducting research? And how might knowledge of these factors be used to better facilitate research? I began to wonder, and thus immersed myself in the teacher-research process.

In the spirit of Duckworth (1987) and Freeman (1989), this study is the product of a university teacher reflecting on her own teaching in a professional development setting. It is one language and literacy professor's attempt to bridge the teaching and research dichotomy while simultaneously realigning the university role as practitioner and researcher by developing scholarship out of the work done by a community of teacher-researchers. **What** teacher educators teach is often contradicted by **how** they teach it (Short, 1993). This work is instead an effort to **live** theory. As a "reflective practitioner" (Schon, 1987) and a "knowing subject" (Freire, 1971), I engaged in the process of learning from teaching. This inquiry was practical and hopefully foundational to formal research that will be useful in improving practice (Richardson, 1994).

I engaged in this process alongside other teachers for many reasons. I hoped that involvement in teacher research would allow us to improve educational practice across levels; contribute to the knowledge base about teacher research; provide insight into staff development programs; encourage teachers' professional and personal growth; generate ideas based on teachers' perceptions and experiences; dissolve barriers separating teachers from teachers; and offer a critical perspective on the teacher-research process.

## Method
### Setting and Participants
This study was conducted in a professional development setting in a suburban school district outside a large, midwestern city. Here, two large-group, in-service meetings were held for four hours each, and two small-group, in-service meetings were held for forty-five minutes each. The time schedules were decided and established by the school district supporting the professional development. During these meetings, the teacher-research process was facilitated. An in-service curriculum, though limited by time constraints, that captured Dewey's (1933) belief that teaching must be an intellectual rather than routine task was developed. While I provided a framework

and guidance for research, no attempts to limit practitioners' freedom to work with issues of importance to them were made. Research became collaborative. Teacher participants opted to work with one another in small groups, sharing in the planning, implementation, and analysis of the research, each contributing her or his unique expertise and perspective (Oja & Smulyan, 1989).

The number of participants in the study fluctuated. Initially, nineteen literacy teachers, eighteen females and one male, elected to embark on the teacher research process. They were paid a small stipend by the district for their participation. At the midpoint of the study, thirteen females and one male were immersed in their research. Ten females and one male completed their inquiries. All teachers were caucasian and their ages ranged from twenty-two to fifty years.

### *Data Collection and Analysis*

The study was qualitative in nature; no impositions or expectations were placed on the data in order to answer the following three questions which emerged naturally from teacher-researcher meetings:

1. What are the attitudes of teacher-researchers as they undergo their first classroom-based research study?
2. What factors, if any, influence the attitudes of these participants when conducting research?
3. How might knowledge of the factors affecting teacher researcher attitudes be used to better facilitate teacher research?

Data were collected from initial, midpoint, and concluding surveys. All meetings with participants were recorded. Extensive interviews were conducted with nine participants three days following the presentations of research. All taped interactions were transcribed. Data were then classified and analyzed at the initial, midpoint, and conclusion of the study.

A qualitative approach to data analysis allowed for the natural emergence of categories. Transcripts and surveys were analyzed through inspection and interpretation (Patton, 1990). Analysis was inductive in nature as I looked for recurring regularities and emerging patterns (Guba, 1978) which were then sorted into categories (Glaser & Strauss, 1967) and ordered. Findings are limited by the specific context of this study.

## Findings
### *Initial*

Teacher-participants reported great concern at the beginning of their research. They experienced anxiety about time issues. "Will I be able to commit to this project enough to obtain worthwhile results? I already feel pulled to the max—personally and professionally," one teacher honestly revealed. Another worried about "Spending more time on this and less time grading papers." The ever-present fear of standardized testing also reared its head as the male participant bluntly asked, "What if our scores drop?" The research process, itself, was equally a nascent concern. Teachers were unsure about "Narrowing the topic." As for their student-participants, they worried they might be "Creating stress for kids at home." Already, teacher-researchers pondered data collection: "I worry that I won't get accurate feedback" and data analysis: "There's so much info . . . how can I sort through it all?" One even contemplated future findings, asking, "Will I like the results I get?"

Less of a concern, but still a source of consideration at the initial stages of research, were perceptions of others (e.g. parents, teachers, administrators, and in-service personnel). For example, teachers demonstrated a desire to please parents: "I worry about reactions from parents" and a need to satisfy "the persons who have organized the staff development." They doubted themselves and their abilities. Teachers admitted feeling "unsure," "insecure," "overwhelmed," "anxious," and "nervous about doing a good job."

### Midpoint

Noticeable changes were evident in teacher attitudes by the midpoint of the study as teachers fully immersed themselves in the process of research. They began to recognize value in their topics as they claimed they were "working on something **I** think is important." As for their student participants, they noticed "the students are benefiting." Data was no longer a source of anxiety: "I find it is very interesting—finding out how the students, teachers, and parents answer questions differently." As for analysis, "it's not so hard," a teacher-researcher asserted. Results were anticipated rather than feared: "I am excited about the results." And a few teachers began to consider the possibilities of disseminating their research, asking, "How can you . . . submit it for publication?" and "How do you present the final product?"

Change in attitude towards the self was noted: "I feel that I am comfortable and more confident;" "I like to be professional;" "I have really immersed myself in this . . . it has become part of my soul." Teachers maintained they benefited from the positive attitude of a co-teacher-researcher during in-service meetings: "You were positive with us; that definitely rubs off." "I'm told, 'this is good,' and I've been helped along the way." "We were led gently down the path." Teachers also admitted that "working as a group has been most beneficial."

Still, there were worries during the midst of the research process. Time remained the primary concern. Teachers needed "time to pull all the information together." They wondered, "When will I finish this project?" They pleaded, "The restraints are too tight." Teachers seemed apprehensive about the amount of reading required for a "good" research project asking, "How many resources are enough?" Another teacher-researcher queried the amount of data necessary for a "solid" study: "Is there a specific amount of data necessary?" Issues of validity were debated as teachers wondered, "How successful has it been?"

### Concluding

Teachers were most positive about the process of research at the conclusion of the study. Teacher-researchers felt quite "comfortable" with their topics. They believed now that "it is better to do the research . . . yourself than read someone else's." They related benefits derived from data analysis: "It made me more organized." And they were quite proud of their final products: "The presentations were also a high;" "I was very impressed with our final product and the other presenters." Teachers recognized growth in themselves: "I think the personal growth was the best part of researching;" "I was so proud of myself;" "It has helped me to grow as a teacher, professional, and individual." At the same time, teachers realized the effects of teacher research on their relationships with colleagues: "It has really brought us together even more as a team" and with students: "It made us more open to our students' needs."

Time was still an unfavorable factor, however. Teacher-research became "one more thing to do" as "it was a lot more work than we expected." The self was still doubted as "we were always worrying if we were doing it 'right.'"

## Discussion

While an analysis of data leads to the discovery of attitudes experienced by new literacy teacher-researchers, a cross-analysis of findings leads to the consideration of those factors influencing and motivating those participants conducting research. Familiarity with these factors might then be used to better facilitate future teacher research in a similar professional development setting.

It is apparent from this study that improved organizational structures, supportive of beginning and experienced teachers' learning and collaboration, are desired. As Mohr (1987) ascertained: "Teacher-researchers need a support system that includes university resources and the backing of their local school system. They need the support of fellow researchers, flexible scheduling, released time to analyze data, and write" (p. 104). Teacher-researchers need to be enabled (Mohr & Maclean, 1987). We must listen carefully and closely, meeting their needs, providing formal and informal support along the research journey.

Specifically, much has been written about isolation in schools (Goodlad, 1984; Lieberman & Miller, 1984; Lortie, 1975). Teaching can be a lonely profession. Time may be spent in a single classroom, and few opportunities to converse with a colleague may present themselves. Perhaps one moment is stolen during a twenty-two minute lunch break or another during the exchange between classes. Teachers need opportunities to interact, Grumet (1989) asserted:

> We must pay attention to the adults who open the doors, ring the bells, hand out the books and the homework assignment. And we need to pay attention not only to teachers' relations to the children, but to their relations to one another as well. What do they know of one another's work? When and how do they work together—if they work together? (p. 21)

In order to support teachers in their research, it is necessary to overcome the serious obstacles caused by teacher isolation (Cochran-Smith & Lytle, 1993). Communities of teacher-researchers consisting of networks of individuals searching for meaning (Westerhoff, 1987) need to be established. A culture of support for visualizing school change needs to be fostered.

Teacher-researcher-participants benefited from such *opportunities for collaboration*: "We just kind of bonded more as professionals and as friends because we spent a lot of time together, and we laughed a lot;" "I gained a lot of insight because of the team work help, and I think it made us closer as a team here. . . . I think it gave a lot of us strength;" "We can all work together. We had a goal in mind and we were able to stumble through it." Interaction with a university-teacher-researcher was also viewed positively: "It was good it was someone from the outside because people didn't know you . . . you had to be prepared. . . . I think the University presence made a difference. I do. I do. I do;" "I think the small-group interaction is a very positive thing because you can zero in on questions that you have, and at the same time you can see where we're having problems and make useful suggestions, and it takes away the anxiety level." Teachers desired interaction with administrators as well, and their lack of participation was duly noted. As Burnaford (1996) reminded, "We cannot ignore the role of school leaders if we are prepared to affirm the value of teacher research as a primary means of professional development in schools" (p. 146). It is apparent that collaboration is also appreciated between schools and communities. Teachers reported learning "a lot about the parents, too, because we interacted with them . . . so it opened up a lot of possibilities." A researcher revealed, "I think they were surprised as to the dedication that many of the staff members had, and I think I also saw that they do support us when we do positive things."

Another factor influencing and motivating teachers involved in the professional development were *experiences with talk*. Teacher-research is fundamentally a social and constructive activity (Cochran-Smith & Lytle, 1993), yet the aforementioned isolation of teachers leaves few moments for sharing teachings and wonderings. Conversational spaces should be created since teachers want to communicate frequently and openly throughout the research process (Cummings & Hustler, 1986; Threadgold, 1985). Discourse communities need to be facilitated and conversations should be sustained. Hollingsworth et al. (1994) articulated those features of conversation that help engagement in reflection about knowledge and experience; these include; creating opportunities for good food, good company, and good conversation; focusing learning on practice-based concerns; discovering biographical connections and differences; and valuing lived experiences and emotions in knowledge. Teacher-participants longed for such interaction, suggesting, "Maybe have a group of people just meet from all over the district to talk about what they're working on."

Teachers especially want occasions to talk about themselves, to swap stories and trade opinions. Participants involved in this research study were surprised by their own abilities, admitting:

"I think I learned personally that I can do more things than I thought I could."

"I'm a really hard worker."

"I can do more than I thought I can do."

"It's really no big deal."

" . . . a little more proud and surprised that I could do it."

Revelations such as these demonstrate lack of knowledge about and confidence in the self. Ray (1993) suggested that most practitioner inquiry begins and ends with personal knowledge, personal knowledge being what teachers construct about themselves, their teaching, and their interactions in the classroom. The teacher research process should begin with self-exploration. Self-reflections and introspections might then lead researchers to challenge beliefs, assumptions, and practices, allowing the personal to intertwine with the practical.

Teacher-researchers were also motivated by the *provision of resources*. Time is recognized by far as a most valuable commodity by teachers. Inflexible work loads and demanding teaching schedules leave few minutes for musing. As early as 1967 Schaefer suggested reduced teaching loads to allow for reflection. Hobson (1996) more recently noted teachers' frustration with time limitations. Teacher-researcher-participants echoed their concerns, requesting "a study-buddy period where you could have gone in and sat down and had a casual place like the lounge that was a study time that you were just there reading" and "subs." Another teacher pondered a more tangible resource: "Financial incentives are usually a good thing."

## Reflection

Since my hopes as a teacher and researcher were clearly stated at the beginning of this article, I am now left reflecting on the process experienced. Yes, contributions were made to the knowledge base about teacher research through the discovery of those factors affecting the attitudes of the participants. Some insight into staff development programs was provided through the description of the study's method and findings. The growth of teachers was encouraged throughout the process. Ideas shared in the discussion were based on teachers' own perceptions and experiences and offered a critical perspective on teacher-research. Through collaborative and communal engagement in the process, barriers separating teachers from teachers were dismantled. Yet one personal goal remains unrealized.

I involved myself in the process of research alongside other teachers, asking questions related to the practice of teacher research as professional development, and engaging in systematic and intentional inquiry about my professional work, but was educational practice improved as a result? Has involvement in teacher research transformed teaching and selves in important ways? Certainly awareness and consideration of the factors affecting participant attitudes can assist teachers as they plan for future research, coordinating better support systems and organizational structures with university and local school systems. But as for the improvement of practice of current teacher-participants, I can only wonder once again. What troubles me is the proven lack of sustained influence of traditional in-service programs (Siedow, Memory, & Bristow, 1985). Will I, will **we**, remain students of learning in our efforts to improve practice, structures, and societies? Will we provide for ourselves those structures which will help to facilitate our research— collaboration, talk, and resources? I can hope so. It is time all teachers take charge of their own professional development. Herein lies the capacity for continual transformation, renewal, and becoming.

---

## References

Bennett, C. K. (1994). Promoting teacher reflection through action research: What do teachers think? *Journal of Staff Development, 15*(1), 34-38.

Branscrombe, A., Goswami, D., & Schwartz, J. (Eds.). (1992). *Students teaching, teachers learning.* Portsmouth, NH: Boynton/Cook, Heinemann.

Burnaford, G. (1996). Supporting teacher research: Professional development and the reality of schools. In G. Burnaford, J. Fischer, & D. Hobson (Eds.), *Teachers doing research: Practical possibilities* 137-150. Mahwah, NJ: Lawrence Erlbaum Associates Publishers.

Cochran-Smith, M., & Lytle, S. (1990). Research on teaching and teacher research. *Educational Researcher, 19*(2), 2-11.

Cochran-Smith, M., & Lytle, S. (1993). Inside/outside: Teacher research and knowledge. New York, NY: Teachers College Press.

Cummings, C., & Hustler, D. (1986). Teachers' professional knowledge. In D. Hustler, T. Cassidy, & T. Cuff (Eds.), *Action research in classrooms and schools* (pp. 36-47). London: Allen and Unwin.

DeGroff, L., & Commeyras, M. (1998). Literacy professionals' perspectives on professional development and pedagogy: A United States survey. *Reading Research Quarterly, 33*(4), 434-472.

Dewey, J. (1933). *How we think: A restatement of the relation of reflective thinking to the education process.* Chicago: Henry Regnery.

Duckworth, E. (1987). *The having of wonderful ideas.* New York: Teachers College Press.

Elliott, J. (1985). Facilitating action research in schools: Some dilemmas. In R. Burgess (Ed.), *Field methods in the study of education* (pp. 235-262).Philadelphia: Falmer Press.

Erickson, F. (1986). Qualitative methods in research on teaching. In M. C. Wittrock (Ed.), *Handbook of research on teaching* (3rd ed.). New York: Macmillan.

Fishman, S., & McCarthy, L. (1993). *John Dewey and the challenge of classroom practice.* New York: Teachers College Press.

Freeman, C. (1989). *The case study method in teacher education: A teacher researcher study.* Paper presented at the Ethnography in Education Forum, University of Pennsylvania, Philadelphia.

Freire, P. (1971). *Pedagogy of the oppressed.* New York: Herder and Herder.

Glaser, B. G., & Strauss, A. L. (1967). The discovery of grounded theory: Strategies for qualitative research. New York: Aldine de Gruyter.

Goodlad, J. (1984). *A place called school.* New York: McGraw Hill.

Goswami, D., & Stillman, P. (1987). *Reclaiming the classroom: Teacher research as an agency for change.* Upper Montclair, NJ: Boynton/Cook.

Grumet, M. R. (1989). *Dinner at Abigail's: Nurturing collaboration.* National Education Association, January, 20-25.

Guba, E. G. (1978). Toward a methodology of naturalistic inquiry in educational evaluation. *CSE Monograph Series in Evaluation, 8.* Los Angeles: University of California, Los Angeles, Center for the Study of Evaluation.

Hobson, D. (1996). Beginning with the self: Using autobiography and journal writing in teacher research. In G. Burnaford, J. Fischer, & D. Hobson (Eds.), *Teachers doing research: Practical possibilities* (pp. 1-17). Mahwah, NJ: Lawrence Erlbaum Associates Publishers.

Hollingsworth, S., et al. (1994). *Teacher research and urban literacy education: Lessons and conversations in a feminist key.* New York: Teachers College Press.

Johnston, P. (1990). *A shift in paradigm: As teachers become researchers so goes the curriculum.* Paper presented at the Ethnography in Education Forum, University of Pennsylvania, Philadelphia.

Lieberman, A., & Miller, L. (1984). *Teachers, their world and their work: Implications for school improvement.* Arlington, VA: Association for Curriculum Development.

Lortie, D. (1975). *The schoolteacher: A sociological study.* Chicago: University of Chicago Press.

McCutcheon, G. (1981). The impact of the insider. In J. Nixon (Ed.), *A teacher's guide to action research* (pp. 186-193). London: Grant Mcintyre Ltd.

Mohr, M. M. (1987). Teacher-researchers and the study of the writing process. In D. Goswami & P. Stillman (Eds.), *Reclaiming the classroom: Teacher research as an agency for change* (pp. 94-107). Upper Montclair, NJ: Boynton/Cook Publishers, Inc.

Mohr, M., & Maclean, M. (1987). *Working together: A guide for teacher-researchers.* Urbana, IL: National Council of Teachers of English.

Noffke, S. E., & Zeichner, K. M. (1987). *Action research and teacher thinking: The first phase of the AR on AR project at the university of Wisconsin, Madison.* Paper presented at the annual meeting of the American Educational Research Association, Washington, D. C.

Oja, S., & Smulyan, L. (1989). *Collaborative action research: A developmental approach.* London: Falmer Press.

Page, E. (1994). Does real research mean teacher research? *English Journal, 83*(6), 51-54.

Patton, M. Q. (1990). *Qualitative evaluation and research methods* (2nd ed.) Newbury Park: Sage Publications.

Ray, R. (1993). *The practice of theory: Teacher research in composition.* Urbana, IL: National Council of Teachers of English.

Richardson, V. (1994). *Conducting research on practice. Educational Researcher, 23*(5), 5-10.

Schaefer, R. J. (1967). *The school as the center of inquiry.* New York: Harper and Row.

Schon, D. A. (1987). *Educating the reflective practitioner.* San Francisco: Jossey-Bass.

Schwartz, J. (1988). The drudgery and the discovery: Students as research partners. *English Journal, 77,* 37-40.

Sheard, D. (1981). Spreading the message. In J. Nixon (Ed.), *A teacher's guide to action research* (pp. 175-185). London: Grant-McIntyre.

Short, K. (1993). Teacher research for teacher educators. In L. Patterson, C. M. Santa, K. G. Short, & K. Smith (Eds.), *Teachers are researchers: Reflection and action* (pp. 155-159). Newark, DE: International Reading Association, Inc.

Siedow, M. D., Memory, D. M., & Bristow, P. S. (1985). *In-service education for content area teachers.* Newark, DE: International Reading Association.

Threadgold, M. W. (1985). Bridging the gap between teachers and researchers. In R. Burgess (Ed.), *Issues in educational research: Qualitative methods* (pp. 251-270). Philadelphia: Falmer Press.

Westerhoff, J. H. (1987). The teacher as pilgrim. In F. S. Bolin & J. M. Falk (Eds.), *Teacher renewal.* New York: Teachers College Press.

# DIVERSE
# VOICES

# Do Academic Centers
# Meet Students' Needs?

**Michele Mits Cash**
**Linda Saumell**

University of Miami

**Marie Tejero Hughes**

Univesity of Illinois at Chicago

## Abstract

*Housing learning assistance programs in one central location on campus can strengthen services through interrelatedness, make it easier for students to locate the services needed, and encourage a sense of unity among staff members. This paper describes the Academic Development Center at a mid-size university that houses a number of student services that had previously existed as separate entities on campus. This paper also discusses what brings students to the center, students' satisfaction with the quality of services, staff and tutors, and recommendations for improvement. The most popular service was tutoring, particularly in mathematics, science, and business. Overall students were satisfied with staff support and tutor quality. Tutors at the center received comprehensive training, which may have contributed to the satisfaction of tutees. Recommendations for enhancing services at the center included extending the hours of operation as well as extending the amount of tutoring time per subject, per week.*

Developmental college reading programs have been a concern of institutions of higher education in the United States since the early 17th century (Leedy, 1958). Throughout the history of higher education in America it has been evident that some sort of learning assistance must be provided for many students to succeed, even at the more prestigious institutions such as Harvard, Yale, and Stanford. Prior to 1900, learning assistance took the form of remedial reading programs conducted by tutors or in secondary education type settings (Enright & Kerstiens, 1980). As the demands associated with domain specific reading requirements have increased over time (Heron, 1989), so too has the need for programs that would foster the development of the type of reading and study skills necessary for academic success. During the 1950's, the institutional belief that good reading and comprehension skills would lead to academic success resulted in an expansion of reading improvement programs. Similarly, increased opportunities for higher education resulting from societal influences such as the Depression, World War II, the GI Bill, the 'Space Race', and the emergence of open admissions policies led to a burgeoning number of students in the 20th century seemingly under-prepared for the rigors of college reading and studying (Enright & Kersteins, 1980; Maxwell, 1997). Changes within the field of college reading programs have evolved slowly, typically more in direct response to what is happening in the institution's community than influences from a more global perspective (Straff, 1985). However, regardless of the etiology or pace of change, what is evident is the important role that learning assistance and developmental reading programs have played in American higher education (Leedy, 1958; Heron, 1989; Straff, 1985).

Today, programs to enhance college academic success may include any form of remedial or developmental curriculum ranging from a single course in reading to a comprehensive program that includes basic skills and counseling. Typical learning assistance programs may deliver services such as tutoring, laboratory instruction, regularly scheduled classes, paired or adjunct classes, supplemental instruction, outreach programs, and distance learning. Ideally, the services offered are those most appropriate to the student population being served. For example, comprehensive reading and study skills courses, paired courses, and supplemental instruction are designed to better serve under prepared and at-risk students who require more structure than that provided by drop-in programs in learning assistance centers (Elliott & Fairbanks, 1986; Johnson & Carpenter, 2000; Roueche, Baker, & Roueche, 1984). On the other hand, outreach programs that include seminars on topics relevant to student success, such as study skills, test taking strategies, and time management may be more appropriate for students requiring less formal structure. Tutoring, one of the most popular services offered (Rouche & Snow, 1977), is most successful when the tutors have received some type of training (Boylan, Bonham, Bliss, & Saxon, 1995). Thus, the provision of formal tutor training courses may be included in the activities of the learning assistance program.

Clearly, learning assistance programs may take different forms, provide different types of services, and go by many different names including learning centers, reading labs, learning assistance centers, academic skills centers, learning skills centers, and academic development centers (Johnson &

Carpenter, 2000). Within this diversity lies a common mission to encourage educational opportunities, develop academic talent and efficiency among diverse students, and provide a bridge between student services and academic services (Boylan, 1983; Cross, 1976; Maxwell, 1997). The clientele of the learning assistance program is not limited to students who are at-risk for failure, but may include students who are underprepared for college level work, English language learners, individuals with disabilities, and adults who have not been in school for many years (Johnson & Carpenter, 2000).

Because institutions of higher education are committed to the academic success of their students, the need for learning assistance programs will likely continue well into the 21st century. However, the existence of such programs depends heavily on institutional philosophy and the perspectives towards learning that are held by each college or university (Johnson & Carpenter, 2000). Organizational resources of the school, the administrator's own academic background, available funding for programs, and administrative policies or governmental mandates all influence and guide the establishment and operation of learning assistance programs.

Important to the expansion of, and continuation of the long-term benefits students receive from learning assistance programs, is the on-going evaluation of services offered by these programs. Boylan, Bonham, White, and George (2000) have cited four major factors that have contributed to both the expansion of learning assistance programs and the need for their evaluation since the 1960's. Coordinating agencies that assess educational activities and monitor student statistics, as well as accountability reports that must be generated in response to federal funds for educational support have both contributed to increases in program evaluation needs. Additionally, as institutions have realized the importance of improving programs, enhancing and maintaining educational credibility assessment has become a critical component of their long-term strategic plans. Finally, the availability of affordable technology that can store, manipulate, and retrieve mass quantities of data and assist in the labor intensive process of evaluation, have encouraged the more frequent evaluation of learning assistance programs. Such evaluations not only meet accountability objectives, but also provide information that facilitates the continual development of the program to meet changing student needs.

To develop our understanding of the Academic Development Center (ADC), a learning assistance program at our university, an evaluation of the center was conducted. It was hoped that this program evaluation would not only assist us in providing services that best met the needs of our students, but also provide other educators with insights into who uses support services and the types of services needed. The purpose of this evaluation was threefold: (1) to discover what brings students to the center, (2) to determine students' level of satisfaction with the quality of services currently offered, as well as their satisfaction with staff and tutors who provide those services, and (3) to solicit recommendations from students about how to improve the center.

## Program Description
### *Description of the Academic Development Center*

The ADC is located in a medium-size private university. Successful student learning is the primary goal of the center. Services offered by the center include content generic programs such as seminars designed to assist students with a variety of study skills and transitional issues and individual assistance for improving textbook reading skills and for refining study skills. Students are also provided with content specific programs such as peer tutoring and supplemental instruction for some of the university's more difficult courses. The ADC also houses the Academic Support Project, which provides ongoing academic support and guidance to first-generation college students from low-income backgrounds and to students with disabilities. The Office of Disabilities Services, which is responsible for the coordination of auxiliary aids and services for students and employees with disabilities, is also part of the center. In addition to assistance provided by the ADC, the University also provides additional assistance through the Writing Center, a Math Lab that provides drop-in math tutoring, a Counseling Center, and tutoring provided by various academic departments.

All students who come to the ADC must complete the Learning and Study Strategies Inventory (LASSI) on their first visit. The LASSI provides information about areas where a student may be experiencing difficulty such as Time Management, Test Strategies, Anxiety, Motivation, Selecting Main Ideas, Concentration, Information Processing, and other study related behaviors. Students then receive a report of their scores, an explanation of each subtest area, and recommendations for activities, such as workshops or individual reading and study skills assistance that can help them to improve in these areas. Students may also receive referrals to other campus entities for certain types of assistance, such as the Counseling Center for help with anxiety problems, or the Career Center if ambiguity regarding career paths is impacting motivation. Within the ADC, students may be referred to a variety of programs as outlined below:

**Peer Tutoring.** Peer tutoring is offered in a wide range of courses, although the primary focus is on lower division courses. Students may receive up to two hours of individual tutoring each week in each subject. Referrals are not required and students do not need to be failing a subject to qualify for tutoring. Undergraduate and graduate students who have completed a tutor-training program, that is certified by the College Reading and Learning Association, conduct tutoring on an appointment basis. The ADC typically employs eighty to ninety tutors.

**Supplemental Instruction.** Supplemental Instruction (SI) provides small group study sessions for the university's most difficult courses. A student leader who has previously completed the course successfully facilitates SI sessions. The SI leaders attend lectures and complete all reading assignments for the course they facilitate. SI courses may be in any discipline, but most often include Chemistry, Math, Psychology, and Biology.

*Smart Start Workshops.* The Smart Start Workshop series consists of seven workshops: Time Management; Note Taking; Textbook Reading; Academic Integrity; Managing Long Term Projects and Papers; Building Productive Relationships with Professors, and Test-Taking/Test Preparation. Workshops are presented at the ADC on a regular rotating basis each semester and by special arrangement, at the residence halls, and for various groups including sororities/fraternities, athletes, multi-cultural student affairs, and others. A variety of strategies are used to encourage student participation in the workshop including table-tent advertising, distribution of schedules to students, placement of schedules in key areas around the University, and inclusion of schedules in student publications. Additionally, students who come to the Center for tutoring or other services complete the Learning and Study Strategies Inventory (LASSI). Based on the LASSI results, students are often advised to attend a particular workshop or workshops for instruction in certain topics.

**Reading and Study Skills Assistance.** Assistance in reading and study skills including textbook reading, note taking skills, test preparation, information organization, and time management is provided by graduate assistants (typically enrolled in the masters program of the School of Education). These assistants, trained by the ADC Director, present the Smart Start Workshops, and work individually with students who either request follow-up after the workshop, or are referred to the Reading/Study Skills Assistants on the basis of LASSI results. Students may also be referred by the Office of Disability Services for assistance with organizational or study skills. Additionally, students may request assistance in these areas on their own.

**Office of Disability Services (ODS).** This office coordinates auxiliary aids and services for students with disabilities, receives and verifies documentation of disabilities, and serves as a clearinghouse for information on disability related items. The ODS often refers students for tutoring or reading and study skills assistance, particularly students with learning disabilities or attention deficit disorders.

**Academic Support Project (ASP).** The ASP provides ongoing academic support and guidance to encourage academic success and persistence of first-generation college students, students from low-income backgrounds, and students with disabilities. The role of the program is to interact with students meeting this criteria, establish a relationship with the student, and act as a liaison with various entities within the ADC to ensure that students access the services they need to succeed.

**First Year Experience.** Transitional classes for incoming freshman are offered on an elective basis. The class explores many campus resources such as Career Planning, Library Research, Wellness Center, Student Organizations, Tutoring, and Study Skills. The Study Skills component is presented through the Smart Start Workshops, which are presented to each class group.

## Students Attending Academic Development Center

All students at the University are eligible to use the services at the ADC at no additional charge to them. During the current academic year, 777 students received individualized services at the ADC. Students were asked to complete the Student Information Questionnaire (see Appendix A) when they first came to the center. This questionnaire provided demographic information about the student, information about the first level of English and math courses taken at the university, and the types of difficulties students might be experiencing. Grade point averages, SAT scores, and other demographic information not provided on the questionnaire were obtained through the university's database. Students attending the center were more likely to be female (64%) than male (36%), and included freshmen (36%), sophomore (30%), junior (18%), and senior (10%) students. Although students were enrolled in a variety of majors, life sciences (34%) and business (18%) majors predominated. The mean grade point average for students was 2.81 on a 4-point scale and the median Scholastic Achievement Test (SAT) score was 1103 (*SD* =139.85).

All students accessing services at the ADC completed the Learning and Study Strategies Inventory (LASSI) (Weinstein, 1987). Students attending the center scored below average on two scales: Test Strategy scores were in the 35th percentile (e.g. items in this section include: "I do poorly on tests because I find it hard to plan my work within a short period of time, and I have difficulty adapting my studying to different types of courses"). Anxiety and Worry scores were in the 40th percentile (e.g. items in this section include: "I worry that I will flunk out of school, and when I begin an examination, I feel pretty confident that I will do well") (see table 1). Scores on all other scales fell within the 50th (+/- 5) percentile. Students were assigned to tutors who would call students to arrange tutoring times or were referred to appropriate services within 24 hours of making a request.

**Table 1. LASSI Profile of Students Attending ADC (n = 777)**

|                              | Percentile | M*    | SD   |
| ---------------------------- | ---------- | ----- | ---- |
| Attitude and Interest        | 50         | 32.68 | 5.19 |
| Motivation                   | 45         | 30.64 | 5.76 |
| Test strategies              | 35         | 28.30 | 5.84 |
| Information processing       | 45         | 26.94 | 5.77 |
| Concentration and attention  | 55         | 26.51 | 6.54 |
| Self testing                 | 50         | 25.44 | 5.67 |
| Use of support techniques    | 45         | 24.90 | 5.41 |
| Anxiety and worry            | 40         | 24.15 | 6.72 |
| Time management              | 55         | 24.10 | 6.91 |
| Selecting main ideas         | 50         | 18.29 | 3.90 |

*scaled scores*

## Evaluation Procedures

At the end of the semester students were asked to complete the Student Satisfaction Survey (see Appendix A). The Student Satisfaction Survey is a 4-point Likert-type scale on which participants indicated their level of agreement (1 = strongly disagree, 4 = strongly agree) to statements relating to the services provided at the ADC and their perceived benefit to the student, such as accessibility and supportiveness of the ADC staff, and improvement of student grades and study skills. The survey also included open-ended questions to solicit comments on most and least beneficial service, value of services, and suggestions for improvement of the ADC and it's services. Both instruments were developed specifically for this evaluation. Student confidentiality was protected by the assignment of coded identification numbers. Data was stored in a Microsoft Access file and was exported to the SPSS statistical program to derive descriptive statistics for reporting purposes. Responses to open-ended questions were written on individual note cards and then sorted into categories. Categories were checked for overlap and completeness and themes established (Lincoln & Guba, 1989).

## Findings from Evaluation
### *What Brings Students to the Center?*

All students attending the ADC were asked to identify the services they used during the past semester. An overwhelming majority (94%) of the students reported that they had come for the one-on-one tutoring available at the center. The students requested mathematics and science tutoring most often which accounted for about 80% of the tutoring at the center. Tutoring was also frequently requested for business (e.g., accounting, economics), English, and social science courses. In addition to tutoring, students came to the center to receive assistance in developing study skills (27%), to meet with supplemental instruction groups (25%), and to participate in Smart Start Workshops (20%). A few students (7%), who were concerned about their reading, came to the center to have their reading ability evaluated.

In addition to determining what services students were utilizing, we were also interested in knowing why students decided to come to the ADC. Students provided us with a variety of reasons for seeking the services of the center. Many of the students indicated that they were failing or doing poorly in at least one of their courses. "I'm currently standing on my last leg." and "I am having trouble in math, and I think a tutor might help." were typical responses from this group. Another large group of students stated that they came to the center as a preventive measure or to improve their grades. Two typical responses were, "I need help in my more difficult classes so I can make the best grade possible" and "To keep up with all my work and help me if I have problems." Students also stated that they came to the center hoping to improve their study skills. "I need to improve my study skills and need tutoring for certain subjects." Free services at the center, and previous positive experiences at the center rounded out the top five reasons for seeking the services offered.

### Are Students Satisfied With the Center?

At the end of the semester students completed the Student Satisfaction Survey to indicate their satisfaction with the center and with their own outcomes attributed to the services they received. The majority of students sought services for tutoring (94%). Other services accessed by students at the ADC included, study skills (27%), Supplemental Instruction (25%), Smart Start Workshops (20%), and to a lesser extent reading tests (7%). Overall, 90% of the students indicated that they were very satisfied or satisfied with the services received. As shown in Table 2, the majority of students rated the various items surveyed very favorably. Students were especially satisfied with the quality (90%), support of staff (94%), and quality of tutors (90%) at the center. Furthermore, students indicated that their academic needs were met, they had become better students, and their grades had improved since attending the center.

When asked what they liked most about the ADC, many students indicated it was the individualized attention received from the staff and tutors. Students made remarks such as, "It was directed specifically to my needs for each course," and "Explanations were specific to my needs and questions." Students were also complementary of the assistance they received to improve their study skills. "Workshops help to develop my study skills and grades." "I

**Table 2. ADC Student Satisfaction Survey (n = 777)**

|  | SATISFACTION | *M* | *SD* |
|---|---|---|---|
| CENTER SERVICES |  |  |  |
| Staff is supportive | 94% | 3.21 | .64 |
| Quality of tutors is sufficient | 90% | 3.11 | .62 |
| Staff is accessible | 79% | 3.20 | .72 |
| Tutoring time is sufficient | 77% | 2.90 | .72 |
| PERSONAL OUTCOMES |  |  |  |
| My academic needs are met | 88% | 3.08 | .61 |
| I am a better student | 82% | 3.06 | .69 |
| My grades have improved | 79% | 2.99 | .70 |
| Self confidence increased | 78% | 2.92 | .71 |
| Helped me stay in school | 74% | 2.86 | .88 |
| Long-range planning improved | 70% | 2.73 | .74 |
| Organization skills improved | 68% | 2.78 | .74 |

*Note: 1 = strongly disagree; 4 = strongly agree*

passed the class I was having trouble in." Overall students were grateful that the center was available to them since it kept them "focused and confident" and "forced [them] to work on a subject [they] need help in."

### *What Do Students Recommend?*

Although the majority of the students who attended the center were satisfied with the services they received, they did provide us with recommendations about additional ways in which the ADC might better meet their needs. Students were most concerned with the times the center was open, which are primarily during normal business hours. Students suggested that the ADC expand their hours into the evenings. They also suggested expanding the amount of tutoring time available to students beyond the current limitation of one hour twice weekly per course. Students suggested that having two-hour tutoring blocks or allowing more frequent tutoring sessions would be helpful. Additional recommendations included allocating tutors more quickly, adding more tutoring space, and having more tutors available for upper level courses.

## Discussion

The ADC opened four years ago and brought together a number of student services that had previously existed as separate entities on campus. According to Johnson and Carpenter (2000), the needs of students accessing learning assistance services are best met when the program is housed in a central location. This model strengthens services through interrelatedness, makes it is easier for students to locate the services they need, and it encourages a sense of unity and teamwork among staff members. Since the services were joined at the center, we have seen a dramatic increase in the number of students utilizing our services. Additionally, the proximity of the Office of Disability Services, the Academic Support Project, tutorial services, reading and study skills assistance, and seminar/workshop series has enabled staff members to work together to make recommendations for the type of assistance students would benefit from, directing students immediately to the staff person responsible for those services, and then following up with other staff members about that student.

As mentioned earlier, typically when a student comes to the ADC, he or she completes the LASSI. The LASSI is then scored and the student receives a report of their scores and what they mean, as well as a list of recommendations that focus on their particular needs. For example, students who did not score well on the "selecting main ideas" scale would be encouraged to attend the Textbook Reading Seminar or obtain individual assistance with these skills at the center. It is likely that the interrelatedness of the services and the team approach to meeting student needs may contribute to the fact that the majority of students viewed the ADC staff as both supportive and accessible.

The majority of students who came to the center did so to obtain tutors. This amounts to approximately 730 of the 777 students. Because we have not undertaken an evaluation such as this previously, we do not know whether there have been variations in this percentage, but we do know that the number of students accessing tutors has risen considerably over the past several years. Our findings indicated that the reasons that students use tutoring vary broadly and include students who are having difficulty in a particular subject, students who are anticipating difficulty in a particular subject that has been problematic for them in the past, and students who are passing a class but are hoping to excel in the subject material or as they put it "earn the best grade possible." The staff of the ADC spends a considerable amount of time attending orientation sessions and meeting with student groups to encourage students to seek tutoring. The staff stresses the notion that students should not wait until they are failing a course to seek tutoring, but that even students who are doing okay can benefit from meeting with tutors. This message seems to have reached students and may account for the variability among the reasons that students are seeking tutoring services.

In keeping with the notion that tutoring is most successful when the tutors have received some type of training (Boylan, et al., 1995), the ADC has recently implemented an extensive tutor-training program. We were encouraged that this training is improving the tutorial program by the fact that 90% of our students felt that the quality of tutors is sufficient. Within the tutor-training program, tutors learn a variety of techniques that they can use to assist students in improving their study skills as well as improving their ability to master the subject matter in which they are seeking help. Again, we were encouraged that quite a few of the students accessing the center felt that they were better students and that their organizational skills and long-range planning had improved through their use of center services. Our tutor-training program requires that tutors attend certain predetermined workshops, and then allows tutors to choose from a menu of other training options including seminars, videos, readings, and other activities. One of the options for tutors is to attend a "Test Anxiety" presentation at the University Counseling Center. We were concerned that the profiles of the students attending the center indicated that they had higher levels of anxiety and worry, and so have decided to move this from the options to the mandatory portion of the tutor-training program to provide additional information for tutors in this area. Since previous researchers (Hancock & Gier, 1991) have demonstrated the benefits of training peer tutors in counseling skills and techniques, this may be an avenue that we might pursue.

A series of study skills seminars ("Smart Start Workshops") was implemented at the ADC during the previous academic year. The results of this evaluation indicated that only about 20% of the students who came to ADC came to attend one or more of the workshops. Since one of the goals of the ADC is to help students to become better learners, we are trying to attract a greater number of students to these workshops. We have altered the time schedule for workshops and have improved our advertising of topics, dates, and times in the hopes of attracting more students during this year.

In soliciting recommendations from students regarding ways that the center might better meet their needs, students appeared most concerned about the times the center is open (normal business hours) and the length of the tutorial sessions (one hour). In response to these recommendations we are exploring the possibility of expanding the hours of operation to include evening hours during which tutoring will be offered as well as study skills presentations. We have also begun placing tutors in the residence halls during evening hours for high volume subject areas such as math and science.

Based on student responses we plan to conduct further reviews regarding changes in the length of tutorial sessions and other services. However, the use of self-report data limits the findings because of what students are willing to tell under the conditions of data collection. It should be also noted that while self-report data provide a view of students' perception of events and conditions, these perceptions may not be an accurate representation of events and conditions as they actually exist. Any question, no matter how simple it may appear, may embarrass the person and encourage him or her to provide a socially desirable response (Fowler, 1988). However, self-reports that are elicited with care and interpreted with an understanding of the circumstances under which they are obtained are a valuable source of information (Ericsson & Simon, 1980, 1993).

During the past few years we have made many changes at the ADC designed to assist students in improving their reading and study skills as well as their grades. Conducting this evaluation has helped us to evaluate these changes within the context of student needs and preferences and have provided direction for changes that we hope to make in the future. In "Teaching and Today's College Students," Upcraft (1996) describes a student body that has changed dramatically from the students of twenty-five years ago. If we compare the students of twenty-five years ago with their predecessors of twenty-five additional years we would again find significant differences among them. Clearly, we could continue this comparison and find many differences between yesterday and today's college student. Changes in American society and schooling are reflected in changing values, expectations, and the levels of preparation of the college students we serve. Maintaining an understanding of the ways in which students are changing and what their needs are for academic support can help those involved in learning support to grow as service providers and to continually adjust and enhance their academic support systems. An on-going evaluation system, such as that implemented at the on-set of this study, can help to inform us about the changing needs of our student population and enhance our ability to meet these needs.

## References

Boylan, H. R. (1983). *Is developmental education working? An analysis of research.* A research report prepared for the National Association for Remedial and Developmental Studies in Postsecondary Education, Appalachian State University, Boone, NC.

Boylan, H. R., Bonham, B. S., Bliss, L. B., & Saxon, D. P. (1995). What we know about tutoring: Findings from the national study of developmental education. *Research in Developmental Education, 14*(1), 1-4.

Boylan, H. R., Bonham, B. S., White, J. R., & George, A. P. (2000). Evaluation of college reading and study strategy programs. In R. F. Flippo, & D. C. Caverly (Eds.), *Handbook of college reading and study strategy research* (pp. 365-402). Mahwah, NJ: Erlbaum.

Cross, K. P. (1976). Accent on learning. San Francisco: Jossey-Bass.

Elliott, M. D., & Fairbanks, M. (1986). General vs. adjunct reading/study skills instruction for a college history course. *Journal of College Reading and Learning, 19*, 22-29.

Enright G., & Kerstiens, G. (1980). The learning center: Toward an expanded role. In O. T. Lenning, & R. L. Nayman (Eds.), *New directions for college learning assistance: new roles for learning assistance* (pp. 1-24). San Francisco: Jossey-Bass.

Ericsson, K. A., & Simon, H. A. (1980). Verbal reports as data. *Psychological Review, 87,* 215-251.

Ericsson, K. A., & Simon, H. A. (1993). *Protocal analysis: Verbal reports as data.* London, England: MIT Press.

Fowler, F. J. (1988). *Survey research methods.* Newbury Park, CA: Sage.

Hancock, K., & Gier, T. (1991). Counseling skills: An important part of tutor training. *Journal of College Reading and Learning, 23,* 55-59.

Heron, E. B. (1989). The dilemma of college reading instruction: A developmental analysis. Unpublished doctoral dissertation, Harvard University, Cambridge, MA (University Microfilms #9014298)

Johnson, L. L., & Carpenter, K. (2000). Evaluation of college reading and study strategy programs. In R. F. Flippo, & D. C. Caverly (Eds.), Handbook of college reading and study strategy research. Mahwah, NJ: Lawrence Erlbaum Association.

Leedy, P. D. (1958). A history of the origin and development of instruction in reading improvement at the college level. Unpublished doctoral dissertation, New York University, New York (University Microfilms #59-01016)

Lincoln, Y. S., & Guba., E. (1989). *Naturalistic Inquiry.* Newbury Park, CA: Sage.

Maxwell, M. (1997). Improving student learning skills: A new edition. Clearwater, FL: H&H Publishing Company, Inc.

Roueche, J. E., Baker, G. A., III, & Roueche, S. D. (1984). College responses to low-achieving students: A national study. *American Education, 20,*31-24.

Roueche, J. E., & Snow, J. J. (1977). Overcoming learning problems. San Francisco: Jossey-Bass.

Straff, W. W. (1985). Comparisons, contrasts, and evaluation of selected college reading programs. Unpublished doctoral dissertation, Temple University, Philadelphia (University Microfilms #8611937)

Upcraft, M. L. (1996). Teaching and today's college students. In R. J. Menges, M. Weimer, & Associates (Eds.), *Teaching on solid ground: Using scholarship to improve practice* (pp. 21-41). San Francisco: Jossey-Bass.

Weinstein, C. E. (1987). Learning and Study Strategies Inventory. Clearwater, FL: H&H Publishing Company, Inc.

## Appendix A. Academic Development Center
## Student Information Form

Welcome to the Academic Development Center. *Services provided by the Center are available to all UM students free of charge.* Completing this questionnaire and the Learning & Study Strategies Inventory will take a few minutes of your time, but will help us to provide the best possible assistance.

1. Name: _____ 2. Date of Birth: _____
3. ID#: _____ 4. Sex: Male   Female
5. Local Address: _____
6. Permanent Address: _____
7. Email Address: _____
8. Local Telephone Number: ___ Permanent Telephone Number: _____
9. How did you hear about the Academic Development Center?

_____

10. Would you like to receive tutoring?                          Yes   No
11. Would you like to participate in Supplemental Instruction?   Yes   No
12. Would you like to take a reading test?                       Yes   No
13. Would you like to participate in our Smart Start Workshops?  Yes   No
14. Would you like to attend our study skills workshops?         Yes   No
15. List the areas in which you feel you need academic assistance.
    Course                    Section              Professor

    _____
    _____
    _____
    _____

16. Describe any difficulties you are presently having at the University:
17. First semester/year enrolled at UM? _____
18. Enrollment Status:    Part-time          Full-time
19. Number of credits enrolled in this semester: _____
20. Classification:  Freshman    Sophomore    Junior    Senior
21. Major: _____ Minor: _____
22. Do you participate in clubs, social activities, Greek life, or athletics?
    Yes   No   If yes, which ones: _____
23. What was the first English class you enrolled in at UM?
    ENG103   ENG105   ENG106   ENG107   Other: _____
24. What was the first Math class you enrolled in at UM?
    MTH099   MTH101   MTH103   MTH107   Other: _____

25. Have you ever been tutored in the past?                    Yes   No
    If yes, what subject(s)? _____
26. Have you ever taken TAL 191?                               Yes   No
27. Did you participate in a Freshman Program,                 Yes   No
    e.g. FYI, Freshman Success, FEX, etc?
    If yes, which program? _____
28. Did you participate in a "Summer Bridge" program?          Yes   No
29. Have you participated in a "Learning Community"?           Yes   No
                        Thank you!

## Appendix B. University of Miami Academic Development Center Student Satisfaction Survey

Student Name: _____ Student ID: _____

*Please help us to provide you with the best services possible by completing this survey.*

| | | STRONGLY DISAGREE | DISAGREE | AGREE | STRONGLY AGREE |
|---|---|---|---|---|---|
| 1. The services I received through the Academic Development Center helped me to stay in school. | | 1 | 2 | 3 | 4 |
| 2. I have more confidence in myself as a student now that I have participated in programs offered at the Academic Development Center. | | 1 | 2 | 3 | 4 |
| 3. The Academic Development Center staff has been very supportive of me in my efforts as a student. | | 1 | 2 | 3 | 4 |
| 4. The Academic Development Center staff is accessible whenever I need their assistance. | | 1 | 2 | 3 | 4 |

5. I would recommend the following Academic Development Center services to other students:

| | | | | | |
|---|---|---|---|---|---|
| Individual Tutoring Program | did not use | 1 | 2 | 3 | 4 |
| Counseling Services | did not use | 1 | 2 | 3 | 4 |
| Mentoring Program | did not use | 1 | 2 | 3 | 4 |
| Academic Advisement | did not use | 1 | 2 | 3 | 4 |
| Financial Aid Assistance | did not use | 1 | 2 | 3 | 4 |
| Cultural Activities | did not use | 1 | 2 | 3 | 4 |
| Diagnostic Services | did not use | 1 | 2 | 3 | 4 |
| Math, Reading and Writing Instruction | did not use | 1 | 2 | 3 | 4 |
| Career Exploration | did not use | 1 | 2 | 3 | 4 |
| Enrollment Assistance for Graduate School | did not use | 1 | 2 | 3 | 4 |
| Smart Start Workshops | did not use | 1 | 2 | 3 | 4 |
| Reading and Study Skills | did not use | 1 | 2 | 3 | 4 |
| Disability Services | did not use | 1 | 2 | 3 | 4 |
| Academic Support Project | did not use | 1 | 2 | 3 | 4 |
| Supplemental Instruction | did not use | 1 | 2 | 3 | 4 |

| | Strongly Disagree | Disagree | Agree | Strongly Agree |
|---|---|---|---|---|
| 6. My long-range planning skills have improved as a result of participating in services provided by the Academic Development Center. | 1 | 2 | 3 | 4 |
| 7. My organization skills have improved by participating in the services provided by the Academic Development Center. | 1 | 2 | 3 | 4 |
| 8. By participating in programs and services offered by the Academic Development Center I am more aware of University and community resources. (Such as, financial aid, daycare, student support services and disability services). | 1 | 2 | 3 | 4 |
| 9. I feel that two (2) hours per subject per week of tutoring time is sufficient. | 1 | 2 | 3 | 4 |
| 10. I feel that the quality (knowledge) of tutors is sufficient to meet my needs. | 1 | 2 | 3 | 4 |
| 11. I feel that my academic needs are being met through the Academic Development Center. | 1 | 2 | 3 | 4 |
| 12. I am a better student since participating in programs and services offered at the Academic Development Center. | 1 | 2 | 3 | 4 |
| 13. I feel my grades have improved as a direct result of programs and services I have obtained from the Academic Development Center. | 1 | 2 | 3 | 4 |
| 14. Overall, I am satisfied with my experiences with the Academic Development Center. | 1 | 2 | 3 | 4 |

**Please provide as much description as possible for the following questions.**

15. My reason(s) for seeking services at the Academic Development Center is/are:

16. The following courses, programs, or services have been most helpful to me:
    Because...

17. My most valuable experience with the Academic Development Center has been:

18. The following courses, programs, or services have been the least helpful to me:
    Because...

19. My suggestions for improving the programs and services offered by the Academic Development Center include:

20. Additionally, I would like to see a program/service in the following area(s):

*Your opinion is important, thank you for your participation in this survey.*

# Enhancing and Reinforcing the Concept Knowledge of English Language Learners Through Children's Literature

**Jane Brady Matanzo**

Florida Atlantic University

## Abstract

*English Language Learners (ELL) are students whose native language is other than English and who are in the process of gaining proficiency in English. For the past three years, undergraduate and graduate elementary education students have administered informal reading inventories and then developed and implemented an instructional literacy program for elementary aged English Language Learners. One of the common patterns shared during subsequent instructional planning discussions was that many of the ELL students had a need for increased conceptual knowledge correlated to English vocabulary to aid comprehension. Since illustrations can be helpful in increasing the content understanding for learners of English, a concentrated search effort and content analysis of concept or informational children's books was made. This article offers 14 criteria to consider when selecting children's literature to develop, extend, and/or reinforce conceptual knowledge, particularly for ELL students. Two bibliographies of analyzed books meeting at least 80 percent of the suggested criteria for 13 expository concept areas and 1 narrative concept area are given in Appendices A and B.*

Flavia*, a fourth grader, needs to learn English and concepts related to her new country, the United States, and her state, Florida. One of the topics studied in her fourth grade curriculum is her new state. Her teacher read *S is for Sunshine, A Florida Alphabet* (Crane, 2000) that is illustrated in detail by Michael Glenn Monroe. At first Flavia was silent; gradually she began to participate. The book provided a visual image of concepts and vocabulary ranging from A for alligator to U for an underwater aquarium where manatees are featured.

Use of this picture book helped Flavia increase her geographic knowledge and her English listening, speaking, and reading vocabularies. As Flavia's knowledge increased, her teacher helped her make connections to the English being heard and the corresponding written words. Next, Flavia drew her own illustrations that reflected her Floridian experiences including information she had gained from the book. She gradually produced contextual vocabulary orally and in writing with both her teacher and peers in ways that demonstrated her understanding. Over time, Flavia became more confident and conversant about her new home and its environs.

The continuum of processes Flavia's teacher practiced is consistent with Krashen's Monitor Theory (1982), which asserts that, especially in the early stages of learning a language, the learner may need stimuli such as illustrations, gestures, and pantomime. Krashen also notes that children may exhibit a silent period when learning a new language.

As the number of English Language Learners in school systems increases (Fleischman & Hopstock, 1993), educators must become more cognizant of specific processes such learners have and materials that might address identified needs. During the past three years, undergraduate and graduate students in our program have administered more than 150 Informal Reading Inventories to third, fourth, and fifth grade students whose native language was not English as part of a university tutoring program. After the assessments were analyzed, the respective classroom teachers of each ELL student recommended two additional comparable students from their classrooms that could participate with the assessed student during the instructional time. It was felt that there would be more language interactions and team collaboration, if small groups could be formed for instruction rather than one-on-one tutoring was used. The university students were expected to plan and implement at least three half-day instructional periods for the three students. In terms of English language competence, the children ranged from new arrivals with little, if any, English knowledge to students who had been exposed to English in the school system for three or more years. The majority of the students came from homes where Spanish was the predominant language.

As part of their course, the university students were asked to look for similarities and differences in the children's assessments and reading performance during the instructional time. One similarity found among many of the children was that they could pronounce English words well but had difficulty with vocabulary meanings, especially when illustrative aids were not present. Illustrations seemed to help the children make connections between concepts they already had learned in their first language and the new English vocabulary (August & Hakuta, 1997; Eastern Stream Center on Resources and Training, 1998; Peregoy & Boyle 2001). Illustrations also may help children understand concepts they encounter for the first time in their new environment (Freeman & Freeman, 1994; Lessow-Hurley, J., 2000).

## Purpose of the Project

Our work with English Language Learners led us to an interest in identifying appropriate children's books for these students. This project is an initial endeavor to establish criteria for selecting concept books for English Language Learners and to offer a bibliographic sampling of titles. The inclusion of informational picture books related to content being taught has been advocated in general (Galda, Cullinan, & Strickland, 1994; Freeman & Lehman, 2001; Freeman & Person, 1998; Norton, 1992) and specifically for English Language Learners (Gopaul-McNicol & Thomas-Presswood, 1998; Peregoy & Boyle, 2001; Perez & Torres-Guzman, 1996).

## Definition of Concept and
## Concept/Non-Fiction Literature

The American Heritage Dictionary (1998) defines a concept as "a general idea or understanding, especially one derived from specific instances or occurrences." Dale (1965) claimed concepts are learned best through direct, purposeful experiences and gave examples of concept progression through his "Cone of Experience" which ranges from direct, purposeful experiences to verbal symbols (p. 304). Vacca, Vacca, and Gove (2000) state that a concept is a "mental image of . . . anything that can be grouped together by common features or similar criteria—objects, symbols, ideas, processes, or events" and can be considered similar to schema (p. 281). This author believes that the greater the degree of concept development, the greater the comprehension and relationship of known concepts to materials viewed, heard, and/or read.

Concept books are non-fiction texts and offer illustrations, realistic photographs, and/or other print media. A brief, accurate text helps to reinforce, and/or extend the understanding of a concept. Hall and Matanzo (1975) state that a "concept book is one which has as its purpose to inform, define, and/or clarify ideas" (p.487). Peregoy and Boyle (2001) note that such books usually focus on one major concept and help to build "vocabulary, provide opportunities for productive language use, and create opportunities for successful participation in classroom activities" (p. 225). The terms, informational books, non-fiction literature, or tradebooks, often are used synonymously to describe more detailed expository books where several concepts or a series of related concepts are presented in greater depth, accompanied and enhanced by the use of illustrations, photos, or other graphic representations which work in conjunction with the more detailed text. These books often feature chronological organization or another given sequence which should aid the understanding of the concept(s) being addressed (Freeman & Person, 1998).

## Criteria to Consider when Selecting Literature to Develop, Extend, and/or Reinforce Concepts

Many children's literature authorities (Cullinan & Galda, 1994; Hillman, 1999; Huck, Hepler, & Hickman, 1993; Norton, 1999) have developed criteria to evaluate concept/informational books. Using this literature base as well as personal professional knowledge based on experience, fourteen criteria for content analysis were chosen. These are listed in Figure 1.

## Content Analysis Procedures

Once the 14 criteria were identified, a procedure for identifying quality and appropriate literature was developed. Recommendations of appropriate books were sought from children's librarians, media specialists, and elementary teachers. In addition, recommendations published in professional books between 1990 and 2001 by children's literature authorities were consulted. Present and past book reviews were also read in *The Horn Book, the Reading Teacher, Language Arts, Book Links, The New Advocate,* and *Bookbird: A Journal of International Children's Literature.*

From these resources, a pool of 975 titles was identified. To make this number feasible, the list was reduced to books published between 1980 and 2001, which narrowed the recommended list to 786 books. A check was made to see which titles were accessible locally through library, school, and bookstore collections and to determine which of the titles were part of a series. It was decided that one book in a series would be analyzed in depth. As a result, 306 books were assembled for analysis.

In the rating process, a cross check was made to ascertain consistency in the decisions made by several raters. Ten concept/informational books were randomly selected from the assembled pool and were evaluated by three raters. Each of the 14 criteria were put on a grid and evaluated on a present/not present scale with page numbers and content documented. Prior to the analysis, the three evaluators agreed on an interpretive stance to guide their analysis of each item (Atkinson, Delamont, & Hammersley, 1988) by analyzing two additional randomly selected books together. After the 10 books were analyzed on the given criteria independently, a comparison of findings was made. There was an agreement of a minimum of 90 percent on the presence of each of the items in the analyzed books.

## Findings

Of the 306 concept/informational books read and evaluated, 94 books met 80 percent or greater of the criteria, with 56 books meeting 100 percent of the criteria. For those books meeting at least 80 percent but not 100 percent of the criteria (total: 38 books), the most frequent criteria *not* met were: "A non-stereotypic multicultural presence is evident in book" (number 3); and "Repetition and/or summary of major concepts using similar and appropriate language are evident" (number 13).

As the books were analyzed, 13 expository concept areas and one narrative concept area emerged. The expository areas are Animal Life: Land and Sea; Clothing; Community/Families/Traditions; Environment/Earth; Language Development; Machines/Tools; Mathematics; Occupations; Plants and Trees; Senses and Body Concepts; Space/Skies; Transportation; and Weather. The narrative category, Adjusting to an English Speaking Environment, was included because a number of narrative books were found among the recommendations and contained many concepts related to learning a new language and culture. One example of the content analysis, *The Great Animal Search* (Young, 1994) is found in Figure 1.

### Figure 1. Criteria and Expository Content Analysis for *The Great Animal Search* (Young, 1984).

1. Topic reflects concepts teachers might expect English language learners to know or conceptual knowledge that would help them cope in/understand new environment. *Yes.*
   *The topic deals with more than one hundred animals around the world that many students from other cultures may be able to identify. North American animals are well represented in this book.*

2. Topic reflects concepts in many curricular/content areas/assessment passages. *Yes*
   *Animal knowledge often is expected by teachers and is addressed in many facets of the curriculum.*

3. A non-stereotypic multicultural presence is evident in book. *Yes*
   *More than 100 animals from such places as Florida swamps, the Arctic, Sahara Desert, Antarctica, and the Great Barrier Reef are included; a world map is given with photographs from many cultures that should help student self-identification and which do not overly exaggerate any given features.*

4. Book is attractively formatted and should interest students. *Yes*
   *Pages feature a double-page spread thematic illustration with the border isolated and labeled with smaller illustrations of animals featured in the*

## Figure 1. Criteria and Expository Content Analysis (continued)

*larger composite illustration. The format invites the learner to revisit the illustrations and discover more illustrated detail with each visit to the book.*

5. Illustrations/Photographs/Graphic representations and/or other media enhance the understanding of the given concept(s) without using the written text initially. *Yes*
*The illustrations and photographs are the major means used for conveying information throughout the book.*

6. Illustrations/Photographs/Graphic representations and/or other media are accurate and correspond to any given text on same or adjoining page. *Yes*
*The labels for the animals and minimal text explanations correspond exactly and clearly to what is being pictured on a given page(s).*

7. Illustrations/Photographs/Graphic representations and/or other media show size, distance, and other relationships as needed. *Yes*
*The sizes of the animals portrayed in a composite illustration are accurate in true to life size comparisons as well as are the flora and fauna found in various parts of the world.*

8. Text information given is accurate. *Yes*
*The animals selected and labeled for the various areas of the world use names given in that locale. Labels are accurate, well placed, and written in lower case letters that would be the usual way the reader will encounter the written form of the word. The directions given on the bordered search pages are simple and clear. For example, the reader might be asked to find three polar bears. Three polar bears are found along with other animals in the illustration and correspond to the likeness of the polar bear found and labeled on the border.*

9. Text information given reflects current knowledge/issues related to concept(s). *Yes*
*The animals and facts presented for a given region reflect a thorough search of the majority of animals for that area and appear current.*

10. Language is written in a clear, understandable manner with few initial clauses. *Yes*
*No initial clauses are used and directions and other information are clearly stated and easily followed.*

11. Language and events in text are sequenced well with concepts building on one another or arranged to encourage thematic or categorical understandings. *Yes*
*This is a definite strength. The book is thematically organized and should*

**Figure 1. Criteria and Expository Content Analysis (continued)**

*help students put animals in geographic categories as well as zonal cat-
egories such as desert animals or sea life.*

12. Examples or explanations are accompanied by illustrations/photographs
    and/or other media to explain or elaborate sub-concepts. *Yes*
    *The illustrations convey most of the meaning of the text and are explana-
    tory and understandable by themselves.*

13. Repetition and/or summary of major concepts using similar and appro-
    priate language is evident. *Yes*
    *Repetition is evident on each composite double spread illustration with
    the border restating through illustration and labeling the specific con-
    cepts stressed for a given geographic area. Readers are actively engaged
    as they search for animals in the composite and match them with a des-
    ignated animal in the border. Repetition is encouraged, as the reader
    needs to find a designated number of a given species between 3 and 12
    times depending on the animal in question. Answer keys are found for
    each of the search pages so the reader can self-check. A summary is given
    by the labeled world map on the final page that is accompanied by ac-
    tual photographs of the animals.*

14. The book is appropriate for an effective read-aloud. *Yes*
    *It is effective for a small group that can gather around the book with only
    one double page spread used in a sitting as a teacher points to features of
    the area and pronounces key words that go with each concept. Readers
    can be guided through the searching game and the teacher can model
    how to use the pictorial answer key. As students learn the concepts and
    how they are pronounced, opportunities to do partner reading and search-
    ing with other students can encourage a student's own aloud reading
    and active use of the given vocabulary.*

A suggested bibliography of the 88 expository books meeting at least 80%
of the criteria is divided into 14 concept areas in Appendix A. If the selection
is part of a series, the series' name is given along with other titles in that series
that were examined and appear to have comparable quality. An additional 214
titles are included in the series' title recommendations. Appendix B presents
a suggested bibliography of six books meeting 80 percent or greater of the
criteria that are written in a narrative style and contain many concepts with
which English Language Learners can identify. All entries also include the ISBN
number to ease reference. These bibliographies are not finite, but recommended examples of titles as a selection resource that might encourage the

language development, concept knowledge, and self-confidence of English Language Learners.

During the analysis, 212 of the examined books did not meet 80 percent of the specific 14 criteria. This does not indicate that these were not quality literature and appropriate for classroom use. However, these books may not be the most effective choices to use initially with English language learners. Many of the rejected titles may be appropriate for these students once their language proficiency develops. The most frequent reasons for their rejection were their not meeting the following numbered criteria: 3) A non-stereotypic multicultural presence is evident in the book; 5) Illustrations/Photographs/Graphic representations and/or other media enhance the understanding of the given concept(s) without relying on the written text initially; 7) Illustrations/Photographs/Graphic representations and/or other media show accurate size/distance and other relationships as needed; 10) Language is written in a clear, understandable manner with few initial clauses; 13) Repetition and/or summary of major concepts using similar and appropriate language; and 14) The book is appropriate for an effective read-aloud so the relative language can be heard in locally pronounced ways and reinforced with given visual impressions.

## Limitations

The major limitation of the project is that only books available within an 80-mile radius of our campus were used from the many books that were recommended. A second limitation is that we have not systematically observed the use of these books with English language learners. The next step of our project will be to use a selection of these books with an ELL population and observe students' literature interactions, their language and concept progression, and their self-selection of expository literature.

## Summary and Recommendations

English Language Learners have many strengths and needs; however, they do not necessarily lack the conceptual experience and knowledge expected by many school districts. They simply may not know the English vocabulary related to their conceptual knowledge. Illustrations picturing a concept with a brief, clearly written text can be beneficial to such a learner. Concept/informational children's literature can be one means to provide that assistance.

Three recommendations for study would give further information about the selected criteria and literature. The first recommendation is to begin to use the books that have met the criteria with English Language Learners in order to observe children's reactions to, retention of, and application of the concepts presented. A second recommendation would be to share the selection criteria with teachers, librarians, media specialists, and others involved with English Language Learners and ask them to do two things. The first would be to apply the 14 criteria to additional concept-oriented books currently available at the school and to see if the criteria are effective and if all items are appropriate. The follow-up step would be to encourage their input to refine the list and to apply "their" list to additional literature selections. They also should be encouraged to replicate the process continuum (Krashen, 1982) used by Flavia's teacher.

The third recommendation is to modify, delete, and add to the given list of identified literature. It is important to remember that this list is a suggested beginning and will be subject to change and additions as teachers use concept/informational literature with their students. In identifying additional literature selections, it is recommended that one be open to including additional subcategories as warranted.

It is important to ascertain, when possible, what concepts particular English Language Learners already possess and determine which literature may be appropriate in helping these students develop, reinforce, and/or extend their conceptual knowledge as well as their English language abilities.

*At the request of parents, the first name of the student has been altered.

---

## References

*American Heritage Dictionary* (1998, 2nd College Ed.). Boston, MA: Houghton Mifflin.

Atkinson, P., Delamont, S., & Hammersley, M. (1988). Qualitative research traditions: A British response to Jacob. *Review of Educational Research, 58* (12), 231-250.

August, D., & Hakuta, K., Ed. (1997). *Improving schooling for language-minority children: A Research Agenda*. Washington, D.C.: National Academy Press.

Crane, C. (2000). *S is for sunshine*. Chelsea, MI: Sleeping Bear Press.

Cullinan, B. E., & Galda, L. (1994). *Literature and the child* (3rd ed.). New York, NY: Harcourt Brace Jovanovich, Inc.

Dale, E. (1965). Vocabulary measurement: Techniques and major findings. *Elementary English, 42,* 895-901.

Eastern Stream Center on Resources and Training (ESCORT) (1998). *Help! They don't speak English starter kit for primary teachers* (3rd ed.). Arlington, VA: Region IV Comprehensive Center at Region XIV Comprehensive Center, Center for Applied Linguistics.

Fleischman, H. I., & Hopstack, P. J. (1993). *Descriptive study of services to limited English proficient students: Summary of findings and conclusions. Vol. 1.* Prepared for the Office of the Under Secretary, U. S. Department of Education. Arlington, VA: Development Associates, Inc.

Freeman, D. E., & Freeman, Y. S. (1994). *Between worlds: Access to second language acquisition.* Portsmouth, NH: Heinemann.

Freeman, E., & Lehman, B. (2001). *Global perspectives in children's literature.* Boston, MA: Allyn and Bacon.

Freeman, E. B., & Person, D. G. (1998). *Connecting informational children's books with content area learning.* Boston, MA: Allyn and Bacon.

Galda, L., Cullinan, B. E., & Strickland, D. S. (1994). *Language, Literacy, and the child* (3rd ed.). New York, NY: Harcourt Brace Jovanovich, Inc.

Gopaul-McNicol, S., & Thomas-Presswood, T. (1998). *Working with linguistically and culturally different children: Innovative clinical and educational approaches.* Boston, MA: Allyn and Bacon.

Hall, M. A., & Matanzo, J. B. (1975). Children's literature: A source for concept enrichment. *Elementary English, 14*(6), 487-494.

Hillman, J. (1999). *Discovering children's literature* (2nd ed.). Columbus, OH: Merrill, Prentice Hall.

Huck, C. S., Hepler, S., & Hickman, J. (1993). *Children's literature in the elementary school* (5th ed.). New York, NY: Harcourt Brace Jovanovich.

Krashen, Stephen (1982). *Principles and practice in second language acquisition.* New York, NY: Pergamon Press.

Lessow-Hurley, J. (2000). *The foundations of dual language instruction* (3rd edition). New York, NY: Addison Wesley Longman, Inc.

Norton, D. E. (1999). *Through the eyes of a child: An introduction to children's literature* (5th ed.). Columbus, OH: Merrill, Prentice Hall.

Norton, D. E. (1992). *The impact of literature-based reading.* Columbus, OH: Merrill, Prentice Hall.

Peregoy, S. F., & Boyle, O. F. (2001). *Reading, writing, & learning in ESL: A resource book for K-12 teachers* (3rd ed.). New York, NY: Addison Wesley Longman.

Perez, B., & Torres-Guzman, M. E. (1996). *Learning in two worlds: An integrated Spanish/English biliteracy approach* (2nd ed.). White Plains, NY: Longman.

Ready, D. (1997). *Doctors.* Mankato, MN: Bridgestone Books.

Vacca, J. A., Vacca, R. T., & Gove, M. K. (2000). *Reading and learning to read* (4th ed.). New York, NY: Longman.

Young, C. (1994). *The great animal search.* London: Usborne Publishing.

## Appendix A. Children's Literature Concept Bibliographic Suggestions: Expository

### *Animal Life: Land and Sea*

Berger, M. (1999). *Chomp! A book about sharks.* New York, NY: Scholastic. ISBN: 0-590-52298-1.

Broekel, R. (1982). *Snakes.* Chicago, IL: Children's Press. ISBN: 0-516-41649-9.

Collard, S.B. (1997). *Animal dads.* London: Dorling Kindersley (DK). ISBN: 0-618-03299-1.

Dowell, P. (1991) *Farm animals.* New York, NY: Simon & Schuster, Little Simon Books. ISBN: 0-689-71403-3.

Fowler, A. (1990). *It could still be a mammal.* Chicago, IL: Children's Press. ISBN: 0-516-44903-6. Another recommended title in the Rookie Read-About Science Series is *Frogs and toads and tadpoles, too.*

Gibbons, G. (1999). *Bats.* New York, NY: Holiday House. ISBN: 0-8234-1637-2.

Jones, F. (1992). *Nature's deadly creatures: A pop-up exploration.* New York, NY: Dial Books for Young Readers. ISBN: 0-8037-1342-8.

Julivert, A. (1991). *The fascinating world of bees.* Hauppauge, NY: Barron. ISBN: 0-8120-4720-4.

Kubick, D. (2000). *The snake book.* London: Dorling Kindersley (DK). ISBN: 7894-6068-8.

Pallotta, J. (1986). *The ocean alphabet book.* Watertown, MA: Charlesbridge Publishing. ISBN: 0-88189-452-1. Other recommended concept books in the Pallotta series include *The icky bug alphabet book; The icky bug counting book (Cienta los insectos); The bird alphabet book; The furry alphabet book; The dinosaur alphabet book; The underwater alphabet book; The Victory Garden vegetable alphabet book; The extinct alphabet book; The desert alphabet book; The spice alphabet book; The butterfly alphabet book; The freshwater alphabet book; The airplane alphabet book; The make your own alphabet book; Going lobstering.*

Parker, S.(1992). *Insects.* London: Dorling Kindersley (DK). ISBN: 0-7894-2215-8.

Parsons, A. (1990). *Amazing birds.* New York, NY: Alfred Knopf. ISBN: 0-679-80223-1.

Rinard, J. E. (1984). *What happens at the zoo?* Washington, DC: National Geographic Society. ISBN: 0-87044-524-3.

Robinson, C. (1999). *In the wild with sharks.* Des Plaines, IL: Heinemann Library. ISBN: 1575-7286-3. Other recommended titles in the In The Wild Series include *Bears; Chimpanzees; Crocodiles; Dolphins; Elephants; Lions; Penguins; Snakes; Whales.*

Taylor, B. (1993). *Forest life.* London: Dorling Kindersley Publishers (DK). ISBN: 0-7894-3475-x.

Tuxworth, N.(1997). *Let's look at animal homes.* New York, NY: Lorenz Books. ISBN: 1-85967-414-3.

Young, C. (1994). *The great animal search.* London: Usborne Publishing. ISBN: 0-7460-1739-1.

### Clothing

Ballard, P. (2000). *Shoes: The sound of sh.* Chanhassen, MN: The Child's World, Inc. ISBN: 1-56766-727-0.

Llewellyn, C. (1991). *Clothes.* Milwaukee, WI: Gareth Stevens Children's Books. ISBN: 0-8368-0677-8. Other recommended titles in The First Look Series include *The airport; Boats; Cars; Changing seasons; Day and night; The forest; Growing food; The hospital; In the air; Keeping warm; Mountains; Rivers; Under the ground; Under the Sea; Using Energy.*

Morris, A. (1995). *Shoes.* New York, NY: Lothrop, Lee & Shepard Books. ISBN: 0-688-136666-4. Other titles in Morris series include *Bread, bread, bread; Hats, hats, hats; On the go; Tools; Houses and homes.*

Smith, W. J. (1989). *Ho for a hat!* Boston: Little, Brown, and Company. ISBN: 0-316-80120-8.

Woods, S. G. (1999). *Sneakers: From start to finish.* Woodbridge, CT: Blackbirch Press, Inc. ISBN: 1-56711-393-1.

### Community/Families/Traditions

Ada, A. F. (1997). *The Christmas tree: El arbol de Navidad.* New York, NY: Hyperion Books for Children. ISBN: 0-7868-2123-X.

Chocolate, D.(1996). *Kente colors.* New York, NY: Walker and Company.

Grossman, P. (1994). *Saturday market.* New York, NY: Lothrop, Lee & Shepard Books. ISBN: 0-688-12177-2.

Isadora, R. (1983). *City seen from A to Z.* New York, NY: Greenwillow Books. ISBN: 0-688-01803-3.

Malam, J. (1999). *Hospital: From accident and emergency to x-ray.* Lincolnwood, IL: Peter Bedrick Books. ISBN: 0-87226-585-4.

Morris, A. (1996). *The daddy book.* Parsippany, NJ: Silver Press. ISBN: 0-362-24696-9.

Morris, A. (1995). *Weddings.* New York, NY: Lothrop, Lee, & Shepard Books. ISBN: 0-688-13272.

Soto, G. (1997). *Snapshots from the wedding.* New York, NY: G. P. Putnam's Sons. ISBN: 0-399-22808-x.

Spier, P. (1980). *People.* Garden City, NY: Doubleday. ISBN: 0-0385-1318-1-x.

Sweeney, J. (1996). *Me on the map.* New York, NY: Crown Publishers. ISBN: 0-5177-0096-4.

## Food

Cook, D. F. (1995). *The kid's multicultural cookbook: Food and fun from around the world*. Charlotte, VT: Williamson Publishing Co., A Williamson Kid's Can! Book.

Ehlert, L. (1989). *Eating the alphabet: Fruits & vegetables from A to Z*. New York, NY: Harcourt Brace & Company. ISBN: 0-15-224435-2.

Morris, A. (1989). *Bread, bread, bread*. New York, NY: A Mulberry Paperback. ISBN: 0-688-12275-2.

Dooley, N.(1991). *Everybody cooks rice*. Minneapolis, MN: Carolrhoda Books. ISBN: 0-87614-412-1.

## Environment/Earth

Baxter, N.(1997). *Our wonderful earth*. Charlotte, NC: C. D. Stampley Enterprises, Ltd. ISBN: 0-915741-77-6.

Butler, D. (1990). *Under the ground*. Milwaukee, WI: Garth Stevens Children's Books. ISBN: 0-8368-0507-0.

Gibbons, G. (1992). *Recycle: A handbook for kids*. Boston: Little, Brown Co. ISBN: 0-316-30971-0.

Gish, M., & Shaw, N. J. (1999). *Fossils*. Mankato, MN: Creative Education. ISBN: 0-88782-987-9.

Pellant, C. (2000). *The best book of fossils, rocks, and minerals*. New York, NY: Kingfisher. ISBN: 0-7534-5274-x.

Vbrova, Z. (1990). *Mountains*. New York, NY: Troll Associates. ISBN: 0-8167-1973-X.

## Language Development

Aliki (1996). *Hello! Good-bye!* New York, NY: Greenwillow Books. ISBN: 0-688-143342 LE.

Boudart, J., Conway, B., & Harkrader, L. (1999). *Picture dictionary*. Lincolnwood, IL: Publications International, Ltd. ISBN: 0-7853-3507-2.

Bryant-Mole, K. (1997). *Is it heavy?* Milwaukee, WI: Gareth Stevens Publishing. ISBN: 0-8368-1727-3. Other recommended titles in the Science Buzzwords Series include *Is it shiny?; Does it bounce?; Where is it?*

Crane, C. (2000). *S is for sunshine: A Florida alphabet*. Chelsea, MI: Sleeping Bear Press. ISBN: 1-58536-012-0. Other recommended titles in this State Alphabet Series are *B is for Buckeye: An Ohio Alphabet; L is for Lincoln: An Illinois Alphabet; M is for Mitten: A Michigan Alphabet*. Additional state alphabet books are forthcoming.

Heller, R. (1990). *Merry-go-round: A book about nouns*. New York, NY: Grosset & Dunlap. ISBN: 0-448-40085-5. Other recommended grammar/concept related Heller books include *Many luscious lollipops: A book about adjectives; Kites sail high: A book about verbs; A cashe of jewels* and other collective nouns.

Hill, E. (1988). *Spot's big book of words/El libro grande de las palabras de Spot*. New York, NY: Putnam's Sons. ISBN: 0399-21689-8.

Hoban, T. (1990). *Exactly the opposite*. New York, NY: Greenwillow Books. ISBN: 0-688-08862-7. Other recommended Hoban concept titles include *Big ones, little ones; A children's zoo; Dig, drill, dump, fill, dots, spots, speckles, and stripes; I read signs, I read symbols, I walk and read; Is it larger? Is it smaller?; Is it red? Is it yellow? Is it blue?; Is it rough? Is it smooth? Is it shiny?; More than one; 1, 2, 3; Round & round & round; Shadows and reflections; Shapes, shapes, shapes; 26 letters and 99 cents; What is it?*

Leventhal, D. (1994). *What is your language?* New York, NY: Dutton Children's Books. ISBN: 0-525-45133-1.

Meider, T., & Goodman, M. (1992). *Let's learn Japanese picture dictionary*. Lincolnwood, IL: Passport Books. ISBN: 0-8442-8494-7. Other recommended language picture dictionaries that likewise have the English counterpart word with each word in the other featured language are *Let's learn . . . Spanish, French, German, Italian, Portuguese,Hebrew*.

Mora, P. (1996). *Uno, dos, tres; One, two, three*. New York, NY: Clarion Books. ISBN: 0-395-67294-5.

Parrish, S. (1998). *ABC of Australian wildlife*. Archerfield BC, Queensland, Australia: Steve Parish Publishing. Other titles in the Nature Kids Australian Early Learning Collection include *My first picture book of frogs; My first picture book of dolphins; My first picture book of kangaroos; My first picture book of koalas; Australian wildlife; Australian birdlife; 123 of Australian wildlife, Australian sea life; Australian rainforest*.

Turner, G. (1986). *New Zealand ABC*. New York, NY: Penguin Books. ISBN: 0-14-050618-7.

Wildsmith, B. (1997). *Amazing world of words*. Brookfield, CT: The Millbrook Press. ISBN: 00-7613-0045-7.

### Machines/Tools

Barton, B. (1987). *Machines at work*. New York, NY: HarperCollins Publishers. ISBN: 0-690-04573-5. Other recommended Barton concept titles include *Bones, bones, dinosaur bones; Dinosaurs, dinosaurs; I want to be an astronaut; Airplanes; Boats; Trains; Trucks; Airport; Wheels*.

Bryant-Mole, K. (1997). *Machines*. Parsippany, NJ: Silver Press. ISBN: 0-382-39588-3. Other recommended titles in the Images series include *Tools, Texture; Materials; Red, Yellow, Blue, and Green*.

Gibbons, G. (1990). *How a house is built*. New York, NY: Holiday House. ISBN: 0-8234-0841-8. Other recommended titles in Gibbons' series include *Monarch butterfly; Farming; Dinosaurs; Trains; Flying; Playgrounds; Tunnels; Boat book; Tool book*.

Hoban, T. (1997). *Construction zone.* New York, NY: Greenwillow Books. ISBN: 0-688-12285-X.

Jennings, T. (1993). *Cranes, dump trucks, bulldozers and other building machines.* New York, NY: Kingfisher Books. ISBN: 1-85697-866-4.

Richards, J. (1999). *Farm machines: Look inside machines to see how they work.* Brookfield, CT: Copper Beech Books/The Millbrook Press. ISBN: 0-7613-0906-3. Other recommended titles in the Cutaway, Look Inside Machines Series include *Diggers and other construction machines; Fire fighters; Jetliners; Racing cars; Space vehicles; Trains; Trucks.*

### Mathematics

Hoban, T. (1998). *So many circles, so many squares.* New York, NY: Greenwillow Books. ISBN: 0-688-15166-3. Another recommended concept title by Hoban is *Animal, vegetable, or mineral.*

McMillan, B. (1991). *Divide and ride.* New York, NY: HarperCollins Publishers. ISBN: 0-06-026777-1. Other recommended titles in the *MathStart Series* include *Too many kangaroo things to do; Give me half!; The best bug parade; Ready, set, hop.*

Pallotta, J., & Bolster, R. (1999). *The Hershey's milk chocolate fractions book.* New York, NY: Scholastic Inc. ISBN: 0-439-13519-2.

### Occupations

Deedrick, T. (1998). *Teachers.* Mankato, MN: Bridgestone Books. ISBN: 1-56065-731-6. Other recommended titles in the Community Helpers Series include *Astronauts; Bakers; Construction workers; Dentists; Doctors; Farmers; Fire fighters; Garbage collectors; Librarians; Nurses; Police officers; School bus drivers; Veterinarians; Zoo keepers.*

Maynard, C. (1997). *Jobs people do.* New York, NY/London: Dorling Kindersley (DK). ISBN: 0-7894-1492-9.

Ready, D.(1997). *Doctors.* Mankato, MN: Bridgestone Books. ISBN: 1-56065-509-7. A recommended title by Ready in the Community Helpers series is *Mail carriers.*

Schaefer, L. M. (2000). *We need mail carriers.* Mankato, MN: Pebble Books/Capstone Press. ISBN: 0-7368-0392-0. Other recommended titles in Our Community Series include *We need dentists; We need doctors; We need farmers; We need fire fighters; We need nurses; We need police officers; We need veterinarians.*

### Plants and Trees

Bunting, E. (1994). *Flower Garden.* New York, NY: Harcourt, Brace & Co. ISBN: 0-15-228776-0.

Burns, D. L. (1998). *Trees, leaves, and bark.* Milwaukee, WI: Gareth Stevens Publishing. ISBN: 0-8368-2043-6. Other recommended titles in the

Young Naturalist Field Guide Series are *Birds, nests, and eggs; Caterpillars, bugs, and butterflies; Seashells, crabs, and sea stars; Snakes, salamanders, and lizards.*

Florian, D. (1991). *Vegetable garden.* New York, NY: Harcourt, Brace Publishers. ISBN: 0-15-293383-2.

McMillan, B. (1988). *Growing colors.* New York, NY: Lothrop, Lee, & Shepard Books. ISBN: 0-688-07845. Other recommended titles by McMillan include *Counting butterflies; Dry or wet?; Fire engine shapes.*

Wexler, J. (1987). *Flowers, fruits, & seeds.* New York, NY: Simon & Schuster Books for Young Readers. ISBN: 0-671-73986-7.

### Senses and Body Concepts

James, R. (1995). *Mouth.* Vero Beach, FL: The Rourke Press, Inc. ISBN: 1-57103-0. Other recommended titles from the Discovery Library Series include *Ears; Eyes; Feet; Hands; Nose.*

Kincaid, D., & Coles, P. (1983). *Touch and feel.* Vero Beach, FL: The Rourke, Inc. ISBN: 0-86625-229-0.

Sandeman, A. (1995). *Breathing.* Brookfield, CT: Copper Beech Books. ISBN: 1-56294-620-X. Other recommended titles from the Body Book Series include *Bones; Eating; Senses; Babies; Blood; Brain; Skin; Teeth; Hair.*

### Space/Skies

Barger, S., Boren, S., & Johnson, L. (1985). *Explore the world of space.* Vero Beach, FL: Rourke Enterprises, Inc. ISBN: 0-86592-942-4.

Gibbons, G. (1993). *The planets.* New York, NY: Holiday House. ISBN: 0-8234-1040-4.

Ingle, A. (1993). *The glow-in-the-dark planetarium book.* New York: Random House.

Simon, S. (1987). *Mars.* New York, NY: Mulberry Books. Other recommended planet/sky titles in the Simon series include *Saturn; Uranus; Jupiter; Stars; The sun.*

### Transportation

Collicutt, P. (1999). *This train.* New York, NY: Farrar, Straus, Giroux. ISBN: 0-374-37493-7.

Gibbons, G. (1987). *Trains.* New York, NY: Holiday House. ISBN: 00-8234-0640-7.

Morris, A. (1990). *On the go.* New York, NY: Lothrop, Lee, & Shepard Books. ISBN: 0-688-06337-3.

Royston, A. (1998). *Truck trouble.* New York, NY: DK Publishing Co. ISBN: 0-7894-2958-6.

Royston, A. (1998). *Boats and ships.* Des Plaines, IL: Heinemann Interactive Library. ISBN: 157572170-8.

Tuxworth, N. (1998). *Let's look at things that go*. New York, NY: Lorenz Books. ISBN: 1-85967-599-9. Other recommended titles in the Let's Look At Series include *Colors; Fruit; Numbers; Animals; Sizes; Opposites; Shapes; My home; Kitchen patterns; Mix and match; Flowers; Bodies; Flying machines; Animal homes; Growing bugs; Nature; Weather.*

### Weather

Butler, D. (1996). What happens when rain falls? Austin, TX: Steck Vaughn Company. ISBN: 0-8172-4151-5. Other recommended titles in the What Happens When Series include *What happens when fire burns?; Flowers grow?; Food cooks?; People talk?; Volcanoes erupt?; Wheels turn?; Wind blows?*

Schulevitz, U. (1998). *Snow*. New York, NY: Farrar, Straus, and Giroux. ISBN: 0-374-37092-3

## Appendix B. Children's Literature Concept Bibliographic Suggestions: Narrative

Adjusting to an English speaking environment:

Aliki (1998). *Painted words; Spoken memories*. New York, NY: Greenwillow Books. ISBN: 0-688-15662-2.

Bunting, E. (1996). *Going home*. New York, NY: Harper Collins Publishers. ISBN: 0-06-026297-4.

Bunting, E. (1988). *How many days to America, A Thanksgiving story*. New York, NY: Clarion Books. ISBN: 0-89919-521-0.

Levine, E. (1989). *I hate English*. New York: Scholastic. ISBN: 0-590-42304-5.

Say, A. (1993). *Grandfather's journey*. Boston, MA: Houghton Mifflin Company. ISBN: 0-395-57035-2.

Williams, K. L. (1991). *When Africa was home*. New York, NY: Orchard Books. ISBN: 0-531-08525-2.

# NETSEARCH STRATEGIES OF PRESERVICE TEACHERS

## Susan Davis Lenski

Illinois State University

## Abstract

*This study investigated strategies preservice teachers used when research-ing using the Internet. Six college seniors in a reading methods course were the subjects for the study. The students were asked to conduct a think-aloud as they searched for sources. As they were searching, the students were prompted to talk about what they were doing and why they were doing it. After the think-alouds, students were asked several debriefing questions. The sessions were transcribed for data analysis. Data were coded based on social and cognitive strategies and were analyzed using the constant comparative method. Reliability was established by an independent reader. Results indi-cated that students used five antithetical strategies: describing their search requests flexibly yet accurately, filtering and evaluating content, becoming distracted and refocusing on topics, working alone and working together, and feeling in and out of control. Conclusions emphasize the need for new ways of thinking about researching using the Internet.*

The purpose of this study was to determine the search strategies preservice teachers used as they researched using the Internet. During a research process using print sources, researchers make both social and cognitive decisions when locating and analyzing information (Flower, Stein, Ackerman, Kantz, McCormick, & Peck, 1990; Lenski, 1998). Currently, little is written about search strategies using the Internet. This study begins that investiga-tion by examining the researching process of technologically experienced preservice teachers and identifying the key strategies they used.

## Background

Conducting research is not merely an academic activity; it is an integral part of life. All of us respond to our natural curiosity by asking questions, forming hypotheses, gathering data, and drawing conclusions. Although researching is an activity in which all of us participate from time to time, there are skills and strategies that make researching more efficient and productive. Researching is usually comprised of the following strategies: generating a research question; locating and evaluating information; selecting, organizing, and synthesizing information; and conveying the findings to the appropriate audience (Spivey, 1997). Researchers, however, do not always move through the steps in the research process in order because the steps in researching are individual. Students may go through the research process in a linear progression, they may spiral back through the research stages, or they may move through the research stages recursively (Lenski & Johns, 1997). Each researching situation is different, and the context of research and students' preferences influence the manner in which they proceed through the stages of research.

As students research, they apply social and cognitive strategies to answer their research questions (Flower, Stein, Ackerman, Kantz, McCormick, & Peck, 1990; Lenski, 1998). Among the social strategies are students' personal interests and the amount of time they have to decide on a research topic. Students also apply cognitive strategies as they research. Cognitive strategies can be divided into two types: process and content. Process strategies consist of understanding the steps to take when researching. An example of a process strategy is the ability to locate sources. Content strategies consist of strategies that enable the researcher to find content that answers research questions. An example of a content strategy is the ability to find a source that has appropriate information. The research about the use of social and cognitive strategies that students use when researching has been conducted using print sources. Now, however, many students use the Internet as they gather information to answer research questions.

Gathering information has changed substantially with the advent of the Internet and other electronic sources. Many of today's students have hours of experiences researching on the Internet and feel most comfortable when searching for information using a computer (McKenzie, 1998; Tell, 1999/2000). Other students have had few computer experiences. Teachers also have differing degrees of Internet experience. We are truly living in a time of overlap (Birkerts, 1994). We do not know to what extent Internet research will replace research using print sources, but the trend has begun.

New technologies are in the process of taking the place of older technologies, but in many cases instructional methods have not yet changed (Jones, 1999). Researching using print sources has been a difficult strategy to teach.

When researching, students are expected to locate appropriate information while reading complex texts and to transform that information into a new text. As new technologies are introduced in schools, the researching process may become even more complex. Therefore, it is a mistake to apply old ways of thinking about research to the newer technologies (Anderson-Inman & Reinking, 1998; Jones, 1999; Mayer, 1997).

One of the reasons why applying research strategies using print texts to Internet research is inappropriate is because of the differences between print texts and Internet texts. When reading a print source, readers recognize the progression of ideas from beginning to end. Print sources, by their very nature, are linear. Even if a reader scans an article reading bits and pieces, the text exists in a linear format. Some authors of print texts have made an attempt to mirror hypertext, such as the novel *House of Leaves* (Danielewski, 2000). This book, however, illustrates the difficulty in making major format changes to a book; print sources are inescapably linear.

Internet sources are not linear, but are multilinear (Bolter, 1998). Multilinear texts have no clear beginnings or endings. Because Internet sources are linked to other sources and sites can be entered through other sites, there are no clear beginnings or endings of Internet texts. In fact "the presumption of reading to the end is replaced by the expectation that the reader will 'explore' and 'surf' to follow the links" (Mitra & Cohen, 1999, p. 186). Internet texts, therefore, are quite different from texts students have traditionally used to conduct research.

Because Internet texts are different from print texts, the role of the reader is changing. Readers play a more active role in reading when using the Internet. Not only do readers construct their own meaning while reading, they actually create their own texts. Since readers of Internet texts can enter sites in different ways, Internet texts are not bounded by the covers of a book. Readers, therefore, can "explode" the meaning of texts (Mitra & Cohen, 1999) by linking to various companion sites. The more active participation of the reader changes the text from reader to reader. Therefore, the role of the reader as constructor of meaning shifts toward the traditional role of the writer, the composer of meaning.

Another difference between Internet texts and print texts is the texts' accessibility. Internet texts are merely a keystroke away from a searcher unlike print sources which are housed in libraries all over the world. Students conducting research have great amounts of information available to them simply by conducting a search on the Internet. The Internet provides access to numerous sources including texts, graphics, photos, and moving images. Sources for this information can include libraries, governmental agencies, private agencies, businesses, and individuals (Ryder & Graves, 1996/1997). Since anyone can publish information on the Internet, the sources students locate may or may not have accurate and unbiased information in them. Because of the availability of information on the Internet, researchers need to use evaluative strategies more often than students using print documents (McKenzie, 1998).

## Methodology
### *Procedures*
This study takes a case study approach using a think-aloud protocol analysis, open-ended questions, debriefing interviews, and audiotaping. I decided to use a case study approach so that I could closely study individual students during the time they conducted research. A case study is a "bounded system" (Stake, 1988) where researchers can observe, record, and describe behaviors as they exist. Since little or no research has described the strategies researchers make as they search electronic sources, a case study approach is the most appropriate type of research to provide general information to answer the research question.

Preservice students from a reading methods class located in a suburban area of a large metropolitan center were invited to take part in the study. Students were asked to determine their facility with searching on the Internet as experienced, novice, and inexperienced. Of the 28 students in the class, 10 students identified themselves as experienced researchers. Six of these preservice teachers volunteered to participate in the study.

I gave the participants a general topic for their search: teaching Internet research strategies in schools. The reason I gave students a research topic rather than having them search self-selected topics was that search strategies are dependent on the depth and width of the topic. Furthermore, the participants in the study were members of inquiry groups in the larger class. During the weeks of the study, inquiry groups were investigating reading/writing connections. The participants of this study used their experiences and reflections about the research process as information for their inquiry groups.

Before the study began, students were given a think-aloud protocol that was modeled after the research conducted by Flower, Stein, Ackerman, Kantz, McCormick, and Peck (1990). Students were asked to talk about their actions as they researched and to describe their reasons for their actions. To practice the think-aloud, the students were given approximately 30 minutes to research a topic while they practiced thinking aloud and speaking into individual tape players. As the students searched, I occasionally asked them for further explanations. Students continued with the think-alouds until they felt comfortable with the activity.

The participants were then given three 45-minute sessions during class to conduct their research with the option of a fourth session. Class was conducted in an elementary school building that had been converted to a building housing a university classroom, computer labs, and offices for a school district's central staff. Students were allowed to work at individual computers that were located in unused rooms or in one of the two computer labs. All of the students choose to work in a computer lab, and all finished the project after three sessions. I conducted debriefing interviews directly after each session using a protocol adapted from Tierney, Soter, and O'Flahavan (1989) and McGinley (1992). During these interviews, I asked the following questions:

1. How did you feel as you conducted research using the computer?
2. How do you think this type of researching is different from using only print sources?
3. Think back to your searching. What else were you thinking as you searched for sources?
4. What have you learned from the activity that you just completed?
5. What is a metaphor for the activity you just completed?

### Data Analysis

The data were transcribed and analyzed using qualitative data analysis. The think-aloud data were used as primary units of analysis and the responses to the debriefing interview questions served as secondary data sources. The coding scheme was based on a unit of analysis called a think-aloud utterance (Kamberelis & Scott, 1992). Think-aloud utterances are comprised of those words spoken aloud by students that are preceded and followed by a period of silence.

The coding was developed based on the constant comparative method of qualitative data analysis (Glaser & Strauss, 1967). After each session, I read the data looking for social and cognitive categories that described the themes and threads of the data. I listed temporary categories, and after successive sessions and additional data, I added more categories. Further readings of data confirmed or disconfirmed categories. Interrater reliability was accomplished by asking an independent rater to review the protocol transcripts and to critique the coding scheme. Suggestions from the independent rater were incorporated into data analysis.

## Results and Discussion

The results of the study indicated that students used antithetical strategies as they searched. They used three pairs of cognitive strategies. First, students described their search requests flexibly yet accurately in order to locate web site listings. Once they found web listings, students rapidly filtered the sites by deciding which ones included content which applied to their topic. While quickly filtering sites, however, students also evaluated the legitimacy of the sites. During this filtering and evaluation process, however, they became distracted by advertisements and other interesting sources and had to continually refocus on their research questions. During their research, students also used social strategies. They worked independently yet easily collaborated with one another, and they ranged from feeling in total control to feeling helpless.

### Describing Search Requests Flexibly Yet Accurately

The first step in Internet research is to locate sources. Internet sources are indexed in two ways: by hierarchical subject directories, such as Yahoo, and by search engines such as Alta Vista or Excite (Pierson, 1997). Sources from these indexes are accessed by inputting search strings using key words about the topic. The search strings call up indexed web sites that have the words used in the search. According to technology experts, surfing is "quite simple" (Bitter & Pierson, 1999). The students in this study, however, did not find surfing the Internet simple at all.

All of the students began their searches by accessing a search engine and typing in a search string. Some of the students used criteria for their choice of search engines as exemplified by Ann's (names are pseudonyms) comments: "The first thing I entered is www.InfoSeek.com. It will give me more information for research, I think, than any other search engine." None of the students successfully found appropriate web sites after their initial search. All of the students rephrased their search strings and continued searching for hits using their initial search engine. They added words to their searches, changed the order of words, and revised searches several times. Matt explains his initial attempts at searching during the think-aloud: "Now I have Yahoo on the screen. For my search topic I am going to type in 'research.' Okay, according to this it has 702 categories and 26120 sites for research. . . . So I need to narrow this down. . . . Instead of just 'research' I am going to type in 'teaching research' and see what I get."

Three students accessed search directories before continuing their searches. Cassie narrowed her search in Yahoo. She noted, "I made a mistake of searching all of Yahoo. So let's see what comes up if we just search 'education.'" Christa changed her search engine immediately. As students continued researching, they moved from one search engine to another, sometimes based on nothing more than whim. Ann stated, "I am sick of Yahoo, so we are going to a different search engine just because I feel like it."

During the inputting of search strings, the students found that they needed to think flexibly about their topics, rearranging words until they found a match. By comparison, during their experimentation of search strings, the students found that they needed to be totally accurate in their search requests. Treva, for example, noted, "We are going to find a web page, then we are going to type in 'researching on the Internet.' Then I press search. I spelled 'research' wrong, only one 'a' not two. Search again." The students, therefore, found that they needed to describe their search requests flexibly yet accurately.

### Filtering and Evaluating Sources

According to recent sources, the Internet contains over one billion sites (Williams, 2000). Because of the sheer volume of sources on the Internet, even using search directories and indexes can make the task of researching overwhelming. As Sudweeks and Simoff note, "the average Internet user is often overwhelmed by the variety and vast amount of information and has difficulty processing and selecting the relevant information" (1999, p. 32). The researchers in this study used two strategies to find information for their project: rapid filtering of sources and evaluating the source's legitimacy.

As students filtered sources, they either sampled a few key sources or they eyeballed their entire list. When their search resulted in many matches, several of the students loaded the first three or four sites that had been identified as most closely related to their search request. For example, Cassie stated, "Oh, there are 50 sites. Let's check the first three." A second strategy they used was to "eyeball" the list for potentially relevant sites. One of Ron's search requests yielded 6,642 sites. He stated, "I mean if it is six thousand different sites, you might have to just eye through them all to find one that you are looking for."

Once students selected sites to access, they used flexible reading strategies to determine whether the site had potential as a research source and should be downloaded for a more careful reading. Ron described his reading strategy as follows: "You can scan or skim or use all those other flexible reading skills to figure out if this is what you really need."

As students skimmed sites for relevancy, however, they also applied evaluative reading skills to determine the authenticity of the site. The students discussed their awareness of the lack of editorial control on most Internet sites. Treva stated, "You kind of got to read through the fluff and you don't necessarily know it is right because maybe there are not as many regulations on the Internet as there are for print sources." As students skimmed sites, they looked at the site's date and publisher, and they noticed authors who published more than one source about the same topic. During her search for sites, Treva reflected, "Last updated November 11, 1999. Oh, hey, that's pretty recently." As Ron searched for sites, he noted the publisher of the site, "I just looked under research, centers for research for learning and teaching. I believe this is a University of Michigan web site."

As Ron continued searching, he found several sites authored by the same person. During this portion of Ron's think-aloud, he indicated awareness of several aspects of authorship. He noticed the publisher and the copyright date, he considered contacting the author, and he actively searched for additional sources with a new point of view. After accessing the first of several Ernest Akerman sources, Ron said, "Okay, this is a Circle A production, copyright 1997, Ernest Akerman. Maybe we should call him." After accessing additional web sites he stated:

> This Ernest Ackerman guy and Karen Harman are really all into this stuff. Let's see. Okay, here are some more articles. Guess who wrote it? Karen Harman and Mr. Ackerman. I just went back and I ended up at the site I was looking at before. Oh brother, there are more books. Okay, more books by Ernest C. Ackerman, department of computer science, Mary Washington College. Is that where he is from? I just clicked on how to get a copy. Popular guy this Ackerman person. I am waiting. Come on, Ackerman. Let's go back. All right, let's find out what somebody else has to say. *Researching on the Internet* by Robin Rolena. I hope that is a woman, because that would be interesting.

### Becoming Distracted and Refocusing on Content

There is no doubt that researching on the Internet is different from research using print sources. Sudweeks and Simoff (1999) describe the differences between the two types of researching by emphasizing the differences between the two types of texts. Print sources have traditionally been located by following a linear search: searching card catalogs and indexes, locating sources, and reading sources. Internet sources are different. A linear search is not the most efficient way to locate texts on the Internet, and Internet texts themselves are not linear. Sidweeks and Simoff explain, "In contrast to the traditional linear search among the shelves of books in a library, the Internet user follows a weblike nonlinear search in which most pages emphasize eye-catching designs and attention-grabbing movement rather than a sequential and logical presentation of information" (1999, p. 31). The students in this study found that as they researched, they were often distracted by the nonlinear aspects of web sites, and they needed to refocus on their projects.

At times students were also distracted by advertisements that popped up on their screens. Even though they were aware of the misleading nature of these advertisements, they were drawn to the distractions. Ron, for example, was distracted when his name appeared on the screen. He stated, "Whoa, on the bottom of this page it says, 'Ron, click here,' and since that is my name, I think I have to." Other students were distracted by news headlines that appeared on their screens. Ann is an example. During researching she interrupted her work to say, "Oh no, a small jet crashed in South Dakota and five are killed. Top stories for today. That is terrible." The students were also distracted by details reported by the web sites as illustrated by Cassie's comment: "Oh, we have visitor 41495 which is good to know, I suppose."

Students were also distracted by sites that personally interested them and sites that they thought would be useful for them as classroom teachers, such as math flash cards, Harry Potter web sites, and lesson plans. Since accessing linked sites is so easy on the Internet, students found themselves lured by the appeal of many sites. Christa summed up the differences between using print sources and searching on the Internet as follows: "Researching on the Internet is very distracting sometimes. So many things [are] on the Internet and everything is so colorful and looks so cool that you wind up getting off your topic and finding so many different things."

### Working Alone and Working Together

Computer networks are social networks, places where a set of people are connected by a set of social relations (Garton, Haythornthwaite, & Wellman, 1999). Experts on the Internet recognize that the Internet has been characterized as a "networked consciousness." On the other hand, Costigan (1999) states that the idea of the Internet being a networked consciousness is "an idea that requires a 'we' that does not exist" (p. xx). Since researching is also a social process (Lenski, 1998), an interesting finding from this study indicated that students made what would be considered a solo endeavor into a collaborative process in three ways: the students included computers in their social network by personifying the computers, they discussed personal ideas with each other while waiting for their computer, and they shared knowledge about appropriate sites with each other.

Researching seems to be an individual process, but students personified their computers in such a way that they assigned the computers partnership in their research. During researching, students talked to their computers politely, thanking their computers for loading files, and vilifying computers for being slow. For example, Matt said, "For some reason this computer is not agreeing with me right now. This is horrible. I don't know if this computer just doesn't like me or what." Four students verbally blamed the computer for the slowness of processing, and they left their computers for what they hoped would be faster computers. Since all of the computers in the lab had the exact same specifications, no one computer worked faster than any other. However, two students tried out three different computers in one research session. Another way students personified computers was by using the first person pronoun "we" during think-alouds when the computer and the student were searching. For example, Treva said, "We are going to go to Infoseek.com. A file came up. I'm reading a list of entries."

When researching on the Internet, students were place-bound. They used keystrokes to locate sources rather than moving to library shelves as they would when researching print sources. Since the students were sitting in front of a computer, they spent much of their time waiting for sites to load. While waiting, the students talked with their fellow researchers and with other students in the computer lab. They engaged in several short communications about personal events. For example, while waiting for her computer to load, Cassie said, "Okay, I am back, having my lovely conversation with Ann about the boys in her high school and whether or not they were dateable." Conversations also encompassed educational topics. For example, Ann told Treva about a web site that she thought would be useful in the classroom. Treva noted that it was easy to become distracted from research. She stated, "It was very easy to get pulled aside to talk to other people that were around in the computer lab, away from what I was doing."

The conversations in which students engaged during their researching also included sharing appropriate web sites about their topic of research. Students discussed the effectiveness of search terms, and asked each other if they had found any interesting sites. They also discussed the usefulness of the sites they had loaded. Occasionally, they printed out information for each other. They seemed completely comfortable sharing information, a collaborative strategy rarely found when students conduct research using print sources (Lenski, 1998). One reason why students were more comfortable collaborating when researching using the Internet may be because Internet researching might be analogous in students' minds to other types of computer play. Researching using print sources may trigger thoughts of schoolwork, which is typically completed alone. Another reason why students may have engaged in more collaborative talk could be because of the ease in sharing information by printing useful material. When using print sources, it is not as easy to share a book as it is on computer because it is far easier to press a key to print a document than to take a book to a copy machine to make duplicate copies.

### *Feeling In and Out of Control*

Researching can evoke intense emotions. For example, Kuhlthau (1988) investigated the research process of high school students who were researching print sources and found that students ranged from feeling frustrated to feeling relieved. The students in this study conducting research using the Internet also experienced intense emotions. Christa illustrated the heightened emotions she had when searching on the Internet by describing Internet research like "running your head into a brick wall, but other times it's just like heaven." Students in this study ranged from feeling in total control to feeling out of control.

When researching using the Internet, the students seemed to be giving control over the process to the computer. All of the students expressed extreme frustration when the computer did not access their commands quickly. Matt said, "This, of course, is loading really slow, slowly, slowly. I am waiting. Maybe another year this page will load."

At times certain sites couldn't be loaded. For example, Ann discussed a situation where a site that she thought would be useful could not be displayed. Ann stated sarcastically, "Of course, the best one doesn't come up. Typical for use of the Internet. There is an error trying to find the file. I take it you have to be of the elite to visit this place." Cassie summed up the feelings many students had: "I learned I am not very patient when it comes to using the Internet."

The research process was not always frustrating. Students also were thrilled and excited when they found a source that could be used in their project or that was of interest to them. For example, when Ron found a site about researching on the Internet, he said, "I am going to look into this. I think this could be very useful, not only for myself but for students." Students were equally enthusiastic when they found sites that interested them personally. For example, when Ann found a web site on the Civil War that was of interest to her she said, "Oh this is great! Civil War Resource of the World Wide Web and since I am such a fan I am going to have to write this one down too. Look at the great things you come across when you are on the Internet."

Why were these students so enthusiastic, yet so impatient and frustrated? One reason may be because students gave control to the computer by virtue of their physical actions. When researching using print sources, students move to reference books, library shelves, and computer catalogues. During this movement, students are taking a proactive stance; they are acting on their environment rather than being held hostage to a machine that may or may not work quickly. On the other hand, researching on the Internet can be very efficient. Treva compared researching on the Internet to researching using print sources. She said, "If I find a whole list of ten things here then I can just click on them real fast and see if I want to use them. I don't have to run all over the library to ten different places to find each one, just to figure out that it is not useful. So it can be a lot faster, and it can also be just as frustrating."

### *Metaphors for Netsearching*

The Internet has been characterized by metaphors. It's called the Web, which brings to mind images of intersecting and far-reaching lines. The Internet has also been called an electronic frontier (Jones, 1999) since it is the most popular unbounded system of the 21st century. Another popular metaphor for the Internet is an information highway. While these metaphors are useful in illustrating an abstract idea, Jones (1999) suggests that the current metaphors for the Internet have caused narrow thinking about the realities of the potential of the Internet in our society.

I asked the students who participated in this study to consider metaphors for researching on the Internet. Each student was asked to think of a metaphor during the debriefing sessions that followed each of the researching sessions. Some of the students offered more than one metaphor during individual interviews, and students occasionally could not think of any metaphors. Students suggested a total of 12 different metaphors from the debriefing sessions. Their ideas fell into two categories, metaphors illustrating the difficulty of searching for specific sites and metaphors for feeling overwhelmed by the amount of information available on the Internet.

The most popular metaphor that students stated was searching for a needle in a haystack. Three of the students mentioned this metaphor at least once during the debriefing interviews. Other similar metaphors that illustrated the difficulty in searching for specific sites were: an investigator looking for clues, searching through a pile of fruit looking for the perfect one, and looking for an ant in a field. Through these metaphors students were highlighting one of the frustrations of their initial stages of searching. After students entered a search, they often received hundreds (or thousands) of hits. They needed to rapidly filter through these hits in order to find one appropriate web site which could link to other related sites. Therefore, when students thought of the researching process, they thought of the difficulties in finding that first good site. Treva explained: "Researching on the Internet is like looking for an ant in a field. But if you're looking for an ant, actually you want a lot of ants. If you're lucky enough to find one ant, more than likely he will lead you to the whole hill of ants. That is what you are looking for, but first you have to be lucky to find one ant."

The second category of metaphors illustrated the students' frustration with the amount of information available to them during their research process. Cassie described researching on the Internet as follows: "It's like driving through a fog. If you are in your car and you are driving through a fog, you are not sure where you are. You are looking very carefully to stay on your side of the road, to look for street signs, or any kind of landmark that might continue to head you in the right direction. Hopefully, at some point, the fog just sort of lifts and everything becomes clear. I was hoping that at some point the fog would lift on my computer and I would discover a heading to look for a site that would give me a ton of other links." Matt described the Internet as being at the center of a web with no limitations as to where to go, and Ann said, "I am in a sea of information." Ann also provided the most unusual metaphor. She said, "I think searching on the Internet is like life because you can't figure it out...because it is going to keep you on your toes for the rest of your life."

## Conclusions and Limitations

Research using the Internet will become an important part of the learning lives of our students. As more students become connected to the Internet, researching on the Internet will most likely replace research using print sources and become an important aspect of being literate. Being literate depends on being proficient in the skills and strategies necessary in a given culture (Warschauer, 1999), and facility with Internet researching is already required in many work situations (Mendrinos, 1997). Therefore, as educators, we need to understand how to research using the Internet, and, as we learn, we need to teach students to become agile researchers. As Christa said, "Maybe that is what we need to focus on, you know, teaching better ways, more effective ways of using the Internet to research."

The premise of this study was that researching using the Internet is different from researching using print sources just as reading hypertext is different from reading books. The conclusions of the study indicated that the students who researched using the Internet used cognitive and social strategies that seemed unique to Internet research. This study, of course, is limited by several factors. First, Internet use was still fairly new to the participants in this study even though they considered themselves to be experienced with Internet research. A study of more adept Internet researchers may reveal different conclusions. A second limitation is the use of a case study. The conclusions of the study may provide a starting point for theory building, but they cannot be generalized at this point. Finally, the strategies used by these preservice teachers may not be useful for developing instruction for students in elementary and secondary school. Future studies of Internet researchers should be conducted to continue to develop knowledge about Internet research strategies.

---

## References

Anderson-Inman, L., & Reinking, D. (1998). Learning from text in a post-typographic world. In C. R. Hynd (Ed.), *Learning from text across conceptual domains* (pp. 165-191). Mahwah, NJ: Erlbaum.

Birkerts, S. (1994). *The Gutenberg elegies: The fate of reading in an electronic age.* Boston: Faber and Faber.

Bitter, G. G., & Pierson, M. E. (1999). *Using technology in the classroom* (4th ed.). Boston: Allyn and Bacon.

Bolter, J. D. (1998). Hypertext and the question of visual literacy. In D. Reinking, M. C. (Ed.), *Doing Internet research: Critical issues and methods for examining the Net* (pp. xvii-xxiv). Thousand Oaks, NY: Sage.

Costigan, J. T. (1999). Introduction: Forests, trees, and Internet research. In S. Jones (Ed.), *Doing internet research: Critical issues and methods for examining the Net* (pp.xvii-xxiv). Thousand Oaks, NY: Sage.

Danielewski, M. Z. (2000). *House of leaves.* New York: Pantheon.

Flower, L., Stein, V., Ackerman, J., Kantz, M. J., McCormick, K., & Peck, W. C. (1990). *Reading-to-write: Exploring a cognitive and social process.* New York: Oxford University Press.

Garton, L., Haythornthwaite, C., & Wellman, B. (1999). Studying on-line social networks. In S. Jones (Ed.), *Doing Internet research: Critical issues and methods for examining the Net* (pp. 75-105). Thousand Oaks, NY: Sage.

Glaser, B., & Strauss, A. (1967). *The discovery of grounded theory.* Chicago: Aldine.

Jones, S. (1999). Studying the Net: Intricacies and issues. In S. Jones (Ed.), *Doing Internet research: Critical issues and methods for examining the Net* (pp. 1-27). Thousand Oaks, NY: Sage.

Kamberelis, G., & Scott, K. D. (1992). Other people's voices: The coarticulation of texts and subjectivities. *Linguistics and Education, 4,* 359-403.

Kuhlthau, C. C. (1988). Developing a model of the library search process: Cognitive and affective aspects. *Reference Quarterly, 28,* 232-242.

Lenski, S. D., & Johns, J. L. (1997). Patterns of reading-to-write. *Reading Research and Instruction, 37,* 15-38.

Lenski, S. D. (1998). Strategic knowledge when reading in order to write. *Reading Psychology, 19,* 287-315.

Mayer, R. E. (1997). Multimedia learning: Are we asking the right questions? *Educational Psychologist, 32,* 1-19.

McGinley, W. (1992). The role of reading and writing while composing from sources. *Reading Research Quarterly, 27,* 227-248.

McKenzie, J. (1998). Grazing the Net: Raising a generation of free-ranging students. *Phi Delta Kappan, 80,* 26-31.

Mendrinos, R. B. (1997). *Using educational technology with at-risk students.* Westport, CN: Greenwood.

Mitra, M., & Cohen, E. (1999). Analyzing the Web: Directions and challenges. In S. Jones (Ed.), *Doing Internet research: Critical issues and methods for examining the Net* (pp. 179-202). Thousand Oaks, NY: Sage.

Pierson, M. E. (1997). The honeymoon is over. Leading the way to lasting search habits. *Technology Connection, 4,* 10-12, 25.

Ryder, R. J., & Graves, M. F. (1996/1997). Using the Internet to enhance students' reading, writing, and information-gathering skills. *Journal of Adolescent & Adult Literacy, 40,* 244-254.

Spivey, N. N. (1997). *The constructivist metaphor.* San Diego: Academic Press.

Stake, R. (1988). Case study methods in educational research: Seeking sweet water. In R. Jaeger (Ed.), *Complementary methods for research in education* (pp. 253-300). Washington DC: American Educational Research Association.

Sudweeks, F., & Simoff, S. J. (1999). Complementary explorative data analysis: The reconciliation of quantitative and qualitative principles. In S. Jones (Ed.), *Doing Internet research: Critical issues and methods for examining the Net* (pp. 29-55). Thousand Oaks, NY: Sage.

Tell, C. (1999/2000). Generation what? Connecting with today's youth. *Educational Leadership, 57,* 8-13.

Tierney, R. J., Soter, A., O'Flahavan, J. F., & McGinley, W. (1989). The effects of reading and writing upon thinking critically. *Reading Research Quarterly, 24,* 134-169.

Warschauer, M. (1999). *Electronic literacies: Language, culture, and power in online education.* Mahwah, NJ: Erlbaum.

Williams, J. (2000, November 21). *Talk of the nation.* Washington, DC: National Public Radio.

# TEACHER EDUCATION VOICES

# Teaching Inquiry Projects: Promoting Reflection and Action in Literacy Education for Preservice Teachers

**Laurie Elish-Piper**

Northern Illinois University

## Abstract

*Teacher educators in literacy aim to prepare reflective practitioners, and the use of teaching inquiry projects with preservice teachers may facilitate this goal. Using a model of action research wherein the preservice teacher identifies a challenge, confirms the challenge, intervenes with a plan, and understands the impact, the researcher worked with two groups of preservice teachers on teaching inquiry projects. The researcher collected data from journals, field notes from class sessions, interviews, focus groups, and project presentations. These data were analyzed using the constant comparative method to identify themes. The findings indicate that the preservice teachers enhanced their knowledge bases and experienced transformations from student to teacher in conjunction with their teaching inquiry projects. The teaching inquiry projects influenced the preservice teachers' future plans in teaching specific aspects of literacy related to their projects. Analysis also revealed "holes" in professional knowledge and preparation to teach literacy, as perceived by the preservice teachers.*

## Introduction

A major goal of teacher preparation is to promote reflection and inquiry into teaching and learning (Goodlad, 1990, 1997). Traditionally, research on teaching has been completed by university faculty who worked in K-12 classrooms to answer their own questions. Recently, a trend toward classroom-based, teacher research has arisen as teachers move toward answering their own questions about their own teaching (Lytle, 2000). As teacher education programs seek to find meaningful ways to help preservice and inservice teachers reflect, connect theory and practice, and implement effective instruction, action research provides a promising option (Dinkleman, 1997; Rearick & Feldman, 1999).

Much has been written in the literature about how action research influences teachers who engage in it (Lytle, 2000). These outcomes include change in theoretical orientation, practice, and professional development (Cochran-Smith, 1994). Lytle (2000) asserts that most action research promotes change in classroom practice for the individual teacher completing the research rather than influencing the field in general. In this process, the teacher examines his/her own beliefs about teaching as well as classroom teaching practices in light of findings of the action research. In addition, as teachers situate their action research projects in the related literature, they begin to make theory to practice connections related to their own classrooms (Cochran-Smith & Lytle, 1993).

A promising route to promoting connections between theory and practice is the use of professional development schools. Within professional development schools (PDS), preservice teachers, university professors, and school-based educators work collaboratively to improve the quality of preservice teacher education, professional development for inservice teachers, and teaching and learning in schools (Holmes, 1990). While professional development schools are touted as one of the most promising practices for improving teacher education, a modest amount of research has been conducted in this area since participants tend to be so busy establishing and maintaining the PDS sites that little times remains to conduct related research (Elish-Piper & Milson, 2000). Furthermore, limited research has been done to document how preservice teachers come to know, understand, and engage in reflective practice in the area of literacy within PDS contexts.

## Research Contexts

Two groups of preservice teachers participated in the research project. These preservice teachers, called the interns, worked in a well-established professional development school. One group participated in the Fall of 1999 and the other in the Fall of 2000. The interns participated in integrated methods courses at the university wherein instructors team-taught some classes, and collaborative assignments were completed across courses (e.g., literacy portfolio to connect reading, language arts, and tests and measurements courses; content area reading strategy lesson to connect reading, language arts, science, and/or social studies courses). Another connection was made by the reading methods instructor who also served as the university supervisor for the clinical experience. A team of clinical faculty (master teachers in the district) worked with the university supervisor to provide support, assistance, and feedback for interns during their clinical experiences. In addition, the university and school district collaborated to create integrated thematic units to serve as models in the methods courses and to be taught in the district. All cooperating teachers participated in a summer workshop to learn about the experiences the interns would have in the coming fall, as well as to contribute to the plans, goals, and experiences for the internship semester.

The district is located just outside a major city in northern Illinois, and the majority of its students are from middle to lower-middle income homes. Most of the students are of European-American backgrounds, but approximately 8% of the students are English language learners. Interns were expected to complete a teaching inquiry project in connection with their semester-long clinical experience which consisted of the first two days of the school year, one day a week for ten weeks, and daily for three consecutive weeks near the end of the semester. The internship semester preceded the final student teaching semester.

The focus of the teaching inquiry project did not have to be literacy since all instructors in the block participated (reading, language arts, tests and measurements, science, and social studies); however, over half of the interns opted to focus on literacy for their projects. In the Fall 1999 group, 17 of the 28 interns completed literacy-related projects, and in the Fall 2000 group, 19 of 31 interns focused on literacy for their teaching inquiry projects. The majority of the remaining interns focused on classroom management questions, another major area of concern for preservice teachers (Farris, 1999; Wiseman, Cooner, & Knight, 1998).

## Intern Participants

The interns tend to mirror the current teaching force, with most of them being female, traditional college-age students of European ancestry (Ladson-Billings, 1994). There were a total of 12 non-traditional students in the two groups. In addition, six males were involved in the study. In the Fall 1999 group, four of the interns were non-native English speakers (i.e., they spoke Thai, Russian, Yugoslavian, and Spanish), and in the 2000 group, two were non-native speakers who spoke Korean and Spanish as their first languages. A total of two African-American and two Latina interns participated in the study.

## The Study

Within this framework, the researcher implemented teaching inquiry projects (TIP) in conjunction with two literacy education courses at the undergraduate level. The following research question guided the study: What are the experiences of preservice teachers who engage in teaching inquiry projects related to literacy?

The researcher documented the experiences and reactions of the preservice teachers throughout the teaching inquiry projects. Data sources included journals, field notes from class sessions, interviews, focus groups, and project presentations. Journals focused on the interns' responses to open-ended questions such as "What are your goals for this clinical experience?" and "What progress are you making toward your goals?" The researcher recorded field notes at the end of each class session to document the interns' responses to topics for discussion, as well as connections they noted between the course and their clinical experiences. Interviews were conducted near the end of the semester to elicit information about the experiences with the teaching inquiry project. All interviews were transcribed. The interviews were conducted by a graduate student rather than the researcher (who was also the reading course instructor and clinical supervisor) so the interns would be more open in sharing their responses. The researcher conducted a focus group at the end of each semester with a sub-set of the interns, and these discussions were transcribed. In addition, the researcher gathered data from the project presentations by video taping the presentations.

Using the constant comparative method (Strauss & Corbin, 1990) the researcher analyzed the data to generate categories and identify patterns and themes to address the research question. Data analysis followed a model described by Miles and Huberman (1994) that included data reduction, data displays, and conclusion drawing/verification. Next, the researcher noted patterns using the techniques of clustering, contrasting, and comparing (Miles & Huberman, 1994). The data analysis categories were corroborated through the assistance of two graduate students who were involved as graduate assistants in the partnership context. In addition, member checks were completed by sharing the findings with a sub-set of interns from each semester to verify the accuracy and validity of the analysis.

## Teaching Inquiry Projects

The teaching inquiry projects followed a basic model for action research wherein each intern collaborated with his/her cooperating teacher to identify a challenge in his/her classroom, confirm the challenge through observation and professional resources, intervene with a plan, and determine the impact. Figure 1 shows the project description sheet that was shared with the interns.

## Figure 1. Teaching Inquiry Project

**General Description:** An important part of teaching is being able to identify problems, develop plans to address problems, and reflect on the success or failure of plans. The Teaching Inquiry Project (TIP) has been designed to help you understand the cycle of reflection and action in which teachers engage. The goal of this project is to help you inquire into your own teaching and reflect on teaching and learning.

### STAGE 1: Identifying the Challenge

Identify a concern, issue, or challenge that you are facing as a teacher. Phrase this in the form of a question such as, "How can I help a struggling reader improve fluency?" or "How do book talks influence student book selection and engagement during SSR?"

### STAGE 2: Confirm the Challenge and Develop a Possible Intervention Plan

Once you have identified a challenge, you will need to gather information that will help explain and confirm the challenge. You will need to collect the following types of information:

1) Personal Observations—might be recorded in a personal journal.
2) Literature Review—read professional journals and magazines to gather more information about the challenge.
3) Technology Resource Review—read on-line resources, participate in professional listservs, and review other technology resources related to the challenge.

You are encouraged to consider collecting the following types of information, if appropriate.

1) Peer Observations—have another teacher observe the situation and provide insights on the problem.
2) Audio and/or Videotape—if appropriate, listen to and/or watch yourself in the challenging situation.
3) Student Work—if appropriate, collect samples of student work that will illustrate the challenge.
4) Student Feedback—if appropriate, talk to students about the challenge.

*You will also propose a possible intervention plan to address your challenge.

### STAGE 3: Intervene with a Plan

Decide what you would like to try as a solution to your problem or to get an answer to your question. Share your plan with other teachers, University Instructors, or anyone you feel might be able to provide you with valuable feedback. Once you have received sufficient feedback and revised your plan accordingly, implement your plan. Gather additional information during the implementation of your plan. The information you collect should allow you to assess your plan.

### STAGE 4: Understand the Impact—Conference Presentation

Review your data and determine the effectiveness of your plan. Your poster presentation for the conference should chronicle each stage of your project, communicate the results of your plan, and make recommendations related to your problem/question.

A planning grid (see Figure 2) was also presented to the interns and intermediate due dates were assigned to help the interns stay focused on the project during the semester. Class time was devoted to discussing the teaching inquiry projects, and university instructors and cooperating teachers served as mentors for interns during the inquiry process.

**Figure 2. TIP Guide: ICIU Process**

| IDENTIFY THE CHALLENGE | CONFIRM THE CHALLENGE | INTERVENE WITH A PLAN | UNDERSTAND THE IMPACT |
|---|---|---|---|
| | Collecting Evidence | Collecting Evidence | |
| | a. | a. | |
| | b. | b. | |
| | c. | c. | |
| | d. | d. | |

Cooperating teachers participated in a half-day workshop on action research before the project was implemented; however, the workshop did not directly involve the teachers in doing action research. Several teachers had engaged in action research for their graduate programs; however, the vast majority of cooperating teachers had not been involved in action research before.

In a hope to disseminate information from the teaching inquiry projects a semester-end conference was held for each of the groups so the interns could present their projects, and findings to their peers, cooperating teachers, university instructors, and other interested persons. For the Fall 1999 intern group, the conference was a professional gathering with over 80 attendees including cooperating teachers, principals, university faculty and administrators, and interns. The interns displayed large posters to detail their teaching inquiry projects and they gave 15 minutes presentations to interested attendees. A similar format was planned for the Fall 2000 interns; however, a large snowstorm caused the conference to be cancelled, and since it was the end of the semester, it could not be rescheduled. As a result, two of the university instructors met with students individually to have them present their projects and findings.

The primary goal for the teaching inquiry projects was to promote reflection and action, and the emphasis was on process rather than just product; therefore, the evaluation of the teaching inquiry projects was designed to reflect this. It was the hope of the instructors that all interns would be successful on their teaching inquiry projects rather than seeking to create a normal curve pattern wherein a specific percentage of students would not succeed with the project. The evaluation rubric for the projects is provided in Figure 3.

**Figure 3. TIP Evaluation Rubric**

**Name:** _____

**Your TIP is worth 50 possible points.**
**Your TIP will be evaluated with the following criteria.**

*Stage 1: Identify the Challenge (5 points possible)*          Your Score _____
    -Stated as question
    -Concern/issue/challenge is meaningful to literacy teaching and learning

*Stage 2: Confirm the Challenge and*
*Propose a Plan (15 points possible)*          Your Score _____
    -Multiple sources of information gathered
    -Personal observations and reflections are included
    -Related, pertinent professional literature is examined
    -Related, pertinent technology resources are examined
    -Information supports and explains challenge
    -Proposed plan is logical and educationally-sound
    -Proposed plan directly addresses challenge

*Stages 3 & 4: Intervene with a Plan and*
*Understand the Impact (30 points)*          Your Score _____
    **Content/Synthesis**
    -Plan is implemented in classroom
    -Plan is implemented for an appropriate duration
    -Clear evidence of plan is included in conference presentation
    -Presentation synthesizes TIP thoroughly
    -Evidence of developing expertise and knowledge related to the challenge
    -Presentation chronicles each stage of TIP
    -Presentation explains the intervention
    -Presentation communicates results of the plan
    -Presentation includes appropriate recommendations related to challenge
    -Documentary evidence to illustrate TIP

    ***Presentation/Communication of Ideas***
    -Evidence of advanced preparation
    -Presentation is well-organized
    -Good eye contact and voice quality
    -Effective use of graphics, technology, and/or other presentation resources
    -Creativity, enthusiasm, and confidence in presentation style
    -Appropriate documentation represented in presentation

Total Possible Points = 50 Points          Your Total Score _____

# Findings and Discussion

Analysis of the data indicated that the teaching inquiry projects were meaningful learning experiences for the interns. Responses clustered in the following areas: knowledge base, transformation from student to teacher, future plans, and "holes" in professional knowledge and preparation. Each of these categories will be discussed in the following sections. All names used for interns are pseudonyms.

## *Knowledge Base*

Overwhelmingly, interns noted that they had enhanced their knowledge base in the areas they studied for the projects. Many projects clustered around working with struggling readers, an area that many interns felt unprepared to address at the beginning of the term. Examples of these projects included "The Struggling Reader: Strategies and Solutions" and "Strategies for Helping a Second-Grade Struggling Reader with Comprehension." These interns reported feeling more knowledgeable about identifying a struggling reader, developing instruction for a struggling reader, and making instructional decisions for this type of reader. While these topics had been addressed in university class sessions, many of the students reported concerns such as, "How will I know what the student's reading level is?" and "How do I work with kids who are so far below grade level?" After completing her teaching inquiry project with a struggling reader, one intern commented, "I am not afraid of working with struggling readers now. I learned a lot of things that do and do not work with these kids. I also know some good resources to help me with struggling readers in my own classroom when I am a teacher." Another intern noted, "It was great to see his progress. I feel like I have more knowledge about working with this type of student, although they are all different. It's good to know that I can teach a low reader to improve."

Several other interns chose to study family involvement in reading for their teaching inquiry projects. Examples of these projects included, "Family Reading Nights to Promote Parent Involvement in Reading," "Using the Internet to Promote Parent Involvement in Reading," and "Strategies for Family Involvement in Reading." These interns indicated that they gained a great deal in terms of their knowledge base about parent involvement and reading through the completion of their teaching inquiry projects. One intern commented, "I was afraid of working with parents. Once I started working on this project, I learned so much. I feel like I know a lot about working with parents now." Another intern noted, "I know so much more about working with parents now that I did this project. Before I had no clue!"

Other interns completed projects related to using literature circles, improving motivation to read, and strategies for using reading across the curriculum. These interns' comments included Leanna's statement about studying literature circles, "I know so much more about lit circles now because of my project. I actually think I could use them in my own room." Liz commented about her project on reading motivation by explaining, "It's amazing how different their motivation is. I learned so much about how to help different kinds of kids want to read. I read some great articles, interviewed teachers, and got to try out my ideas. I learned so much from this project. I wish I could say the same for everything I did this semester!" At the conclusion of her TIP on using reading across the curriculum, LaTonya explained, "Now it makes so much sense that I need to teach reading all day. Before it just seemed like they should know how to read their books. Now I have some strategies that work so I can help them understand science or social studies, or whatever they need to read. Now I actually know how to teach reading across the curriculum. That's a good feeling since I want to teach middle school."

### Transformation from Student to Teacher

Many of the interns reported that the entire semester had helped them begin to make the shift from student to teacher in preparation for their full-time student teaching experience in the following semester. The one element of the semester that they reported as having the greatest influence on this transformation was the teaching inquiry project experience. They noted the empowerment they felt with identifying their own topics, developing and carrying out their own intervention plans, and "thinking like a teacher." Furthermore, the interns expressed the power of the final presentation as part of the transformation from student to teacher. Each of these areas is discussed below.

### Empowerment of Identifying Own Topic.

Many interns noted that with the exception of being allowed to choose a topic for a library research paper, or to select from a group of options for projects, this was the first time in their professional education courses that they had full control over selecting what they would study and how they would proceed. Their responses to this openness ranged from elation to fear, as evidenced in the following quotes which were characteristic of many interns. Kayla exemplified the group of students who were extremely pleased to have a chance to select their own inquiry topics. She commented, "It's about time. I know what I need to learn, and I finally got a chance to do it. It was hard figuring out a topic to study, but it meant so much more to me since it was something I really wanted to learn about." At the other end of the continuum were students like James who expressed concern, "I didn't know what to study. It was scary. I was worried I'd pick the wrong topic or something stupid. I spent way too much time trying to figure out what to study. I kept wishing someone would say, 'do this.'" The largest group of students fell somewhere in-between these two extremes, meaning that they were pleased but worried about identifying their own topics. Vali's comment characterizes these types of responses, "It was weird at first. I mean, I didn't know where to begin or what to study. I was kind of angry, I mean you guys are the professors and teachers, why can't you just tell me what to study. After a few weeks in my clinical, I started to have questions about what was going on. I was glad I got to choose what to study. Then I was glad I got to pick my topic, but I wasn't at first!"

### *Developing and Carrying Out Plans.*

In the inquiry process, the interns had to develop an intervention plan to address their question. The plan required that the intern do something on a consistent basis, whether that was implementing a specific teaching strategy or using a procedure on a regular basis. For example, Leanna implemented literature circles daily for two weeks as part of her teaching inquiry project, and Janie implemented 15 different tutoring sessions with a struggling reader over a three-week period. Marisol sent home a weekly newsletter, developed a family reading night program for her grade level, and developed several activities to send home for parents and children to complete together. The interns reported that their intervention plans allowed them to do something on a consistent basis so that they felt they developed more confidence and skill than they did when just implementing a lesson or project here or there. For example, Marisol explained, "I got into the flow of thinking about working with parents. I got more confidence. It got easier because I was working on it all semester." Janie described her experience by saying, "I got to work with Sinisa every day so I became the expert. My teacher even asked me about how he was doing and what I thought she should do with him next. It was really good to get into the flow rather than jumping from this to that."

### *Thinking Like a Teacher*

Many of the interns identified changes in thinking about classroom situations, students, teaching, and learning during the teaching inquiry projects. Evidence of thinking like a teacher included Jaimie's insight, "I used to just worry about how my lesson was going, what I was doing. Because I was using running records with my struggling readers, I started to worry more about them and if they were learning." In this example, Jaimie realized that the focus of her teaching should be on learning rather than just on her delivery of the lesson. Marcus had a similar experience when he noted, "I really got to know the kids I was working with in my class. I wasn't just thinking what can I get from this clinical. I started thinking what can I give to the kids and my teacher during this clinical?"

Other interns showed evidence of thinking like a teacher in terms of exercising diagnostic teaching or responsive teaching stances (e.g., Rasinski & Padak, 2000; Roller, 1996; Edwards & Pleasants, 1998). For example, Tiffanie noted, "I got so I was making changes in my lesson right there on my feet like my teacher does. That was so amazing. I used to just cling to my lesson plan, but I saw the kids weren't getting it so I changed what I was doing. I think I got to this point because I was doing strategy lessons every day with my group." Greg explained, "I was thinking just a minute or two ahead of my students. I was anticipating their responses and thinking about what I would do next to help them understand better. I felt more confident than I did in my single lessons. The intervention was mine so I felt like it was okay to move away from what I had written in my lesson plan if the kids already knew what I was teaching or they had no clue."

### *Final Presentations.*

The Fall 1999 interns participated in a formal conference setting to present their teaching inquiry projects. Using break-out sessions, each intern presented his/her project to small groups of teachers, university faculty, district administrators, and peers. Each intern prepared a large poster display and a 15-minute presentation. Each intern did his/her presentation two times to allow conference attendees to participate in as many presentations as possible. The presentations were evaluated by at least one instructor from the semester. The interns noted that the stakes were high for the conference, as was the stress level. James explained, "I was scared to death to be presenting in front of these teachers with all of their experience and the principals, too." Gina explained, "I must have practiced a thousand times because I was so stressed out about my presentation. I was going through it in my sleep!" While not explicitly instructed to do so, the interns showed up in suits and professional clothing suitable for interviews. All but a few of their presentations were well-prepared, informative, and interesting. Many of the interns had expressed concern that the conference attendees would be bored by their presentations. As Greg stated, "I think they'll be bored. It's big stuff for me to learn about this, but they've been teaching for years. I'm sure they already know all of this." Many of the interns were surprised to find out about the interest level of the attendees, and one intern noted, "I was shocked to see the teachers taking notes from my presentation. They really liked my parent homework journal idea. I felt so proud that they thought of me like a teacher. It was great!"

During the Fall 2000 semester, a major snow storm closed the school district and university so the conference had to be cancelled. Because it was the end of the semester, the conference could not be rescheduled. As a result, two of the instructors met with the interns for individual appointments to share their teaching inquiry projects. All but a few of the interns expressed regret that the conference had to be cancelled. Ann summed up these feelings with her statement, "I was really nervous, but I wanted to learn about everyone's project. I wish we could have had the conference. I heard how great it was last year, and I really wanted to be part of it this year."

### Future Plans

Most of the interns noted that the teaching inquiry projects influenced and directed their future plans for teaching. Many of the interns identified specific plans related to their TIPs in terms of activities, approaches, or strategies they would use. This outcome is illustrated by Katie's statement, "I will definitely use this in my own classroom because I know it works." Veronica explained, "I am going to use making words in my own class. It worked great and the kids loved it. I was skeptical at first, but it is a great approach!" Beyond these basic conclusions about using a specific strategy or approach, some interns developed a deeper insight about what they planned to do in the future related to their teaching inquiry projects. Greg concluded, "I am going to approach struggling readers in a much different way than I would have a semester ago. I realize that they can do a lot, but they need tons of modeling, scaffolding, and encouragement. Before I doubted that some kids could really answer higher level questions and understand what they read, but now I realize that is not true." Ian explained his future plans by stating, "I'm so happy about how the parents responded to the class website and e-mail. I worried that they wouldn't have time or be interested in doing this at the sixth-grade level. *Boy was I surprised.* I now realize that most parents are really interested and want to get involved, but it's my job to find ways to make this happen. Before I thought I wouldn't really do parent involvement since I want to teach upper elementary or middle school. Now I know I'll promote parent involvement no matter what grade I teach."

### Holes in Professional Knowledge and Preparation

Many of the interns used the reflective writing and focus group sessions to share concerns and observations about what Kelly called "holes" in professional knowledge and preparation. Kelly commented, "I realized how little I did know about reading when I did my TIP. I didn't know how to make one lesson build off of another. I didn't know how to differentiate instruction for students. I didn't know how to use assessment to inform my instruction. I'm a good student. I've gotten all A's in my education courses and I had a great first clinical. I'm glad I got to do my TIP because I know a lot more about teaching reading now, but I wonder if I should have learned some of these things in other classes earlier." Marisol explained, "I knew lots of the 'what to do' but I didn't know the 'why to do it' or the 'when to do it' of teaching reading. I mean I had lots of ideas for teaching strategies and activities, and I knew some good assessments, too. I just didn't know what I was supposed to do with them in a real classroom. I learned some of this in my clinical and as part of my TIP. I still feel really weak in this area of using the things I learned in my methods classes. Maybe that will come with student teaching." Many of the "holes" focused on classroom management and organization issues, as is a common criticism of teacher education programs (Farris, 1999; Wiseman, Cooner, & Knight, 1998). Leanna explained, "I had no idea how to keep the kids under control in their literature circles. We talked about these in my methods classes, but I had only seen them done with adults. It was chaos the first couple of days. I went home crying, but I kept trying. I wish we could learn more about how to implement these great new ideas in classrooms with real kids. I learned through trial and error, which is okay, but I'd like to have more basic knowledge about how to manage the classroom, especially for cooperative learning and group work." Vali expressed a common "hole" for the interns, that of time management in and outside of the classroom. Vali commented, "I was swamped with journals from my TIP. It never dawned on me that I could stagger the due dates until I talked to my teacher and supervisor. It seems like I should have known this before I got to my second-to-last semester." Vali went on to note, "Maybe I did hear some of these things about managing time in my classes, but it never mattered until now. I think the program should focus more on practical concerns like time management, stress, classroom management, and organization during the last couple of semesters when we really need this."

Another type of concern focused on the professional development and knowledge of some cooperating teachers who one intern described as, "clueless about TIPs and action research." While a summer workshop had been provided for the cooperating teachers, several had been absent that day. Furthermore, the workshop had focused on talking about action research, but the cooperating teachers did not have the opportunity to engage in action research themselves. With the exception of a few teachers who had completed action research as part of their graduate programs, the concept was new to them. Some of the interns felt frustrated by the lack of expertise and knowledge of their cooperating teachers. Sara explained, "My cooperating teacher doesn't get what I'm trying to do with this project. She talks about my lessons, but she doesn't seem to understand how I'm trying to evaluate the outcomes of my intervention plan, or why I'm doing that other than because it is an assignment." Many of these interns sought out other mentors for their projects in university faculty, the university supervisor, or clinical faculty within the district.

## Limitations

The teaching inquiry projects were completed within the framework of a well-established professional development school. Furthermore, the team of university instructors and school-based educators was committed to collaborating and facilitating the teaching inquiry projects. The outcomes of this approach most likely would differ greatly in a non-PDS setting. The findings are based mainly on anecdotal and self-reported data, and as such, they should be interpreted with caution because of the limitations of these types of data. In addition, the interns in the study self-selected to be part of the PDS program, known on-campus as a more demanding route than taking a traditional block of courses. These interns may have been more motivated and engaged in the process of becoming teachers than typical preservice teachers. These distinctions should be noted when considering the findings of the study.

## Remaining Questions and Future Research

As was noted earlier, the interns were part of a well-established professional development school, and the research did not attempt to separate out the effects of the PDS on the interns' development as compared to the teaching inquiry projects themselves. Future research in non-PDS settings is needed to determine if this approach will have positive benefits for preservice teachers in those settings. Further research is also needed to determine if plans for instruction result in actual teaching practices once the interns become certified teachers. Both groups also reported concern that the many responsibilities of teaching would likely prevent them from engaging in other action research studies in their own classrooms in the future. Examination of these concerns and strategies for implementing action research in a time-efficient manner warrants further consideration.

A number of questions and obstacles remain related to the implementation of teaching inquiry projects with preservice teachers. First, what degree of knowledge and experience must cooperating teachers possess about action research to be able to support preservice teachers engaged in the process? Furthermore, how can this knowledge and experience be developed and nurtured in cooperating teachers? Because of the power of the final conference, strategies need to be put in place to ensure that the conference will happen, even if bad weather or other extreme circumstances arise. This could be as simple as scheduling a make-up date in advance, or pursuing options such as holding the conference after the end of the semester or on a weekend.

## Conclusion

As the partnership team reflected on its outcomes, goals, and plans for the future during a recent meeting, one member of the team explained, "The TIP is the best thing we do. It is the one thing I know makes a difference in how we prepare our interns as compared to the traditional courses. It is the one thing that helps them think like a teacher and begin to reflect on their own practice." A comment by one of the interns captures the power and promise of the teaching inquiry projects best, "It was one of the hardest things I ever did, and it was also one of the best things I ever did. I really feel like a teacher now. I am thinking like a teacher now. I think professors should include TIPs in their courses and programs because they do make a difference . . . at least they did for us this semester."

## References

Cochran-Smith, M. (1994). The power of teacher research in education. In S. Hollingsworth & H. Sockett (Eds.), *Teacher research and educational reform* (pp. 142-165). Chicago: University of Chicago Press.

Cochran-Smith, M., & Lytle, S. L. (1993). *Inside/outside: Teacher research and knowledge.* New York: Teachers College Press.

Dinkelman, T. (1997). The Promise of Action Research for Critically Reflective Teacher Education. *Teacher Educator, 32,* 250-274.

Edwards, P. A., & Pleasants, H. M. (1998). How can we provide for culturally responsive instruction in literacy? In S. B. Neuman, & K. A. Roskos (Eds.), *Children achieving: Best practices in early literacy.* Newark, DE: International Reading Association.

Elish-Piper, L., & Milson, A. J. (200). Harlem-NIU Partnership: Continuing Connections. *Thresholds in Education, 26,* 12-18.

Farris, P. J. (1999). *Teaching, bearing the torch (2nd ed).* Boston: McGraw Hill.

Goodlad, J. I. (1990). *Teachers for our nation's schools.* San Francisco: Jossey-Bass.

Goodlad, J. I. (1997). *In praise of education.* New York: Teachers College Press.

Holmes Group (1990). *Tomorrow's schools: Principles for the design of professional development schools.* East Lansing, MI: Author.

Ladson-Billings, G. (1994). *The dreamkeepers: Successful teachers of African American children.* San Francisco, CA: Jossey-Bass Publishers.

Lytle, S. (2000). Teacher research in the contact zone. In M. L. Kamil, P. B. Mosenthal, P. D. Pearson, & R. Barr (Eds.), *Handbook of reading research: Volume III* (pp. 691-718). Mahwah, NJ: Lawrence Erlbaum Associates.

Miles, M. B., & Huberman, A. M. (1994). *Qualitative data analysis* (2nd ed). Thousand Oaks, CA: Sage.

Rasinski, T., & Padak, N. (2000). *Effective reading strategies: Teaching children who find reading difficult (2nd ed.).* Upper Saddle River, NJ: Merrill.

Rearick, M. L., & Feldman, A. (1999). Orientations, Purposes and Reflection: A Framework for Understanding Action Research. *Teaching and Teacher Education, 15,* 333-49.

Roller, C. M. (1996). *Variability not disability: Struggling readers in a workshop classroom.* Newark, DE: International Reading Association.

Strauss, A., & Corbin, J. (1990). *Basics of qualitative research: Grounded theory procedures and techniques.* Newbury Park, CA: Sage.

Wiseman, D. L., Cooner, D. D., & Knight, S. L. (1998). *Becoming a teacher in a field-based setting.* Belmont, CA: Wadsworth Publishing Company.

# RELEASING RESPONSIBILITY FOR ASSESSMENT OF THEIR LEARNING TO PRE-SERVICE TEACHERS

## Betty L. Goerss

Indiana University East

## Abstract

*This article describes the results of a two-semester pilot in a Secondary Reading Methods course at a regional campus of a state university. Three goals guided this pilot: integration of reading theory and strategies with Interstate New Teacher Assessment and Support Consortium (INTASC) principles and classroom instruction in a field experience, modeling of the use of authentic assessment, and modeling of gradual release of responsibility to pre-service teachers. Pre-service teachers determined their own assessment plan to demonstrate competency of course outcomes. They were encouraged to work with peers from their content field to develop this plan, which could include requirements from other methods courses or their field experience.*

Future teachers need the opportunity to implement what they learn in college classrooms through application in real teaching situations. A report by the National Commission on Teaching & America's Future (1996) called for improving teacher preparation and professional development by connecting theory to practice. They note that teachers often teach the way they were taught rather than applying what they learned in college when university learning occurs apart from practice.

This report and others encouraged teacher educators to relate theory to practice, often through such means as professional development schools (Abdal-Haqq, 1998; Lyon, 1995). This makes the role of teacher educators more complex as they prepare future teachers to meet high standards. They must model and provide realistic experiences to prepare them for the classroom while building a theoretical basis for their instructional decision making. To achieve these lofty goals, teacher educators must constantly find new ways to integrate theory with practical applications that pre-service teachers may use in the classroom.

In addition to connecting theory and practice many universities, including ours, must prepare teachers to meet the Interstate New Teacher Assessment and Support Consortium (INTASC) Principles adopted in thirty-seven states as standards for new teachers. These are the competencies that we want our pre-service teachers to have when they enter the teaching field, thus they must be integrated throughout our teacher-education program. Just as K-12 classrooms cannot meet all the new standards without integration, neither can teacher educators include everything that pre-service teachers need in a few methods courses. This requires rethinking methods courses to provide models connecting theory to best practice across content fields.

The use of performance-based assessment in methods classes provides an excellent model of best practice for pre-service teachers applicable in their classrooms (Wiggins, 1996). Performance-based assessment involves tasks closely related to those found in the real world, which demonstrate proficiency for a given topic. It is valid, assesses the learning for which it was intended, is rigorous, involves meaningful learning, and is often judged by rubrics, teacher feedback, and peer evaluation (Wiggins & McTighe, 1998). To provide an adequate model for pre-service teachers, assessment should provide the opportunity for them to demonstrate what they have learned as they engage in the learning process (Viechnicki, Barbour, Shaklee, Rohrer, & Ambrose, 1993). Furthermore, assessment should be part of a continuous process in which the teacher is reflective for the purpose of growth (McLaughlin & Voyt, 1996).

Another best practice that pre-service teachers may apply to their classroom is the gradual release of responsibility model. The model as described by Pearson and Gallagher (1983) was designed for reading experiences in which the teacher provides a model and instruction, then through guided practice, the teacher gradually releases the responsibility to the student. Students move from situations in which teachers are almost totally in charge of students' success through a gradual progression toward students taking charge of their own learning. It has been used successfully in many different grade levels with a variety of tasks. The extent to which teachers provide scaffolding and release responsibility to students is largely dependent on the specific task and the texts that are used (Brophy, 2000; Collins, Brown, & Holum, 1991).

## Rationale and Goals of the Pilot Process

Our state requires that every pre-service teacher complete a course in reading before he/she is certified to teach. Many secondary pre-service teachers do not see the need for a reading course since they believe they will not teach reading. One way in which I help them realize the value of the course is to provide opportunities to integrate reading methods content with content area in their methods within a field experience. Our Division of Education supports this idea so secondary pre-service teachers take reading methods at the same time as their specific content area methods (science, math, social studies, or English). The block includes a pre-student teaching field experience in which pre-service teachers are teaching in a school for two class periods or one block daily. INTASC principles are identified within this integration of content, reading strategies, and classroom experience. This provides the opportunity for pre-service teachers to make connections by using what they learn in their reading and content methods courses in a field experience classroom while developing competency in INTASC principles.

In an effort to provide a process for pre-service teachers make these connections in my reading methods course, pre-service teachers were allowed to select their own performance-based assessment (Wiggins, 1987) to demonstrate learning outcomes for my course. They were encouraged to use requirements from their content methods course and field experience to demonstrate these outcomes. There were three goals for having pre-service teachers determine their own performance-based assessment.

The first goal was to provide the opportunity to integrate reading methods with their course content and their field experience. It was based on the desire to help pre-service teachers learn to select and use effective reading strategies in their classroom instruction. In past experiences, pre-service teachers in my course often failed to apply what they learned when the course was taught apart from a field experience component. My belief was that if they planned and taught a lesson in a school setting that included reading strategies then received credit for doing so in my course, they were much more likely to continue this practice.

The second goal was to provide a model of authentic assessment that they could use when they became teachers. This is based on the belief that if pre-service teachers do not attempt authentic assessment while they are pre-service teachers, they may revert to assessment that they experienced when they were in high school (Short & Burke, 1989).

A third goal was to provide a model of students taking responsibility for their own learning that pre-service teachers could use in their own classrooms. The format for this goal came from the gradual release of responsibility model by Pearson and Gallagher (1983) as described previously. I adapted this model of instruction in an effort to help them understand how it might work in their classrooms.

The opportunity for pre-service teachers to choose the performance-based assessment that would demonstrate their competency of course outcomes in reading methods seemed an appropriate means to meet all three goals. For pre-service teachers, performance-based assessment is evaluation using

products or tasks as similar as possible to what they will use in their classroom. Teaching a lesson or writing a lesson plan are examples of performance-based assessment that could demonstrate competency of an outcome
such as integrating writing into the curriculum, one of the outcomes for my
reading methods course.

## Introducing this Process to Pre-Service Teachers

To introduce this approach, I used the following format. At the beginning of the semester I related how each course outcome met the identified
INTASC principle. For example, one outcome of my secondary reading

### Figure 1. Course Outcomes: Reading Methods Syllabus –M464

**Course Description:** Methods and materials are presented for teaching students to
read and write more effectively in the content areas in middle school, junior high,
and senior high school. The reading process, the reading-to-learn and writing-to-
learn processes, and the relationships among reading, writing, language, and thinking are examined.

**Objectives:** This course will prepare you to be a teacher that is:

**A Reflective Scholar**, demonstrated by explaining your understanding of the
processes of reading to learn and writing to learn, supporting them with theory
and research.

**An Instructional Leader,** demonstrated by describing the approach you would
use to integrate reading and writing in your content area, basing your approach
on your beliefs.

**A Global Citizen,** demonstrated by planning how you would use reading and
writing to develop students' critical thinking skills, applying it to a local, national or global issue.

In addition, this course will help you to become an educated person who:
* Is able to express himself/herself clearly, completely, and accurately
* Has the ability to think rationally, to develop informed opinions, and
  to comprehend and create new ideas.
                                    **—IUE Student Learning Objectives**

| **Course Outcomes:** | **INTASC Principle** |
|---|---|
| Pre-service Teachers will: | |
| A. understand the reading process | 1 |
| B. be able to use a variety of techniques, strategies, and approaches for instruction | 4 |
| C. be able to select materials for classroom instruction | 7 |
| D. be able to integrate technology into instruction | 6 |
| E. be aware of a variety of methods for assessment | 8 |
| F. be able to provide scaffolding to improve learning | 3 |
| G. be able to teach students to become metacognitive | 2 |
| H. be able to integrate writing into your content | 4 |

methods course is: "Pre-service teachers will be able to use a variety of techniques, strategies, and approaches for reading instruction." This helps pre-service teachers meet INTASC Principle 4 that states: "The teacher understands and uses a variety of instructional strategies to encourage students' development of critical thinking, problem solving, and performance skills." We discussed the outcomes of the course and some possible artifacts that would meet each one, such as a thematic unit demonstrating the integration of several reading strategies. Figure 1 is the first page of the syllabus that identified the outcomes for the course and the related INTASC principle.

Following this introduction, pre-service teachers met with others from the same content areas to discuss a specific plan to meet the outcomes. At this point I answered questions and made suggestions. Pre-service teachers were given two weeks to submit a performance-based assessment (PBA) plan for meeting course outcomes that included their choice of artifact(s) to meet each outcome, due dates, and the point value. An example of one such PBA plan is found in Figure 2. The two math education pre-service teachers who developed this PBA plan selected a variety of artifacts to demonstrate their learning and each one came from their field experience.

## Figure 2. Secondary Math Proposed Performance-Based Assessment Plan

| Due Dates | Outcome | Points | PBA's |
| --- | --- | --- | --- |
| March 23 | Understand the Reading Process | 40 | Learning Log Word Problem Lesson |
| March 30 | Use variety of strategies and approaches | 125 | Series of lesson plans |
| April 1 | Become familiar with professional journals | 50 | Summarize response to journal articles |
| April 1 | Select materials for classroom instruction | 125 | Lesson plans with student work |
| March 2 | Integrate technology into instruction | 75 | Graphing calculator demonstration |
| March 30 | Able to use a variety of assessment tools | 125 | Teacher-made tests student samples |
| March 30 | Provide scaffolding to improve instruction | 40 | Lesson plan with group, individual work |
| March 30 | Teach students to become metacognitive | 40 | Administer and analyze Metacognitive Reading Awareness Inventory |
| March 30 | Integrate writing into the curriculum | 50 | Exit cards, journaling— student samples |

I provided suggestions and encouraged them to use requirements for their content area methods courses and the field experience, thus helping them to integrate reading methods into their teaching. For example, a thematic unit prepared as a requirement for English methods could be used as part of the PBA plan if it included reading strategies or integrated writing or other course outcomes. Furthermore, one artifact such as a thematic unit might meet several outcomes while another artifact might just partially meet one outcome. A lesson taught in the field experience, along with one or two other artifacts, might meet the outcome of integrating writing into their curriculum. Student work could provide a demonstration of competency when included as part of a lesson taught in a field experience.

To make the connection between reading methods and the artifacts chosen from a field experience or content methods requirements, pre-service teachers had to explain how each selected artifact met the outcome for which it was intended. This explanation provided the connection, a reflective component of integrating the theory with practical application (Tierney, Carter, & Desai, 1991).

Figures 3 and 4 are examples of artifacts from two pre-service teachers and their explanations of how the artifacts met specific course outcomes.

## Figure 3. Sample Artifact by Pre-service Teacher

**Outcome: Be able to teach students to become metacognitive**

To show students how to be more metacognitive I administered the Metacognitive Reading Awareness Inventory. It is hoped that by completing the inventory, they will be more aware of how they are learning.

I had a total of 45 students participate in the survey. A few of the students chose more than one answer on each question. However, because most of the students chose only one I am only going to indicate the answer that occurred most frequently along with how many times it was chosen.

| | | | |
|---|---|---|---|
| 1. | A–32 | 6. | A-24 |
| 2. | C-26 | 7. | A-20 |
| 3. | D-23 | 8. | A-22 |
| 4. | A-18 | 9. | B-22 |
| 5. | A-26 | 10. | A-24 |

After looking at the responses the students gave, I was not at all surprised. This is what the students were doing in class. I think they have learned several reading techniques just through experience. However, I do not think they have been taught how to "read." They know how to recognize words and their meaning but they have never been taught how to pre-read, skim, look back . . . they don't know how to approach different reading materials. This is shown in their responses to number 4 and number 10. Other than that I think the students are right on and doing pretty good with their concept of reading. There is definitely room for improvement but at their age they are doing pretty good.

## Figure 4. Sample Artifact From Secondary Science Education Major

**Explanation**: The following lesson plan is submitted as partial completion of the following two outcomes: use a variety of techniques, strategies, and approaches for instruction and integrate writing into the curriculum.

This lesson introduced a new unit in my physical science field experience classroom. I activated prior knowledge about the states of matter through the use of a picture and related vocabulary. Another technique used in the lesson was student participation in an exercise in which they become states of matter followed by a discussion of the experience. Then, think-aloud was used to introduce the chapter, walking them through the entire chapter. To monitor understanding, I used an Exit Slip at the end of class (writing).

### Lesson Plan

**Goal:** Introduce the unit, discuss broad terms, and relate it to the previous unit, energy
**Outcomes Obj**: Students will be able to:
- Describe and give examples of the three states of matter
- State the kinetic theory of matter and describe how it relates to states of matter

**Course:** Physical Science
**Time:** 50 minutes
**Title:** States of Matter
**Ref No:** PS_3_a_1

| Activity | Description | Time | Type* | Materials Required |
|---|---|---|---|---|
| **Camera & TV** | Display the section picture of states of matter with some terms for the section | 5 | 1 | Camera, TV, pictures |
| **Discussion & Participation** | Clear out middle of floor for "human states of matter" Solids: Get 10 students standing close together, with movement—vibration Crystals: Arrange in geometric pattern Show example of salt crystals Amorphous: Arrange in no pattern Show wax Liquids: Keep 6 students. Move a little faster No structure. Shape of container Gas: Keep 2 people:   Move faster. Heat up Move people even faster | 20 | 3,4 | |
| **Reading Strategy** | Use "**Think-Aloud**" to introduce chapter Summarize chapter headings. Review chapter highlighting: kinetic theory, class. Map, property | 15 | 8 | Textbook |
| **Writing** | Assign an "**Exit Slip**" with attached questions | 10 | 8 | Question Sheet |

**\*Types:**
1 Lecture; 2 Lab; 3 Demo; 4 Group; 5 Guided Practice; 6 A/V Comp;
7 Experiment; 8 Reading/Writing

Figure 3 includes data the pre-service teacher collected from administering the Metacognitive Reading Awareness Inventory (Miholic, 1994) to her class. The explanation demonstrates the pre-service teacher's ability to use this tool to assess student awareness of their metacognitive abilities and relate it to observations of student behavior in the field experience.

In Figure 4, a secondary science education major uses a lesson plan for partial completion of two course outcomes. His explanation indicates that he has integrated instructional strategies from reading methods into a lesson he taught in his field experience. He also used a writing activity to gather information about what students learned in this lesson.

### Positive Results—First Semester

Involving pre-service teachers in the assessment process was a challenging goal. In the first semester when I instituted the process, I made progress and experienced several difficulties. There were four content areas in the course (math, science, social studies, and English) and all four groups determined their PBA plan as a content group (each one in the group would use a similar artifact to demonstrate competency). For example, each science pre-service teacher chose to use a lesson plan from the field experience to demonstrate integrating writing into the curriculum. In some instances I made recommendations and suggested different due dates than pre-service teachers had set, but generally I found that they set high expectations for themselves and their plan was adequate for meeting the outcomes of the course.

The process of determining their PBA plan was probably just as powerful as the plan that resulted. For example, pre-service teachers were given some opportunity in class to complete their PBA plan—select their artifacts, determine the points for each one (within the total points allowed), and the dates that each artifact would be due. The process involved consensus decision-making and teamwork (Johnson & Johnson, 1996). Several groups prepared presentations involving all of them so planning and decision-making were results of that process as well. Secondary English and math majors completed their entire PBA plan as a group. The science and social studies majors developed their plan as a group but the science group submitted each artifact individually and the social studies group only had one group artifact (a power point presentation).

### Difficulties Encountered—First Semester

During the first semester PBA plans were implemented, as mentioned above, the English and math content groups completed their entire PBA plan as a group. There were only two math pre-service teachers and they were team teachers in their field experience. They selected all of their artifacts from their field experience, thus they were authentic and each pre-service teacher contributed equally. Their artifacts and explanations were excellent examples of how reading strategies and math content can be effectively integrated.

On the other hand, the English content group chose to do one power point presentation as a group to demonstrate all the course outcomes. It was an extensive and excellent presentation, however, it did not meet all the outcomes effectively nor did it include any work from individual field experiences. Therefore, the application into practical teaching was minimal.

The science and social studies content groups' plans were more effective than the English group. The primary problem was that some pre-service teachers did not meet their own deadlines for completion. Furthermore, every pre-service teacher had difficulty explaining how the artifacts met the course outcomes. Since this was a pilot effort I provided some instruction and allowed them to revise these explanations once, without penalty.

### Learnings From the First Semester

To improve the process for future classes, I asked pre-service teachers at the end of the semester to tell me specifically how they felt about determining their own performance-based assessment plan and to make suggestions for improvement. Only one person in the class was negative. Typical comments follow:

- I thought this was a great learning experience. At some point in my career, I'm sure I will have to do something similar to this. Now I know how to do one and I won't have to waste time being taught, only reviewing.
- I felt it made the class a lot more individualized and personal.
- At first, I did not like determining my own PBA's because I was not familiar with the concept. Now, as I reflect back I did like establishing my own PBA's. It was challenging but worthwhile.

The primary suggestion from the first class was to provide more information about what they were expected to do. Therefore, the fall syllabus included one page of directions for PBA plans (see Figure 5) and appropriate explanations. I also spent class time modeling and practicing how to write effective explanations.

The first semester experience was an initial step in involving pre-service teachers in making decisions about their own performance-based assessment. I learned much about planning and implementing a process such as this, especially the extra time and flexibility required. I determined to try a second pilot in the fall semester before implementing it as a permanent part of the course.

## Figure 5. Instructions in Syllabus for Performance Based Assessment

### *Performance-Based Assessment of Learning Outcomes*

In this course you will choose your own performance-based assessment (PBA) artifacts to indicate competency in learning outcomes for the course. You may work with those in your content area to develop your PBA plan or you may work alone. You or your group are also responsible for deciding the point values within the total points of 700 and for setting due dates. These dates can be changed with one week notice, but points will be deducted for assignments turned in after due dates that you set and do not amend.

You may also work with your content group in completing your PBA plan, but no more than half the outcomes can be met through group projects. For example, you might do a power-point presentation to meet some of the outcomes, but at least four of the outcomes must be completed alone. Furthermore, three or more of your outcomes must be met through your field experience, i.e. a lesson plan with student work, an activity that you used, or perhaps a thematic unit that you taught.

You may use assignments from your specific methods course to meet outcomes for this course. For example, you might develop a thematic unit for your methods course and integrate several reading strategies. It would then meet outcome B for this course.

Below are ideas for artifacts that were used by pre-service teachers in this course in the past:

- **Variety of techniques, strategies, approaches . . . (B)** Lesson plans with student work, video taped lesson with lesson plan and self-evaluation, thematic or unit plan
- **Be able to select materials for classroom instruction (C)** Thematic or unit plan, content presentation in class
- **Integrate technology into classroom (D)**—student work, lesson plan, thematic or unit plan, power point presentation in class
- **Reading Process (A)**—Learning Log, short paper on the reading process
- **Scaffolding instruction (F)**—lesson plan, thematic or unit plan with adaptation
- **Variety of methods of assessment (E)**—teacher-made tests, student work that is analyzed and evaluated, thematic or unit plans with assessment, lesson plans
- **Teach students to be metacognitive (G)**—administer, analyze, and report results of Metacognitive Awareness Inventory, lesson plan on metacognitive strategy
- **Integrate writing (H)**—Student writing, thematic or unit plans, lesson plans

**Note: one artifact might demonstrate several outcomes. For example, a thematic unit could be used for several learning outcomes. Each artifact must have an explanation of how it meets the intended outcome(s). It will not be accepted without an explanation. An example of such an explanation is on the next page.**

### Positive Results—Second Semester

Providing more information and examples for the second semester pilot made the process work more smoothly. Pre-service teachers understood the expectations and were very positive toward determining their own PBA plan. The modeling and practice improved explanations and fewer problems resulted. The content groups used class time efficiently and only two short meetings were held during class.

### Difficulties—Second Semester

The difficulties with the PBA plans encountered in the second semester were quite different than those the first semester. The English group again decided to do all their work together and they selected a variety of artifacts that was extensive enough to demonstrate competency in all outcomes. However, in this particular group, it seemed apparent that one student in the group completed most of the work. I spoke with each person individually about the inequity of this arrangement, but since it was a group decision, each one received the same grade for the PBA plan.

The social studies group completed about half of their PBA plan individually and together they had a power point presentation. Although they each shared the responsibility, one student was much stronger than the others. They all received the same grade for the shared presentation, nearly half of the grade for the course.

The science group did not collaborate even on determining their PBA plan to meet the outcomes. Each one submitted a separate PBA plan, which took much more time for me to evaluate and provide feedback. Furthermore, it eliminated the decision-making and teamwork, powerful components of the first semester's pilot.

### Summary of Results

Based on the quality of student work and attitudes toward the process in two semesters of implementing the gradual release of responsibility model for assessment in my secondary reading methods course, the positive results were:

- Team-work and decision-making were practiced among like content pre-service teachers in their efforts to determine and implement their PBA plan.
- Pre-service teachers experienced a process for taking responsibility for learning.
- Overall, they worked harder with a more positive attitude toward the course than pre-service teachers in classes prior to use of this model.
- Secondary majors learned how to integrate reading methods into the teaching of their content.

- There was opportunity for reflecting on their learning by writing explanations.

The negative elements of this process include:
- It is time consuming for the professor and the pre-service teachers and requires class time that is already limited.
- There are potential opportunities for pre-service teachers to gain from other's work without contributing.
- Without providing restrictions, pre-service teachers could complete the PBA plan without meeting all the goals of the process.

## Future Changes

Having pre-service teachers determine their own performance-based assessment plan is a valuable process and model for them. It provides a framework for pre-service teachers to become responsible for their own learning and is a model they can use in their own classrooms. Pre-service teachers expressed how much more thought and planning it took to select their own artifacts than when they were told what to do. The opportunity to select an artifact and explain how it demonstrates their learning is good preparation for the portfolios required as entrance to our student teaching and for graduation. Furthermore, it helps them make connections and understand the INTASC principles they are required to meet for state licensure.

It is important to change this procedure to keep the previously mentioned problems from occurring again. One idea implemented into the syllabus for next semester is that no more than half the PBA plan can be met through a group project. This provides the opportunity for collaboration among content groups but also requires that each student demonstrate individual competence. To meet the goal of integration with their content area and teaching experience, at least three of the outcomes must be met through teaching in the field experience rather than lesson plans or papers that have not been used. Figure 5 reflects the changes in instructions for the next class.

I preferred giving pre-service teachers total openness in choosing their own documentation to meet course outcomes that was provided during the two-semester pilot. However, it is necessary to provide some guidelines and restrictions to assure each student is graded on his/her own merit and that integration of reading into content teaching occurs. In reflecting on my goals, the format that evolved seems to follow more closely the gradual release of responsibility model while my pilot efforts tended to lack adequate guidance before giving pre-service teachers total responsibility. These two pilot semesters have helped define the level of support that pre-service teachers, almost ready for student teaching, need for determining their own assessment plan.

# References

Abdal-Haqq, I. (1998). *Professional development schools: Weighing the evidence.* Thousand Oaks, CA: Corwin Press.

Brophy, J. (2000). Teacher influences on student achievement. *American Psychologist, 41,* 1069-1077.

Collins, A., Brown, J. S., & Holum, A. (1991). Cognitive apprenticeship: Making thinking visible. *American Educator 15,* 6-11, 38-46.

Johnson, D. W., & Johnson, R. T. (1996). Conflict resolution and peer mediation programs in elementary and secondary schools: A review of the research. *Review of Educational Research, 66,* 459-506.

Lyon, N. (1995). Creating a professional development school. *Quality Teaching, 4,* 4-6.

McLaughlin, M., & Voyt, M. (1996). *Portfolios in Teacher Education.* Newark, DE: International Reading Association.

Miholic, V. (1994). An inventory to pique students' metacognitive awareness. *Journal Of Reading, 38* (2), 84-86.

Pearson, P. D., & Gallagher, M.C. (1983). The instruction of reading comprehension, *Contemporary Educational Psychology, 8,* 317-344.

The National Commission on Teaching and America's Future. (1996). *What matters most: Teaching for America's future.* (Research Report No. 395931). New York: National Commission on Teaching and America's Future.

Short, K. G., & Burke, C. L. (1989). New potentials for teacher education: Teaching and learning as inquiry. *Elementary School Journal,* 193-206.

Tierney, R. J., Carter, M. A., & Desai, L. E. (1991). *Portfolio assessment in the reading-writing classroom.* Norwood, MA: Christopher-Gordon Publishers.

Viechnicki, K., Barbour, N., Shaklee, B., Rohrer, J., & Ambrose, R. (1993). The impact of portfolio assessment on teacher classroom activities. *Journal of Teacher Education, 44* (5), 371-377.

Wiggins, G. (1987). Creating a thought-provoking curriculum. *American Educator 11,* 10-17.

Wiggins, G. (1996). Practicing what we preach in designing authentic assessments. *Educational Leadership, 54* (4), 18-25.

Wiggins, G., & McTighe, J. (1998). *Understanding by design.* Alexandria, VA: Association for Supervision and Curriculum Development.

# IMPROVING PRESERVICE TEACHERS' LEARNING FROM TUTORING STRUGGLING READERS: LESSONS FROM THE FIELD

**Helene M. Anthony**

The College of New Jersey

**Deborah Lee Harris**

Florida Atlantic University

## Abstract

*The authors are two instructors of reading methods of diagnosis and remediation courses that have a required tutoring component. This article describes three changes in both the practicum and courses that appeared to make significant improvements in the quality of the tutoring experience for our preservice teachers. The three changes were establishing and maintaining a true school partnership, designing authentic course assignments, and fostering collegial relationships between school and university participants.*

## Introduction

Although there is a growing body of research on the effects of volunteer tutoring programs on *children's* reading achievement (e.g., Juel, 1996; Rimm-Kaufman, Kagan, & Byers, 1999; Wasak & Slavin, 1993), there is relatively little information on literacy tutoring experiences that routinely occur as part of remedial reading methods courses in professional teacher education programs (Hedrick, 1999) and their effects on the *tutors'* learning. Since these practicum experiences are intended to teach the tutors as much as the tutees, it is surprising that we know so little about their impact on developing teachers (Aiken & Day, 1999; Rogers, 1995; Worthy & Prater, 1998). How do novices view these experiences? In what ways do they see the tutoring situation as contributing to their growing understanding of the reading process and to their increased competence in designing appropriate literacy instruction for individuals and small groups of children? What knowledge, beliefs, and practices do they "take" from these experiences for possible application in their future classrooms? How might teacher educators maximize students' opportunities to learn from their work with struggling readers?

As instructors of undergraduate methods courses in diagnosis and remediation of reading difficulties, we began to raise these questions after initially assuming that the required tutoring practicum would have a significant impact on our students' learning. To our dismay, we had found that while our students generally enjoyed having a chance to work with children, citing the value of having "real-life, hands-on" opportunities in schools, they talked mainly about the value of the experience for their tutees, not for themselves and their own professional learning. They liked being in a school setting, as well as the feeling that they were helping a child, and potentially "making a difference" in his or her life. Students often viewed their role as tutor as being more of a "buddy" than a teacher, however, and because of this, Helene found that students could not speak precisely about how they could relate instructional strategies used in tutoring to a subsequent practicum she taught. Supervising former tutoring practicum students during their student teacher semester, Deborah learned that they tended to see what they had done when tutoring one child as unrelated to teaching reading to small or large groups of children.

Concerned, we began talking together about our respective courses (Helene taught special education majors in New Jersey, and Deborah taught special education and elementary education majors in Florida) and the structure of the existing tutoring practicums. We looked to the literature for insights on how other course instructors had attempted to make the literacy practicum an educative experience, only to find that few definite solutions exist (Hedrick, McGee, & Mittag, 2000; Koals, 1994). Other educators have written of similar limitations related to course-related field experiences (Arends & Winitzky, 1999; Knowles & Cole, 1996) and many have pointed to the Professional Development School as a promising site for addressing those concerns. Lacking access to fully operating professional development schools, we sought to modify the course practicum in order to incorporate features of successful school/university partnerships. Among the issues that we considered in doing so were: the importance of selecting a site conducive to learning (Carter & Andes, 1996); the need to ensure that course and field experiences are mutually reinforcing (Kidd, Sanchez, & Thorp, 2000); the need to have student and faculty presence in a school and to engender students' relationships with a range school personnel (Grisham, Laguardia, & Brink, 2000); and the need to provide students with feedback and opportunities for reflection (Knowles & Coles, 1999).

This paper describes our initial frustrations with the practicums as they had historically been implemented at our sites, then details the changes we made to improve the effectiveness of this experience. We draw from detailed surveys that our students completed at the beginning and ending of our courses, our observations of their lessons with children, reports from classroom teachers and principals, and an analysis of their written work.

## A Sampling of the Practicums' Shortcomings

One of the most serious problems we noted was the lack of consistency in our students' experiences. At Deborah's site, the elementary education students had traditionally been expected to find their own placements. This meant that some used family members or neighbors' children, a situation that sometimes caused tension or even disagreements that lasted beyond the length of the course. Other students found placements in schools, but it was not uncommon for them to arrive at the school ready to tutor, only to be told by their tutees' teachers that the session had to be cancelled. Sometimes there was an assembly or field trip that the teacher had "forgotten" to tell the tutor about, or the child had unfinished work that needed to be finished up—the reasons given were numerous and usually legitimate—but conveyed to the tutors a message that what they were doing was tolerated but not valued by the school personnel.

In Helene's case, the students were all placed at the same school, yet even then had qualitatively different experiences. Their general education teacher hosts varied to such a degree that sometimes tutors were given no guidance at all for working with their tutees, while others were asked to implement highly scripted reading programs. Moreover, the tutors held their sessions in a range of locations, everywhere from a corner of the classroom, to hallways, even in a materials storage room. Again, the message sent to the students was that their presence was a burden, not an asset to the school. Since the preservice teachers (at both campuses) were working with children of all ages, it was also more difficult to tailor class sessions so as to address all students' tutoring needs.

Working both separately and together, the authors made a number of changes to their courses and their approach to the tutoring component. Of these improvements, three in particular appeared to make the tutoring experience significantly more meaningful for students: (1) establishing a true partnership with a school; (2) designing more authentic course assignments; and (3) fostering collegial relationship development between school and university participants. Each of these will be described in more detail below.

## Establishing a True Partnership

Both of us made deliberate decisions about the practicum setting. We each wanted to locate a school that had a diverse population where the staff was committed to serving the needs of all learners. Finding a site where the administration was not merely willing to cooperate, but was enthusiastic and convinced that the program offered valuable opportunities for all participants. Finally, we also sought to find schools where family involvement was encouraged and appreciated.

Enlisting a high level of support from the principal and other key contact people (e.g., the special services coordinator, the reading specialists, the librarian) was instrumental in developing a true partnership with the selected schools. In both cases, we met at length with these individuals and explained our program needs while also discussing their specific school needs so that we could develop a tutoring program that benefited everyone. At the NJ site, Helene actually changed the tutoring time from mid-morning to a before-school program to eliminate the problems teachers experienced when children were pulled from class during instructional time. In the FL site, Deborah held her classes at the school building and worked the class time around the teachers' preferred tutoring time. Planning discussions also addressed issues related to tutee selection and space. At one site it was decided that the tutees would all come from the third grade, while at the other, the focus was on first and second graders who had been identified by teachers as "at-risk" for literacy failure. In both cases, tutors and their tutees were placed more centrally in the school (no more storage closets). This allowed the instructors to have a real presence in the building on tutoring days.

In each location, the principal officially welcomed the preservice teachers into the building and made statements to them about how much their tutoring work was appreciated. The fact that the principals routinely spoke to the tutors when they were in the building impressed many of them and made them feel part of the school community. One student commented about how valued she felt, noting that, "Even the principal thanked us on a daily basis!" There was also a wider awareness of the program among the school faculty than had existed in the past that lent more support for the tutors. For example, if a tutor needed extra time with a child who had arrived late for tutoring, the teachers were more willing to honor that tutor's request.

## Designing Authentic Course Assignments

As instructors, we advocated to our students the importance of using authentic literacy assessments and developing authentic literacy tasks with children. We therefore felt compelled to reexamine our own course assignments in relation to the tutoring practicum. Revisions were made in three specific areas: assessment, planning, and reflection. All students were required to use appropriate assessment instruments to determine their tutee's literacy strengths and weaknesses, to develop lesson plans for each tutoring session, and to reflect on each session before developing the next lesson.

### Assessment

Because the tutees were of similar ages, both instructors were able to focus class instruction on the specific assessment measures that the tutors would be using. The preservice teachers were prepared during the first few weeks of class to begin their tutoring sessions with a variety of informal literacy assessments in order to identify specific literacy goals for their tutoring. Among the assessment instruments used were Marie Clay's (1993) Observation Survey, a commercial informal reading inventory, observation checklists, and interest interviews. Each student wrote a diagnostic report summarizing her tutee's performance on assessments before and after tutoring sessions, reviewed the teaching methods used during tutoring, indicated where her tutee had made progress, and made recommendations for future interventions. While this task did not differ dramatically from ones the instructors had used before, the audience for the reports broadened to include not only the instructor but also the classroom teacher and/or reading specialist working with the student's tutee. In fact, in the FL setting, the principal provided substitute coverage so the teachers could meet with the tutors to discuss their reports at the end of the tutoring experience. The quality of the reports was noticeably improved from previous semesters and students' comments indicated that they came to see the diagnostic report as an important teaching tool, not merely as a class assignment. One student noted that, "The reports gave me a good starting point [for tutoring] and helped me see the changes in my tutee's literacy skills." Another saw the value of writing the reports in contributing to her understanding of children's literacy development: "Although they were long, I believe that doing them was really important— Writing about it helped me understand it."

In the NJ site, where the tutors met twice a week with their tutees, the students were also required to produce a literacy portfolio for the tutees, giving them a real-life context for understanding this type of assessment (Farr, 1994; Koals, 1994). However, what made the project truly authentic was the fact that it was presented to the tutee's parent/guardian at the celebration day at the end of tutoring. Orchestrating occasions for preservice teachers to offer their insights to parents and teachers provides them with the opportunity to experience a more professional role. Students seemed a bit apprehensive and anxious when these assignments were first given, focusing on their novice status and role as learners. After completing them, however, their confidence and increased sense of competence were evident. One student noted on her survey that, "As I wrote the final report I was surprised to realize exactly how much I did know about literacy development and instruction." Another commented that ". . . it was not only a good learning experience, but for me, it was one to prove to myself that I was capable of doing it. And somewhat successful at it too!"

### *Planning*

Once tutors were meeting in central locations, the instructors could be present at tutoring sessions and have the opportunity to closely monitor each tutor's planning and instruction. Every tutor was required to submit his or her lesson plan to us at the start of the tutoring session. The tutors met with their tutees either twice a week for an hour for fifteen weeks (NJ site), or once a week for an hour and twenty minutes for seven weeks (FL site). Since one-on-one literacy tutoring is different from whole-class instruction, we developed a lesson plan format that more closely matched the nature of a tutoring session. The format required tutors to (1) identify a specific literacy goal (or goals); (2) describe what materials and strategies they were using to meet that goal; (3) outline the procedure they were following; and (4) explain why they were using those particular materials in that particular way. We asked the tutors to design literacy experiences for their tutees using text at all three reading levels (independent, instructional, and listening), and to structure their time so that at each session, the tutor read to the child, the child read to the tutor, and they read another text together. Within the given time frame, they were also encouraged to include other activities as appropriate, such as drawing, writing, puppetry, games, or creating visual displays of text content. Even though the format was stipulated, it was made clear to students that the goals/objectives, teaching strategies and materials had to be tailored to the tutee's needs. The Johns and Lenski (1997) text, *Improving Reading: A Handbook of Strategies*, was used in both courses as a resource book for students. Everyone was expected to use the book, but in different ways depending on their tutoring goals. This flexible structure for lesson development was greeted positively by the students. There were many comments on the post surveys like the following, "We had the freedom to create lessons of choice/necessity rather than follow strict guidelines," and "I learned how to build a lesson around a student."

In addition to the lesson planning format for individual sessions, we also expected our students to work within a diagnostic teaching framework (Wixson, 1991). That is, students needed to be mindful that each teaching session was also an assessment opportunity. While tutors were to have developed thoughtful and detailed plans based on their tutee's individual needs, we discussed in class the necessity of keeping plans flexible and interacting in a way that is responsive to the child's performance. After each session, students were required to write a response to the question, *What did you learn about your tutee's literacy processes today?* We found that our students' anticipation of this question did encourage them to see their tutoring as ongoing assessment and to expect to make on-the-spot changes to their original plans. When describing what was learned from tutoring, one student revealed her awareness of this aspect of diagnostic teaching by stating: "I had the chance to practice making adjustments and to use my tutee to judge how I am doing and what I need to do more of."

### *Reflection*

A critical aspect of diagnostic teaching is being reflective. As teacher educators, we felt it was important for our students to reflect on their teaching on two levels. In terms of their role as tutor/diagnostic teacher, we wanted them to analyze the sessions in ways that would inform them about their tutee's strengths and needs, as well as the efficacy of their instructional choices. Past experience had taught us that preservice teachers tended to focus on more superficial aspects of the tutoring experience. When asked to reflect on their sessions, for example, a student might glibly comment that it was successful "because the tutee had fun," or because "I learned I have to be more patient." We also felt that it was important for the students to reflect on their developing knowledge of self as a teacher, both their own understanding of the reading process and their role in promoting children's literacy growth. In addition to the question described above regarding their tutee's literacy processes revealed during the session, students were also asked to write a response to the following: *What did you learn about yourself as a teacher? How will today's session influence your future planning?* Students shared their responses in small groups and also got written and verbal feedback from us. We both feel that focusing our students' attention on these specific questions resulted in a more thoughtful and substantive analysis of the tutoring sessions and also helped make the idea of diagnostic teaching more concrete. Students' written reflections also helped us better to guide them in their planning. For example, one student wrote, "When I walked away from my child today I felt like a failure as a teacher. He did okay, but I guess I was expecting instant results, an instant fix. Later after we talked I realized that sometimes growth is very slow and incremental. I can't take out my frustration on the child but have to go back to the drawing board for the next session." Comments like these allowed us to begin a discussion about the importance of looking for and building on progress, and the need to remain flexible when designing instruction.

## Fostering Collegial Relationships

Previous placements had, all too often, isolated the tutors from the rest of the school. We believe that future teachers, both special educators and general educators, need to understand the larger picture of remedial reading instruction, and develop a holistic view of a struggling reader. With that goal in mind, we both incorporated into the design of the tutoring practicum opportunities for tutors to interact with other professionals in the building. For example, tutors were required to make contact with either the tutee's classroom teacher or reading specialist during the experience. Some exchanged notes, others spoke in person or on the telephone. While not all of the teachers responded, some very productive sharing did occur. Students made comments such as the following "She [the classroom teacher] provided some extra materials and gave me some guidance. She made it clear that I had her support," and "This contact [with the tutee's reading teacher] allowed me access to her strategies and some literature." A few students even observed in their tutee's classroom. One believed that this enabled her ". . . to see how I could help my tutee based on what his teacher did in the classroom."

In addition, communication with parents was considered an important goal of the practicum. Helene required tutors to send a note home with tutees to explain what they were doing and to solicit information that would be helpful to them. Deborah had students fill out a daily feedback form that went home to parents. In both cases, we were trying to model ways that teachers could establish positive, on-going communication with parents. As with the classroom teachers, responses from parents varied and this provided real-life lessons about parental involvement. Some students were surprised at how involved some of the parents were, as one noted, "Her mother said she practiced her sight words at the dinner table with her." In the before-school program, a few parents were seen when they dropped off their children and informal conversations took place between parents and tutors on a regular basis: "She [the child's mother] told me about my tutee's progress in class and also asked me to work on certain tasks. It really helped to know she supported my work as well as worked with my tutee at home."

At the NJ site, the celebration at the completion of the tutoring program was intended to provide a formal opportunity to meet parents, as every tutee's family received an invitation to come have rolls and coffee and meet their child's tutor. This was the setting for the sharing of the tutoring portfolio. This past semester the celebration also included readers theater performances by all the children. All but two children had at least one parent or family member present at the celebration.

While we frequently have objectives in our college courses related to parental involvement, we are rarely able to provide our students the opportunity to speak substantively with a child's parent prior to student teaching. This aspect of the tutoring experience gave the preservice teachers the chance to begin to understand the role of families and also the complicated lives of many families: "Because of (the tutee's) lateness, I had many uncompleted lessons, but she is one of ten foster children all getting ready for school." There was also evidence of a developing sensitivity in some of the students' comments about their tutee's family involvement. One student noted that she had had difficulty communicating with her tutee's non-English speaking parents: "I sent a couple of notes home and received no response." While she may have initially interpreted this as parental lack of concern about her tutee's involvement in the program, she came to realize that that was not the case, "On the last day her mother seemed very interested in everything we had done together."

## Conclusions

Both of us believe the implemented changes had a significant impact on our students' learning. At both sites, all tutors reported that the experience was a positive one. As reported in other studies of reading tutoring, our students also found the experience to be personally rewarding (Hedrick, McGee, & Mittag, 2000; Rogers, 1995; Worth & Prater, 1998). In addition, our students commented about how they grew as teachers. We believe that setting up the practicum to allow for more consistency in placements (i.e., tutors tutoring on the same days in a centralized location, or tutees coming from a narrow range of grade levels) resulted in a more coherent course, one in which information was presented specifically targeted to the needs of the tutoring placement, as well as information that was intentionally outside the parameters of the practicum (i.e., unique needs of the struggling adolescent reader, published remedial reading programs, and so forth).

We also have some evidence that the students perceived themselves to be much better prepared to provide appropriate literacy instruction to struggling readers. Between developing lessons, writing reports, and meeting with teachers and/or parents, the students felt that they had developed both skills and confidence for future teaching. They learned the value of coming to know children as individual literacy learners. Whereas past students had seen the practicum as not connected to future teaching in a whole class setting, comments such as the following were common amongst our current students: "I got to focus on the details with one student that I can now use when looking at a group of students." Another wrote:

> One thing I began to realize during the tutoring sessions was the importance of one-on-one experiences with each student. If a teacher does not make that extra effort to get to know a student as an individual and try to uderstand some things that can be used as motivating factors for that particular kid, then many children will be lost along the way.

While we feel we have made some great strides in improving our students' learning from the tutoring experience, there are areas in which we will continue to work. For example, many students indicated that they would have liked a more structured interaction with the classroom and reading teachers throughout the tutoring, as well as more opportunities to communicate with parents. We see it as a positive sign that the students were requesting this type of interaction for future tutoring practicums. They had clearly seen the potential value of these types of contacts. One student reflected: "I should have spoken with the reading specialist sooner because she is a valuable resource and has lots of materials." In addition, more structured and/or regular contact with classroom and reading teachers could help the course instructors better address another area of concern, the selection of appropriate children's literature. It became clear that students had a more difficult time than we had anticipated in translating the grade levels identified in the IRI for independent, instructional and frustration level text into appropriate children's literature choices. While both instructors discussed characteristics of books for emergent, early and fluent readers, as well as the concept of leveled books, and brought materials into the classroom to demonstrate both of these ideas, individual students noticeably struggled to make these material selections for their tutees. Discussing material selection with a teacher as part of tutoring, with all the classroom materials and library titles available in that setting, seems a wonderful learning opportunity. We need to think of ways to make that time available to both teachers and tutors.

Additionally, even though tutors administered interest inventories during their very first meeting with their tutees, not all of them took the child's interests and other strengths into account when planning tutoring sessions. Even though they had been instructed to build on the child's strengths to develop areas of weakness, they sometimes missed these opportunities, for example, not using a third-grader's interest in snakes to introduce him to the great variety of types of informational text, or not using the well-developed verbal skills of an early emergent first-grader to develop brief language experience stories to "read." Perhaps more structured communication with parents would help keep the tutors focused on those aspects of the child's personality and talents that are not literacy-dependent. What to do in those very few cases where parental involvement is unlikely, remains a challenge. As the special services coordinator at Helene's site said, "We're making a special effort to identify children for tutoring who are really at-risk for literacy failure. For a few of those children, their home situation is part of their risk." We clearly don't want to make decisions that eliminate children from participating in a beneficial program because of lack of parental involvement.

Finally, both of us learned the challenge of maintaining the partnership with the school. It is ironic that we (the instructors and the program) became so much an accepted part of the school (i.e., no longer guests) that the potential for taking the tutoring program for granted existed. School faculty need to realize that every group of preservice teachers should receive the same demonstrations of enthusiasm and appreciation as the first group, for example, welcome sign and refreshments, opening orientation, closing celebration, and so forth. College instructors need to continually evaluate whether the program is meeting the expectations of the school. In order to facilitate this, the authors have a formal debriefing meeting with their school contact people at the conclusion of each semester to reflect on the tutoring experience and decide on changes for future semesters.

The tutoring practicum is such an integral part of many remedial reading courses and its potential impact on what students take away from the course is significant. The selection of the tutoring site, as well as decisions about pupil participation, space and time need to be made with great care. Additionally, course instructors need to thoughtfully align class content and assignments with the practicum experience in order to capitalize on the tutoring as an opportunity to promote substantive growth in novices' ability to become skilled diagnostic teachers.

---

# References

Aiken, I., & Day, B. (1999). Early field experiences in preservice teacher education: Research and student perspectives. *Action in Teacher Education, 21*(3), 7-12.

Arends, R. & Winitzky, N. (1996). Program structures and learning to teach. In F. Murray (Ed.), *The teacher educator's handbook* (pp. 526-556). San Francisco: Jossey-Bass.

Carter, K., & Anders, D. (1996). Program pedagogy. In F. Murray (Ed.), *The teacher educator's handbook* (pp. 557-592). San Francisco: Jossey-Bass.

Clay, M. (1993). *An observational survey of early literacy achievement.* Portsmouth, NH: Heinemann.

Farr, R., & Tone, B. (1994). *Portfolio performance assessment: Helping students evaluate their progress as readers and writers.* Fort Worth, TX: Harcourt Brace.

Grisham, D., Laguardia, A., & Brink, B. (2000). Partners in professionalism: Creating a quality field experience. *Action in Teacher Education, 21*(4), 28-41.

Hedrick, W. B. (1999). Pre-service teachers tutoring 3rd, 4th, and 5th graders one-on-one within the school setting. *Reading Research and Instruction, 38*(3), 211-219.

Hedrick, W. B., McGee, P., & Mittag, K. (2000). Pre-service teacher learning through one-on-one tutoring: Reporting perceptions through e-mail. *Teaching and Teacher Education, 16*(1), 47-63.

Johns, J. L., & Lenski, S. (1997). *Improving reading: A handbook of strategies.* Dubuque, IA: Kendall/Hunt Publishing Company.

Juel, C. (1996). What makes literacy tutoring effective? *Reading Research Quarterly, 31,* 268-289.

Kidd, J., Sanchez, S., & Thorp, E. (2000). Integrating language and literacy through projects: An applied internship experience. *Literacy at a new horizon: The Twenty-Second Yearbook of the College Reading Association.* Commerce, TX: The College Reading Association. 206-225.

Knowles, J. G., & Cole, A. (1996). Developing practice through field experiences. In F. Murray (Ed.), *The teacher educator's handbook* (pp. 648-688). San Francisco: Jossey-Bass.

Koals, M. B. (1994). *Portfolio assessment for pre-service teachers: Two hands-on techniques to familiarize students in a reading methods course with this form of assessment.* Paper presented at the Annual Conference of the National Council of Teachers of English, Portland, OR, March 10-12.

Rimm-Kaufman, S. E., Kagan, J., & Byers, H. (1999). The effectiveness of adult volunteer tutoring on reading among "at-risk" first grade children. *Reading Research and Instruction, 38*(2), 143-152.

Rogers, S. F. (1995). *Field-based research: When preservice practicum teachers make a difference for themselves and their students.* Paper presented at the Annual Meeting of the College Reading Association, Clearwater, FL, November 4-6.

Wasak, B. A., & Slavin, R. E. (1993). Preventing early reading failure with one-on-one tutoring: A review of five programs. *Reading Research Quarterly, 28,* 179-200.

Wixon, K. (1991). Diagnostic teaching. *The Reading Teacher, 44*(6), 420-22.

Worthy, J., & Prater, S. (1998). Learning on the job: Preservice teachers' perceptions of participating in a literacy tutorial program. Forty-seventh Yearbook of the National Reading Conference (pp. 485-495). Chicago: The National Reading Conference.

# Examining the Literacy Beliefs and Change Processes of Pre-service Teachers With Reading Specializations in a Field-Based Teacher Education Program: Critical Dissonance Factors

**Brenda Smith**
**Mary Beth Sampson**
**Wayne M. Linek**
**I. LaVerne Raine**

Texas A&M University-Commerce

## Abstract

*This qualitative study builds on previous studies that described types of dissonance experience by preservice teachers enrolled in their initial literacy courses. The current study reports on the beliefs and practices of preservice teachers at the end of their field-based teacher education program. Specifically, the types of dissonance experience by preservice teachers in their fifth field-based literacy course will be described.*

## Introduction

For public school students to achieve their maximum potential in reading, teachers must implement teaching and learning strategies that reflect best practice (Cunningham & Allington, 1999; USDOE, 1987). Research indicates that teachers' beliefs concerning such practice have an intense impact on their behavior in the classroom. Teachers tend to use the same methods of instruction that they experienced during their own schooling regardless of whether or not they have a basis in research (Britzman, 1991; Lortie, 1975). Wells (1994) has noted that change in teachers is the prerequisite to educational change. Since beliefs are primarily based on one's prior experience, it is necessary to experience reflection (Risko, Roskos, & Veukelich, 1999) and some type of disequilibria (Dressman, Graves, & Webster, 1999; Wolf, Hill, & Ballentine, 1999) or dissonance for change to occur (Azjen, 1988; Festinger, 1957). Thus, it becomes critical to investigate dissonance and the factors in change in preservice teacher beliefs. This qualitative study builds on previous studies that described types of dissonance experienced by pre-service teachers enrolled in their initial literacy courses.

Recent research (Linek, Nelson, Sampson, Zeek, Mohr, & Hughes 1999; Zeek & Wickstrom, 1999) has described changes in pre-service teachers' beliefs about literacy and factors contributing to those changes in a variety of settings, i.e., a university based literacy methods course with no field experience, a university-based literacy methods course with unsupervised field experience, and a field-based literacy methods course. Factors contributing to the changes common to all programs were instructor modeling, course assignments/readings, cognitive dissonance, and reflection. Although pre-service teachers in each program experienced change, students participating in the field-based program described a greater variety of dissonance factors impacting their beliefs about literacy instruction. Factors unique to field-based courses include cultural dissonance, emotional dissonance, experiential dissonance, and political dissonance. Implications of this research support a field-based model of teacher education for development of a complex view of the process of literacy teaching.

Since the field-based model has become an accepted and increasingly widespread mode of pre-service teacher education, it is critical to explore how beliefs are formed and changed within this type of program. Current research on pre-service teachers has mainly described what occurs in early childhood programs (Martin, Martin, & Martin, 1999) and initial literacy methods courses (Sampson, Walker, & Fazio, 1999). However, little is still known about how that dissonance changes as pre-service teachers with reading specializations move through their final field-based literacy courses. The objectives of this study were to: a) better understand literacy beliefs and change processes in pre-service teachers with reading specializations engaged in a field-based teacher education program, b) ascertain factors influencing their change processes during the course of one year, and c) describe categories of dissonance based on multiple data sources.

## Methods

The present inquiry took place during the fall semester of 1999. The population consisted of eleven pre-service teachers majoring in reading education while engaged in a field-based teacher education program during the final year of preparation. The field-based program at Texas A&M University-Commerce is designed to incorporate university and public school collaboration in order to increase the educational opportunities for public school students and pre-service teachers. The first semester students are designated as *interns,* and spend two full days per week in the public schools and one day per week at the university for instructional seminars which are designed to help pre-service teachers develop conceptual knowledge of core curriculum components as well as focusing on collaborative group discussions that interweave effective teaching strategies. During their second semester, students are classified as *residents,* and spend five days in the public schools. They return to the university for instructional seminars once every two weeks.

The researchers collaborated to devise a formal study to explore the literacy beliefs and change processes in pre-service teachers. Questions guiding this study were:

1. What are pre-service teachers' majoring in reading education beliefs about literacy, literacy instruction, and assessment before and after their semester-long field-based teacher education experience?
2. What changes occur in the beliefs of pre-service teachers majoring in reading education?
3. What factors influence the change process?

The researchers in the current study have been exploring pre-service teachers' beliefs in their own respective literacy methods courses (the fifth and sixth courses in a reading specialization sequence) utilizing self reported data and artifacts, responses from various class activities, produced by students in public school classrooms. Similar trends were perceived to be common across the students and the courses, which were different than described in the previous research about initial literacy methods courses.

The conceptual base of courses utilized in this study were learning how to plan and implement various vocabulary and strategic instructional reading strategies, as well as to assess the students' acquisition of content knowledge being taught by the pre-service teacher in the public school classroom. After the course instructor modeled various vocabulary and reading strategies, the pre-service teachers were required to plan and implement six lessons incorporating vocabulary strategies to be taught in their respective field classrooms. Additional course requirements included using a spelling features word list to assess the developmental spelling stage of their classroom students. Based upon this analysis, the findings were used to plan and organize appropriate word study activities. After the pre-service teacher taught a lesson, a reflection form was completed and analyzed to identify patterns of perceptions concerning their teaching of each of the six required lessons. "Through self-knowledge a teacher can begin to see how life experiences shape behavior in the classroom. Self-knowledge is essential to good teaching" (Draper, 1994, p. 3).

## Data Sources and Analysis

Eleven pre-service teachers majoring in reading education completed pre- and post- semi-structured, open-ended questionnaires exploring their beliefs concerning literacy/literacy instruction prior to beginning a semester of field-based experience and at the end of the semester long experience (see appendix). Reflection forms addressing the experiences that the prospective teachers completed throughout the semester were also utilized as data sources. In addition, researchers conducted instructor interviews, and collected artifacts, collected student responses from various class activities and from the field-based experiences to more thoroughly explore the perceptions of the pre-service teachers, shifts that occurred and factors.

Constant comparative analysis (Strauss & Corbin, 1990) was selected to analyze data. Codes and categories were identified and modified as the analysis proceeded (Bogdan & Biklen, 1992) in order to: 1) identify the pre-service teachers' beliefs about literacy at the beginning and end of the field-based experience; 2) identify changes in beliefs; and 3) identify factors that influenced changes in beliefs. As the categories from the data emerged, areas that were constant across multiple data sources were explored, verified, and corroborated by the research team until a consensus was reached. After the categories were established, the researchers reexamined the data and sorted the responses into various categories. The responses were tallied using a frequency count and percentages of the total comments were computed for each category. Some students gave answers that fell into more than one category, thus total percentage is not reported. Credibility of the study was further strengthened through team collaboration and prolonged and persistent observation.

## Results

The semi-structured, open-ended questionnaires were analyzed to determine the pre-service teachers' beliefs about literacy, literacy instruction, and assessment before and after their semester of field-based teacher experiences. Responses were coded and six broad domains emerged: 1) beliefs about good readers; 2) beliefs about how to teach beginning readers; 3) beliefs about reading expository text with unfamiliar vocabulary; 4) beliefs about organization and management; and 5) beliefs about assessment. Percentages addressing the specific belief patterns categorized under each of the six domains are represented in the respective tables (see Tables 1-5).

Categories and percentages addressing the prospective teachers' beliefs concerning good readers are shown in Table 1. Calculation and comparison of the percentages of total comments were distributed over 10 factors. Some students gave answers that fell into more than one category, thus total percentage is not reported.

### Beliefs About Good Readers

Prior to their field-based experiences, pre-service teachers tended to have a limited view of good readers with only five categories emerging from the data describing good readers (see Table 1). These addressed a reader's ability to "say the words correctly," "understand what they read," and "like to read." In addition, their responses indicated a belief that good readers "read at grade level."

### Table 1. Beliefs about Good Readers

| BELIEFS | PERCENTAGE | |
|---|---|---|
| | PRE | POST |
| Focus on Word Level | 73 | 9 |
| Focus on Comprehension Level | 54 | 73 |
| Non-Specific Focus on Affect | 36 | 18 |
| Ability at Grade Level | 27 | 45 |
| Fluency Does Assure Comprehension | 9 | 0 |
| Ability to Decode Does Not Mean the Child Understands | 0 | 27 |
| Uses Strategies | 0 | 18 |
| Reads for Different Purposes | 0 | 9 |
| Growth Equals Success | 0 | 36 |
| Gain Information | 0 | 36 |

After being in public schools for one semester, students' responses shifted. Only two of the original categories showed an increase in responses. These categories addressed comprehension and the ability to read material on grade level. The pre-service teachers grew in their beliefs that the ability to read on "grade level," and comprehension of material were indicators of a "good reader." Their comments concerning comprehension expanded into specific areas that dealt with expository text. A new category emerged indicating their belief that good readers "gain information" from text they are reading. Additional new categories addressed beliefs that "fluent" reading does not always equal comprehension; growth in reading should be an indicator of success or "good" reading, and the importance of the use of strategies and varying purposes for different texts. Interestedly, the prospective teachers demonstrated an increased belief in the importance of comprehension, as the beliefs addressing a non-specific view of affect decreased.

## Beliefs About How to Teach Beginning Readers

When categories were identified and percentages calculated addressing the prospective teachers' beliefs concerning how to teach beginning readers, a variance of percentages of the categories under four domains where prominent (see Table 2). For example, when asked prior to the field-based course what she would do to teach beginning readers to read one pre-service teacher said, "I would teach the children how to sound out each letter. I would then teach them how to combine letters to form words, teach the meaning of words, and make sure they are aware of vowels and consonants and how they are used. With the use of phonics I would teach the children to read. I think if taken step by step reading can be a simple, successful task." After the field-based experience this same pre-service teacher said, "Teach them phonics and how to make meaning from words. They need syntax and semantics. Lots of strategies and activities." The shift illustrated in this case is from focusing on letters, words, and teaching to integrating the three cueing systems and helping children learn how to make meaning from words.

**Table 2. Beliefs About How To Teach Beginning Readers**

| Beliefs | Percentage | |
|---------|:---:|:---:|
| | Pre | Post |
| Sound | 0 | 9 |
| Letter | 36 | 9 |
| Word | 18 | 45 |
| Text | 36 | 36 |

A further illustration of the beliefs before and after the field-based course follows in the words of this pre-service teacher who initially said, "I would begin with letter/sound relationships starting with consonants, then move to vowels. After that, I would use the CVC pattern to introduce word families. By using word sorts, I would gradually advance to the more difficult sorts." After the field-based course the same pre-service teacher said, "For beginning readers I would first get them excited about reading by reading aloud to them wonderful books, including pattern books and rhyme. I would use big books, journal writing, and create their own books. I would use as many different ideas as possible to show the students that reading is everywhere. I also want my writing program to share an equal part of my reading instruction."

## Beliefs About Reading Expository Text with Unfamiliar Vocabulary

A shift also occurred in beliefs about what one should do when facilitating the reading of expository text with unfamiliar words (see Table 3). Initially, almost half of the pre-service teachers saw little or no need to do anything prior to the reading of expository text to facilitate student understanding. For example, prior to the field-based course, when asked if she would do anything with unfamiliar words in a fourth grade passage on how a forest develops, one pre-service teacher said, "No, I would allow them to read it and then allow time for sharing aloud so maybe they could discover what the passage means from the help of each other." After the field-based course the same pre-service teacher said, "Yes, I would. One strategy that could be done prior to reading the story is 'Question My Word Knowledge.' It gives the students an opportunity to be introduced to the word, have the opportunity to give their definition to the word, and then visit a dictionary to check for the meaning."

**Table 3. Beliefs About Reading Expository Text with Unfamiliar Vocabulary**

| BELIEFS | PERCENTAGE | |
|---|---|---|
| | PRE | POST |
| No need to do anything prior to reading | 27 | 0 |
| Might be a need for doing something prior to reading | 18 | 0 |
| Would do something prior to Reading | 54 | 100 |

### *Beliefs About Language Learning*

The pre-service teachers in this study were also able to better articulate their beliefs about language learning after the field-based course. Prior to the course 45% articulated self-assurance of how children learn language; after the course a significant growth occurred showing an 81% variance in beliefs. For example, prior to the course when presented with the question, "Children learn language and learn about language by being a language user. What does that mean to you as a teacher of readers, writers, speakers, and listeners?" One pre-service teacher said, "It means modeling to the students proper grammar when we talk or read to our students. We should communicate to our students in the same way we want them to be able to communicate to us as well as others. Skills for listening, speaking, comprehending, and writing must be taught in order for children to be successful complete language users." After the field-based course the same pre-service teacher said, "Experience makes the difference in development, not just the age. Students that have been stimulated and motivated to speak, read, write, listen, bloom, and grow. Students that have not may seem to be stifled or behind, yet they are just at an earlier developmental stage due to their experiences with language." The "pre" comments focus on the teacher and teaching whereas the "post" comments focus on what children actually experience. As far as understanding how children learn language, there was significant growth in pre-service teachers' understanding of how language obviously is a central aspect of learning to read.

### *Beliefs About Organization and Management*

Domain 5 focuses on the pre-service teachers' beliefs of organization and management (see Table 4). Prior to the field-based course, prospective teachers had very general beliefs. For example, one pre-service teacher said, "Life is not divided into subjects that we separate and work on for a certain amount of time each day. Our classroom routines should not be divided into content areas that we cover separately and independently." After the course the same pre-service teacher said, "I would choose to use integrated units across the curriculum. Create thematic units for a book or topic and include all learning areas in this study/lesson." Prior to the course another pre-service teacher said, "I think you should try to integrate subjects as much as possible. I think that there will be more time for reading and writing if the subjects are integrated." After the course the same pre-service teacher said, "I want to integrate the subjects as much as possible. For example, with the Civil War I'd have them write about it and have them add up dates or figure out how old those people would be today." Thus, initially emphases were placed on a general theory of organization. After the course, these pre-service teachers were able to articulate specific ways to manage and organize instruction.

### Table 4. Beliefs About Organization and Management

| Beliefs | Percentage | |
|---|---|---|
| | Pre | Post |
| General | 54 | 9 |
| Specific | 45 | 91 |

### *Beliefs About Assessment*

Table 5 represents the change in pre-service teachers' beliefs about formative and summative assessment as they moved through their fifth reading specialization course. At the beginning of the course, almost half (45%) of the pre-service teachers could give no specifics about how they would assess or evaluate students in reading and writing. For example, one pre-service teacher said, "I will use my knowledge of reading and writing." Another pre-service teacher said, "I will hear them read and evaluate their writing." The remaining pre-service teachers (55%) gave answers indicating some awareness of formative and/or summative assessment strategies. After the field-based course all of the pre-service teachers could identify specific formative assessments that they would employ. For example, the first pre-service teacher said, "Running records, reading strategies, tests, group or individual activities. Through research and a whole lot of time. [sic]" The second one said, "I can do spelling inventories that would give me great data to use for my reading groups."

## Table 5. Beliefs About Assessment

| BELIEFS | PERCENTAGE | |
|---|---|---|
| | PRE | POST |
| Formative | 45 | 100 |
| Summative | 36 | 18 |
| No Specifics | 45 | 0 |

After determining the shifts pre-service teachers had made in beliefs during the semester long experience, their written reflections completed after teaching a lesson were analyzed. Students responded to the following open-ended prompts:

What went well with the strategy lesson?
What did not go well with the strategy?
How did the students benefit from this strategy?
I wish I had . . .or the next time I will make these changes.
What did you learn?

### Categories of Dissonance and Accompanying Realizations

Reflections indicated that pre-service teachers began to experience sufficient dissonance as they attempted to implement the strategies into their lessons to force them into ownership of the teaching process. They began to focus on what was making their lesson effective more than on just completing an assignment. A careful review of the collective reflections revealed six categories of dissonance and realizations (see Table 6).

## Table 6: Categories of Dissonance and Accompanying Realizations

| | FREQUENCY | PERCENTAGE |
|---|---|---|
| | TIMES REPORTED | |
| Appropriate match of instructional materials to developmental level of children | 12 | 21 |
| Time management during a lesson | 10 | 17.5 |
| Behavior management during a lesson | 10 | 17.5 |
| Self-monitoring focused on value of strategies | 10 | 17.5 |
| Adequacy of the modeling step of the lesson | 8 | 14 |
| Self-monitoring focused on use of manipulatives. | 7 | 12 |
| Total reflections collected | 57 | |

The following are specific pre-service teachers' comments to support each of the six areas identified in Table 6:

### Factor: Appropriate match of instructional materials to the developmental level of the children

When working with 3rd grade resource students one pre-service teacher commented: "I modified the material to fit my students and they were all successful."

### Factor: Time management during a lesson

One pre-service teacher suggested using a timer to help keep the children on task while doing the independent phase of the lesson. Another pre-service teacher said, "I had to modify the strategy to fit into the allotted time."

### Factor: Behavior management during a lesson

Some of the pre-service teachers tied their comments of keeping the children on task to their own preparation. For example, one pre-service teacher said, "Be more organized. Have a better closure."

### Factor: Self-monitoring focused on the value of strategies

"I learned that when they find out the importance of a technique, they will use it more on their own."—"These strategies really work!!" "Simply reading the chapters in a text will not ensure that actual learning has taken place. Strategies should be used to facilitate real-life learning."

### Factor: Adequacy of the modeling step on the lesson

"I did not explain the sort very well and they had never done those before. I will have sorts on overhead transparencies and do the sorts with them as guided practice."

### Factor: Self-monitoring focused on use of manipulatives

"Once again, I saw first hand, how having something (other than a worksheet) in their hands—works! The students really learn better when they can manipulate it!"

## Factors Influencing the Change Process

The analysis of multiple data sources revealed the strongest influencing factor in the change process as being the combination of both field and seminar experiences (see Table 7). Pre-service teachers noted the value of both university seminars and field experiences with comments such as:

"I have a better understanding of how important reading and writing is for the students and how reading and writing is taught in the classroom. I also have more strategies to go to for ideas."

"The most important aspect of this course was the modeling of the strategies and the discussion of implementing the strategies."

"I think the strategies are a plus. I have used them and they work. I feel *every* child can be successful if given the proper tools."

"It's not just phonics, but everything else. It is a whole world, not just rote reading. The on-hands practice and the ability to use our information made the biggest difference for me."

Thus, the most valuable component for learning how to develop and implement literacy instruction and assessment of students in the classroom proved to be the combination of the university seminar experience and more focused field experience for pre-service teachers majoring in reading education.

### *Factors Influencing the Change Process*
**Table 7: Factors Influencing the Change Process**

| Factors | Percentage |
|---|---|
| University Seminar Experience | 9 |
| Field Experience | 9 |
| Combination of University and Field Experience | 81 |

## Discussion

Overall, the results of this study emphasized the pre-service teachers change of focus in how to make reading/language learning relevant and effective for students in the classroom. The percentages showed a strong focus on language functions in real-life context when pre-service teachers considered literacy and literacy development at the end of their fifth reading specialist course. The pre-service teachers were more specific in their planning and teaching of appropriate instructional goals. They also recognized the power of combining university seminar instruction with actual implementation of literacy lessons in public school classrooms. These findings support the identification of the field-based model of teacher education as critical in the effective preparation of teachers (Goodlad, 1991; Holmes Group, 1990 & 1995).

Kagan (1992) reported that cognitive dissonance is needed for pre-service teachers to confront their own beliefs and acknowledge that modification is necessary for instructional effectiveness. The reflection and disequilibria that occur while experiencing the act of teaching appeared to be the primary initiator of dissonance. Although the public school classroom experiences triggered the dissonance, the seminar experiences provided the scaffolding to facilitate assimilation and accommodation. This aligns with schema theory, which identifies dissonance as the trigger for assimilation and accommodation (Anderson, 1994). In addition, Upitis (1999) notes that in order to talk about effective teaching practices, one has to have actual teaching experiences to reflect upon while Vygotsky's (1976) theory of Zone of Proximal Development (ZPD) purports that learning can be scaffolded through a learner's collaboration with a more knowledgeable person. Thus, scaffolding occurred as opportunities to reflect and discuss with knowledgeable others were provided in the university seminar.

## Significance

The results of this study support Vygotsky's theory of ZPD, schema theory, and the need for field-based teacher preparation. Additionally, since the beliefs of pre-service teachers formed at this stage of their preparation were linked to hands-on practice in public school classrooms; it is logical to assume that they will carry these beliefs into their first year of teaching. This information is critical in raising the level of awareness of the importance of planning the amount of time spent in field experiences in order that pre-service teachers will be prepared to approach their first year of teaching with the necessary competences and skills needed for success as school university partnerships become the norm in teacher education programs (Donovan, 1999; Wiseman 1999). Cognitive dissonance is necessary for novices who must confront their on beliefs and images and acknowledge that they need adjustment (Newton & Smolen, 2000). Consequently, the results of this study further confirm Wildman and Niles (1987) findings that teachers and pre-service teacher must pass through a stage of "disequilibration" in order to resolve conflicting classroom experiences to gain new understandings. It is critical that we as researchers explore our own practice and the role it plays in the development of these pre-service teachers with reading specializations beliefs and practice. Results of this study support dissonance as a critical factor in the change of pre-service teachers' beliefs concerning practice in literacy instruction and assessment.

## Limitations and Implications

This study was limited by the number of students in the courses required for a specialization in reading education. Further study might include the interconnection among the categories and the survey instrument used to gain insight into pre-service teachers' thinking processes and the occurrence of dissonance factors. The collection of data for this research was limited to a questionnaire, instructor interviews, and a collection of students responsive from various course assignments. Additional means for collecting data may define further categories of dissonance. Finally, the investigation of the necessity of experiencing reflection of disequilibria in order for change to occur in pre-service teachers' beliefs concerning literacy and literacy instruction needs to be further explored before ascertaining final conclusions. Thus, by following these students through their residency semester and sixth reading course, the conclusions could be refined.

# References

Anderson, R. C. (1994). Role of the reader's schema in comprehension, learning, and memory. In R. Ruddell, M. Ruddell, & H. Singer (Eds.) *Theoretical Models and Processes of Reading (4th. Ed) (pp. 469-482)*. Newark, DE: International Reading Association.

Azjen, I. (1988). *Attitudes, personality, and behavior*. Chicago: Dorsey.

Bogdan, R., & Biklen, S. (1992). Qualitative research for education: An introduction to theory and methods (2nd ed.) Boston: Allyn & Bacon.

Britzman, D. (1991). *Practice makes practice: A critical study of learning to teach*. Albany, NY: SUNY.

Cunningham, P., & Allington, R. (1999). *Classrooms that work: They can all read and write*. New York: Longman.

Donovan, C. (1999). Learning to teach reading/language arts: Considering the impact of experiences on understanding. In T. Shanahan & F. Rodriguez-Brown (Eds.) *National Reading Conference Yearbook 48* (pp. 451-465). Chicago: NRC.

Draper, D. (1994). Reflections on practice: Taking the time to think. Unpublished doctoral dissertation, San Francisco State University.

Dressman, M., Graves, C., & Webster, J. (1999). Learning to read the research: How preservice teachers come to terms with cognitive versus holistic model of reading. In T. Shanahan & F. Rodriguez-Brown (Eds.) *National Reading Conference Yearbook 48* (pp. 437-450). Chicago: NRC.

Festinger, L. (1957). *A theory of cognitive dissonance*. Stanford, CA: Stanford University Press.

Goodlad, J. (1991). Why we need a complete redesign of teacher education. *Educational Leadership, 48*(4), 4-10.

Holmes Group (1990). *Tomorrow's schools of education*. East Lansing, MI: Holmes Group.

Holmes Group (1995). *Tomorrow's schools: Principles for the design of professional development schools*. East Lansing, MI: Holmes Group.

Kagan, D. M. (1992). Professional growth among pre-service and beginning teachers. *Journal of Educational Research, 62*(2), 129-169.

Linek, W. M., Nelson, O. G., Sampson, M. B., Zeek, C. K., Mohr, K. A. J., & Hughes, L. (1999). Developing literacy beliefs about literacy instruction: A cross-case analysis of pre-service teachers in traditional and field-based settings. *Reading Research and Instruction, 38*(4), 371-386.

Lortie, D. (1975). *Schoolteacher: A sociological study*. Chicago: University of Chicago Press.

Martin, M., Martin, S., & Martin, C. (1999). Pre-service teachers constructing their meanings of literacy in a field-based program. In J. Dugan, P. Linder, W. Linek, & E. Sturtevant (Eds.) *Advancing the World of Literacy: Moving into the 21st. Century* (pp. 55-66). Carrollton, GA: CRA.

Newton, E., & Smolen, L.A. (2000). From theory to practice: A qualitative case survey of TEFL peace corps volunteers in America. In P. E. Linder, W. M. Linek, E. G. Sturtevant & J. R. Dugan (Eds.) *Literacy At a New Horizon* (pp. 241-255). Commerce, TX: College Reading Association.

Risko, V., Roskos, K., & Veukelich, C. (1999). Making connections: Pre-service teachers' reflection processes and strategies. In T. Shanahan & F. Rodriguez-Brown (Eds.) *National Reading Conference Yearbook 48* (pp. 412-422). Chicago: NRC.

Sampson, M., Walker, C., & Fazio, M. (1999). Collaborative research, reflections and refinement: The evolution of literacy coursework in a professional development center. In J. R. Dugan, P. Linder, W. M. Linek, & E. G. Sturtevant (Eds.) *Advancing the World of Literacy: Moving into the 21st Century* (pp. 67-80). Commerce, TX: College Reading Association.

Strauss, A., & Corbin, J. (1994). Basics of qualitative research: Grounded theory procedures and techniques. Newbury Park, CA: Sage.

Upitis, R. (1999). Teacher education reform: Putting experience first. *Teacher Education Quarterly, 26*(2), 11-19.

USDOE. (1987). *What works: Research about teaching and learning.* Washington, DC: Author.

Vygotsky, L. S. (1978). *Mind in society: The development of higher psychological process.* Cambridge, MA: Harvard University Press.

Wells, G. (1994). *Changing schools from within: Creating communities of inquiry.* Toronto: OISE.

Wildman, T. M., & Niles, J. A. (1987). Essentials of professional growth. *Educational Leadership, 44*(5), 4-10.

Wiseman, D. (1999). The impact of school-university partnerships on reading teacher educators: Important conversations we must have. In J. R. Dugan, P. Linder, W. M. Linek, & E. G. Sturtevant (Eds.) *Advancing the World of Literacy: Moving into the 21st. Century* (pp. 81-93). Carrollton, GA: CRA.

Wolf, S., Hill, L., & Ballentine, D. (1999). Teaching on fissured ground: Preparing pre-service teachers for culturally conscious pedagogy. In T. Shanahan & F. Rodriguez-Brown (Eds.) *National Reading Conference Yearbook 48* (pp. 423-434). Chicago: NRC.

Zeek, C., & Wickstrom, C. (1999). The making of a teacher: The influence of personal literacy development on pre-service teachers' current teaching practices. In T. Shanahan, & F. Rodriguez-Brown (Eds.) *National Reading Conference Yearbook 48* (pp. 479-490). Chicago: NRC.

## Appendix A. Exploring Preservice Teachers' Philosophical Orientation To Literacy Learning (Pre Poll)

Student Number _____

Sex _____ Age _____ Today's Date _____

1. What is a good reader? Why do you say that?
2. What do students need to know about letter/sound relationships? How would you teach that?
3. Consider children's initial encounters with print in a school setting.
   a) What would you do to teach beginning readers to read? Why would you do that?
   b) What materials would you use to teach beginning readers? Why have you decided to use these materials?
4. There are some unfamiliar words in a fourth grade narrative passage on how a forest develops, will you do anything to familiarize students with the vocabulary before reading the passage? If so, What would you do? and Why would you do that?
5. Children learn language and learn about language by being a language user. What does that mean to you as a teacher of readers, writers, speakers, and listeners?
6. How would you organize and manage subjects such as reading, math, science, social studies, and other subjects in your classroom?
7. What would you use to assess or evaluate students in reading and writing? How will you collect and use what you have assembled?
8. Describe your own current attitudes toward reading and writing, that is, do you see reading and writing as positive or pleasurable activities you do or do you have some negative feelings toward them? Describe your attitudes and the kind of materials, reading and writing activities, or topics/subjects about which you have strong feelings on way or another. Have your attitudes changed since the beginning of the semester as a result of this course? How? Why do you think so?
9. As you are working through this class, have your thoughts and feelings about teaching reading and writing to elementary students changed from the beginning of this class? If so:
   a) Explain how your thoughts and feelings have changed.
   b) What particular aspects of this course do you believe are making the biggest difference for your? Why do you say that?
10. If you could change anything about this course, content, components, etc. what would you suggest?

## Appendix B. Philisophical Orientation To Literacy Learning (Post Poll)

Student Name_____ Course #_____

SS#_____ Sex_____ Age ____ Today's Date _____

1. What is a good reader? Why do you say that?
2. What do students need to know about letter/sound relationships? How would you teach that?
3. Consider children's initial encounters with print in a school setting.
   a) What would you do to teach beginning readers to read? Why would you do that?
   b) What materials would you use to teach beginning readers? Why have you decided to use these materials?
4. There are some unfamiliar words in a fourth grade narrative passage on how a forest develops. Would you do anything before presenting the passage to the students? If so, What would you do? Why would you do that?
5. Children learn language and learn about language by being a language user. What does that mean to you as a teacher of readers, writers, speakers, and listeners?
6. How would you organize and manage subjects such as reading, math, science, social studies, and other subjects in your classroom?
7. What are your current attitudes toward reading and writing?
8. What would you use to assess or evaluate students in reading and writing? How will you collect and use what you have assembled?
9. As you are working through this fourth reading class, have your thoughts and feelings about teaching reading and writing to elementary students changed since you began taking reading courses? If so:
   a) Explain how your thoughts and feelings have changed.
   b) What particular aspects of this course, its components, or content do you believe will make the biggest difference for you? Why do you say that?

# FAMILY
# VOICES

# QUESTIONS PARENTS ASK: THE FAQ PROJECT

**Maryann Mraz**
**Danielle Gruhler**
**Nancy Padak**
**Jackie Peck**
Kent State University

**Jodi Dodds Kinner**
University of Illinois, Chicago

**Chris McKeon**
Walsh University

**Evangeline Newton**
University of Akron

## Abstract

*Parental involvement in literacy fosters children's reading achievement. To maximize the impact of this involvement, parents and school personnel must share concepts about what is important in children's literacy and language development. By actively addressing parents' questions about literacy learning, teachers and administrators can help parents understand the pedagogical practices that support a variety of instructional practices. This study, the first phase of a larger project, sought to gather and categorize questions about literacy and literacy learning that parents ask elementary school principals.*

*Mail surveys invited principals in Ohio to share the questions parents ask them. More than 1650 questions were submitted. Collaborative inductive analysis yielded 18 categories of questions. The conclusion of the article offers speculations about the origins of these questions and their potential impact on the nature of home-school relationships. In addition, some possible uses of the questions are suggested.*

"How can I help my child comprehend what s/he is reading?" "Should I teach my child to sound out unfamiliar words?" "Taxpayers spend a fortune on text books. Why do I have to pay for trade books, too?" These are a small sampling of questions reported by principals in a study that investigated the nature of the questions parents ask them. The purpose of this article is to present our research thus far on what we have dubbed the "Frequently Asked Questions" (FAQ) Project.

## Why Address Parents' Questions?

Research supports the notion that parental involvement in literacy learning fosters reading achievement (Baker, Afflerbach, & Reinking, 1996; Durkin, 1966; Morrow, 1995; Rasinski & Fredericks, 1989). Moreover, parents' attitudes and beliefs about literacy suggest that they truly want their children to succeed (Spiegel, 1994). Spiegel's review of the literature suggests that parents of successful readers share a sense of the importance of education and that they value reading aloud to their children. Indeed, many teachers urge parents to read aloud to their children because research supports this as an effective literacy development practice (Morrow, 1995; Rasinski & Fredericks, 1990).

Today's parents, however, find themselves immersed in the politics of literacy lingo, achievement test results, advertised home-teaching phonics games, and school program adoptions that go far beyond a teacher's recommendation to read aloud at home. The field of literacy has received recent unprecedented national publicity. Reading test scores appear regularly in newspaper headlines across the nation; politicians mandate reading benchmarks for specific grade levels; school districts purchase costly programs in hopes of preventing reading failure among their students. Needless to say, national attention to literacy has sparked a wide range of questions by parents: "Will my child fail the third grade if he can't pass the test?" "Do you teach phonics?" "Why is my child struggling in reading?" Often such questions evolve from local newspaper headlines that draw attention to literacy concerns (Goodman, 1998; Watson, 1998); additionally, the questions parents ask frequently reflect beliefs and attitudes about how they were taught to read (Zemelman, Daniels, & Hyde, 1998).

Regardless of the source of parents' questions, we believe that they are important for several reasons. First, parents deserve answers to their questions. It is well documented that parental involvement in education contributes to the academic achievement of their children (Henderson, 1988; Thorkildsen & Stein, 1998; Zemelman et al., 1998). Additionally, home-school connections that demonstrate a meaningful commitment to parents have a positive impact on student learning (Baker, Allen, Shockley, Pellegrini, Galda,

& Stahl, 1996); hence, it behooves us as literacy educators to take a vested interest in the questions parents ask about reading and writing.

Second, the success of home-school cooperation efforts that revolve around reading and writing rests, in part, on parents and school personnel sharing concepts about what is important in the literacy and language development of children. As Baker, Allen, et al. (1996) aptly comment, this is significant because "if parents and teachers have different beliefs and goals for children, it may be difficult for the two parties to reach a shared understanding of children's needs" (p. 27). By actively addressing parental questions about literacy, teachers and administrators can help parents understand the pedagogical principles that support a variety of instructional practices.

Third, although there are a variety of ways in which literacy educators can foster positive relationships between home and school, clear communication is a core ingredient of all successful home-school connections (Baker, Afflerbach, & Reinking, 1996; Fredericks, 1995). Effectively communicating with parents by genuinely addressing their concerns about literacy is one way in which teachers and principals can foster positive home-school connections. However, while most administrators and teachers intuitively know how to communicate with parents, they often lack resources that can systematically help them address the questions that parents ask about reading and writing instruction (Fredericks, 1995). Indeed in a study of 75 reading educators, Fredericks and Taylor (1984-1985) found that although "most reading professionals are aware of the variety of ideas, suggestions, and information that could be shared with parents . . . [they] need an operational framework upon which to build a successful outreach program" (p. 186). Another large-scale survey study (Jacobson, Reutzel, & Hollingsworth, 1992) of elementary principals concluded similarly that principals "may need readily accessible and practical information" about current innovations in reading education (p. 370). We concur that knowledge of current literacy research can provide teachers and administrators with important background information for answering parents' questions about reading programs and practices. However, knowledge about the nature and types of parents' questions is also needed.

Our study addressed the following question: What are the questions parents ask most frequently regarding the literacy education of their children? By investigating the nature of parental concerns, this research serves as a beginning framework for educators as they strive to ensure that parents are informed on a variety of literacy issues that often spark lively discussions beyond the classroom walls.

# Method

The researchers were university faculty members, doctoral students, and classroom teachers. Letters explaining the project were mailed to all public and private elementary school principals in Ohio. The principals were invited to participate in the project by listing the questions that parents most frequently ask regarding literacy learning. Thus, data for the study consisted of principals' renderings of parents' questions.

Over 2000 letters were sent with return envelopes; 256 (approximately 10%) principals replied. Because of the return rate, the results presented here should not be viewed as representative of parents' questions throughout Ohio. Nevertheless, we received 1,679 questions, which provides ample information for beginning to explore the nature of parents' questions.

The questions were typed and entered into a database using the computer software "Ethnograph" (Seidel, Friese, & Leonard, 1995). Using inductive analysis (Glaser & Strauss, 1967), initial categories were sought that addressed the question: "What are the questions that parents ask most frequently regarding the literacy education of their children?" Six initial categories emerged based on a preliminary analysis independently conducted by three of the researchers: a) concerns regarding how to help and support children at home, b) questions regarding the best approaches to teaching reading, c) specific queries about instructional strategies for teaching spelling, writing, grammar, and phonics, d) questions regarding reading assessment, e) concerns about classroom organization, and f) technology related queries.

Two researchers coded all questions according to these initial categories. This process happened simultaneously but separately in order to address issues of credibility and dependability in the analysis. Each question was coded as belonging to one or more of the categories. For instance, the question "Which is better, basals or whole language?" was coded as a question regarding the best approach(es) to teaching reading, while "why do you teach spelling when we have computers to spell-check?" was coded as a question related to both technology and language arts instruction. This continued for each of the 1,679 questions, resulting in many of the questions having numerous codes. Other categories that emerged during this first coding were noted for later discussion. These included additional as well as more specific categories and subcategories within broader ones.

The researchers then met to discuss the analysis that had been completed up to that point. They went through the questions one by one and agreed on the code(s) for each. Any areas of disagreement were discussed until consensus was reached. In addition, the other emerging categories were discussed at this time. These new categories were described, defined, and affixed to the appropriate questions.

The researchers then worked separately to code the data again, this time using the more specific category and subcategory codes. Broad categories were related to: Motivation, Technology, Phonics, Organization and Grouping, Remediation, Handwriting, Grammar, Early Literacy, Books, Testing and Assessment, Writing, Home Concerns, Language Arts Programs, Instructional Strategies, Spelling, and an "other" group for those questions not fitting into any of these categories. Subcategories within each of these 15 broad categories described the more specific questions that parents asked. For instance, the Spelling category had within it the following subcategories: invented spelling, spelling instruction, developmental expectations, importance of spelling, and the impact of technology on spelling.

The researchers met a second time, this time with a third researcher, to review the questions and codes. As part of this conversation, the group decided to create 3 smaller categories, Children, Reading, and Schools, to accommodate questions in the Other category. Agreement was reached, and the data were modified, again using the "Ethnograph" (Seidel et al., 1995) program. The final set of 18 categories accounted for all questions. Finally, descriptive information about the 18 categories of questions was developed.

## Results

Tables 1 and 2 show results of the study.[1] Table 1 shows both the raw numbers and percentages of questions within each category and the numbers (and percentages) of distinct issues raised in each category. For example, the

**Table 1. Categories, Frequencies, and Issues**

| CATEGORY | QUESTIONS | | DISTINCT ISSUES | |
|---|---|---|---|---|
| | N | % | N | % |
| Books | 128 | 8 | 22 | 6 |
| Children | 24 | 1 | 14 | 4 |
| Early Literacy | 59 | 4 | 15 | 4 |
| Grammar | 27 | 2 | 4 | 1 |
| Handwriting | 16 | 1 | 6 | 2 |
| Home Concerns | 272 | 16 | 39 | 11 |
| Motivation | 57 | 3 | 11 | 3 |
| Organization/Grouping | 65 | 4 | 12 | 4 |
| Phonics | 167 | 10 | 16 | 5 |
| Programs | 170 | 10 | 34 | 10 |
| Reading | 7 | 0 | 4 | 1 |
| Remediation | 58 | 3 | 13 | 4 |
| Schools | 23 | 1 | 14 | 4 |
| Spelling | 192 | 11 | 22 | 6 |
| Strategies | 142 | 8 | 51 | 15 |
| Testing/Assessment | 124 | 7 | 30 | 9 |
| Technology | 67 | 4 | 12 | 4 |
| Writing | 81 | 5 | 20 | 6 |
| **Total** | **1679** | | **340** | |

**Table 2. Most Frequently Cited Categories**

| CATEGORY | SUMMARY | EXAMPLES |
|---|---|---|
| Strategies | How to teach particular aspects of reading: comprehension, word attack, fluency; general instructional issues, including classroom management. | How can I tell if my child is comprehending? How do children develop fluency? What's the best way to teach reading? What is a strategy? Which ones are best? |
| Home Concerns | How to support reading and language learning at home; issues related to time. | How do I encourage love of reading at home? How can I help my child? What should I do if my child gets stuck/ makes a mistake with a word? How much should my child read beyond the school day? |
| Programs | The "great debate"; information about specific programs and methods of teaching; general curriculum questions. | Do children learn skills (including phonics) in "whole language" classrooms? How? What is Reading Recovery? Is it worth the cost? How do you teach reading? Should children be reading and writing in all subjects? |
| Testing/Assessment | Mandated testing in Ohio; how reading is assessed and graded; how children can improve their reading grades; benchmarks/ grade-level expectations. | How does the school prepare my child for the Ohio Proficiency Tests? How do you grade reading without worksheets? What should be assessed? What are grade level expectations in reading? Are they the same for all children? How (and how often) do you evaluate my child? |
| Writing | Writing growth; writing instruction, including "process writing" and specific instructional routines (e.g., journals); at-home writing activities; reading-writing connections. | What should be "counted" (i.e., spelling, grammar) in different types of writing? What is the writing process? What's included? How often should my child write in school? What is the relationship between reading and writing? |

**Table 2. Most Frequently Cited Categories (continued)**

| Category | Summary | Examples |
|---|---|---|
| Spelling | The what and why of invented/ temporary spelling; teaching strategies; expectations; spell-checkers. | How will my child ever learn to spell conventionally? Why is my child encouraged to invent spelling? Won't this just confuse him/ her? What happened to the lists and spelling books? When will schools begin to "demand" correct spelling? Isn't it OK just to teach children how to use spell-checkers? |
| Books | Selecting books for children/ parents to read; role of trade books in the reading program; using the public library. | How do I find the right book for my child? Is it OK for my child to reread books/ read only one kind of book (e.g., scary story)? How do teachers teach reading without a basal? How do I find appropriate books at the library? |

question "How do I find appropriate books at the library?" was included on 18 survey forms (raw number) but represents only one distinct issue in the Books category.

Both the breadth and depth of parents' questions is apparent from inspecting Table 1. Principals reported parents asking 340 separate questions about literacy and literacy learning within the 18 broader categories.

Table 2 provides summaries and sample questions for the 7 categories that contained the most questions. These are presented according to frequency of distinct issues, e.g., the "Strategies" category had the most distinct issues (15% of total; see Table 1). These 7 categories accounted for 65% of all questions and 63% of the distinct issues represented among the questions.

In general, parents' questions focus on several types of issues: a) what happens at school and why. Here we note attention to both broad curricular decisions (e.g., "What is the relationship between reading and writing?") and specific, child-centered concerns (e.g., "How [and how often] do you evaluate my child?"); b) how to support children's learning at home; c) requests for information, which often included educational terminology (e.g., "whole language," "invented spelling," "Reading Recovery"); and d) "then-and-now" types of requests (e.g., "How do you grade reading without worksheets?", "What happened to lists and spelling books?").

## Discussion

This study has convinced us that parents do, indeed, have an astonishing variety of questions related to literacy, literacy learning, and their children's growth as literate people. That being the case, the brief, conventional "school open house" conversations or "tea and dessert" Title I presentations are unlikely to address all parents' questions. One implication from this work, then, is a strong suggestion that school personnel conduct their own inquiries into questions of concern to their own parent communities. The broad categories uncovered in our research may provide a framework for this effort. For example, a beginning-of-the-year newsletter could include a page that asks parents for their questions within the 7 categories listed in Table 2. School personnel could then use the results to plan ways to respond to parents' questions.

Having determined the questions of concern to their own parent communities, school personnel then need to develop ways to address the questions. Toward that end, the types of questions across categories may suggest possible approaches. Parents' questions went far beyond the typical "how do I help at home?" types of concerns. For example, many parents in our study had broad, curricular questions. They wanted to know about the school literacy curriculum, and they were interested in the rationale for literacy program decisions as well as the impact of these decisions on the education of their children. They were also interested in changes over time, in how and why today's classroom differs from classrooms of the past. An implication of these findings relates to home-school communication surrounding innovations in literacy programs and practices. Educators need to help parents understand the reasons for change.

Vehicles for addressing parents' questions could include user-friendly brochures or "fact sheets" with research-based answers to common questions. These could be sent home in school newsletters, distributed at parent meetings, or shared at parent-teacher conferences. Indeed, the next phase of our study will be to develop and share such products.

As we began planning these, however, more questions emerged. In other words, the data analysis phase of our study has produced additional topics of inquiry based on what the patterns within parents' questions might tell us about their literacy perceptions and concerns. For example, the broad continuum of experience and polar beliefs underlying the questions were often striking. For example, the question, "Why don't you teach phonics?" from one parent, was followed by, "Why DO you spend so much time teaching phonics?" (emphasis added) from another. "Why do you use whole language?" on one survey was countered with, "Why don't you use whole language?" on another. Perhaps these parent questions reflect a preoccupation with finding the "right" methodology that has dominated teacher preparation in the twentieth century. In fact, one byproduct of the "great debate" may be that it has misled parents into thinking that the complex process of learning to read can be unlocked with a simple prescriptive formula or the "right" method.

Broad questions such as, "How can I help my child?" and "How do you teach reading?" underscore this impression and strongly suggest parents' need for basic information about how children learn and how they can support that effort. Other questions were highly specific and implied that, although a parent may have possessed general information about children's reading and writing, more sophisticated explanations were required in order to clarify issues of concern.

The breadth and depth of questions within categories left us wondering how the personal experiences of parents, in terms of both their own literacy development and that of their children, might have influenced the nature of the questions they posed. Learning is schema-driven, constructed through personal experience within a sociocultural context. Were certain questions more likely to be asked by parents whose children needed support with reading and writing? What do parents believe are the purposes of reading? How did their school experiences influence these views? The answers to these questions, which are beyond the scope of our study, have the potential to influence the type of information that parents actually need. Consequently we also face a challenge in trying to provide useful and easily understood information about a process that is, by its nature, somewhat idiosyncratic.

Even the issue of what "counts" as research-based answers to parents' questions can be problematic. There is a growing concern among educators and scholars about whose research is used to defend particular positions and about how research related to literacy instruction is interpreted and presented to the public (e.g., Allington, 1999; Coles, 2000; Taylor, 1998). For example, in his book, *Misreading Reading: The Bad Science that Hurts Children*, Coles (2000) cautions against placing too much confidence in certain research findings. His own inquiry found that studies with findings termed "indisputable scientific evidence" (p. ix) that one teaching method was superior to another often assumed causal relationships where simple correlations were actually found. Coles' analysis provides further evidence of the complexity involved in the search for simple answers to parents' questions.

As researchers, then, we have become increasingly aware that the answers to many of the FAQ Project questions are complex and often dependent on the sources used to address them. Although we see a clear need to provide parents with answers that do not simplify or evade their questions about literacy education, we have a renewed understanding of the enormity of this task.

---

## Note

[1]The entire data set, organized by categories, subcategories, and distinct questions is 12 single-spaced pages in length. Those interested in obtaining a copy may contact Nancy Padak at npadak@literacy.kent.edu.

## References

Allington, R. T. (1999). Crafting state educational policy: The slippery role of research and researchers. *Journal of Literacy Research, 31,* 457-482.

Baker, L., Afflerbach, P., & Reinking, D. (Eds.) (1996). *Developing engaged readers in school and home communities.* Mahwah, NJ: Erlbaum.

Baker, L., Allen, J., Shockley, B., Pelegrini, A. D., Galda, L., & Stahl, S. (1996). Connecting school and home: Constructing partnerships to foster reading development. In L. Baker, P. Afflerbach, & D. Reinking (Eds.), *Developing engaged readers in school and home communities* (pp. 21-41). Mahwah, NJ: Erlbaum.

Coles, G. (2000). *Misreading reading: The bad science that hurts children.* Portsmouth, NH: Heinemann.

Durkin, D. (1966). *Children who read early.* New York: Teachers College Press.

Fredericks, A. D. (1995). Community outreach. In S. B. Wepner, J. T. Feeley, & D. S. Strickland (Eds.), *The administration and supervision of reading programs* (2nd ed.) (pp. 178-193). New York: Teachers College Press.

Fredericks, A. D., & Taylor, D. (1984-1985). Parent involvement in reading: What educators want to know. *The Reading Instruction Journal, 31*(2), 17-20.

Glaser, B. G., & Strauss, A. L. (1967). *The discovery of grounded theory: Strategies for qualitative research.* Chicago: Aldine.

Goodman, K. S. (1998). Who's afraid of whole language? Politics, paradigms, pedagogy, and the press. In K. S. Goodman (Ed.), *In defense of good teaching: What teachers need to know about the 'reading wars'* (pp. 3-37). York, ME: Stenhouse.

Henderson, A. T. (1988). Parents are a school's best friends. *Phi Delta Kappan, 70,* 148-153.

Jacobson, J., Reutzel, D. R., & Hollingsworth, P. M. (1992). Reading instruction: Perceptions of elementary school principals. *Journal of Educational Research, 85,* 370-380.

Morrow, L. M. (Ed.). (1995). *Family literacy: Connections in schools and communities.* Newark, DE: International Reading Association.

Rasinski, T., & Fredericks, A. D. (1989). Can parents make a difference? *The Reading Teacher, 43,* 84-85.

Rasinksi, T., & Fredericks, A. D. (1990). The best reading advice for parents. *The Reading Teacher, 43,* 344-345.

Seidel, J., Friese, S., & Leonard, D. C. (1995). *The ethnograph v4.0: A program for the analysis of text based data.* Amherst, MA: Qualis Research Associates.

Spiegel, D. L. (1994). A portrait of parents of successful readers. In E. H. Cramer, & M. Castle (Eds.), *Fostering the love of reading: The affective domain in reading education* (pp. 74-87). Newark, DE: International Reading Association.

Taylor, D. (1998). *Beginning to read and the spin doctors of science. The political campaign to change America's mind about how children learn to read.* Urbana, IL: National Council of Teachers of English.

Thorkildsen, R., & Stein, M. R. S. (1998). *Is parent involvement related to student achievement? Exploring the evidence.* (CEDR Research Bulletin No. 22). Bloomington, IN: Phi Delta Kappa.

Watson, A. (1998). The newspaper's responsibility. *Phi Delta Kappan, 79,* 728-734.

Zemelman, S., Daniels, H., & Hyde, A. (1998). *Best practice: New standards for teaching and learning in America's Schools* (2nd ed.). Portsmouth, NH: Heinemann.

# "Do You Want Me to Read to You?": A Case Study of Older Siblings' Literacy Teaching

### Lisa A. Lenhart

The University of Akron

## Abstract

*Research on siblings teaching siblings shows there is a teaching-learning process that goes on when one sibling serves as the teacher and the other serves as the learner. The goal of this qualitative, naturalistic case study was to observe a set of siblings during literacy events and then describe the older sibling's behaviors as she interacted with her younger sibling. The study found that the older sibling played a crucial role in their younger sibling's literacy development. The older sibling knew a great deal about literacy learning, was a constructivist teacher, and created zones of proximal development for the younger sibling.*

## Introduction

Literacy learning is a highly social activity; it does not occur by itself. The key social group in which most young children's learning takes place is the family. More able family members—usually the parents—are seen as the child's first literacy teacher. Although many parents attempt to assist literacy development in some way, they do not all do it in the same way, to the same extent, with the same materials, or with the same concept of what literacy means (Heath, 1983; Taylor, 1983; Taylor & Dorsey Gaines, 1988; Weinberger, 1998).

## Purpose

The purpose of this study, one portion of a larger investigation, was to provide an in-depth description of an older siblings' interactions with a younger sibling when reading and writing together in their environment. It describes the literay interactions between two sisters- Hannah, age 5, and Emma, age 18 months. The overarching question that guided this part of the research was: What patterns of behavior does the older sibling exhibit during literacy events?

## Review of the Literature

We know that the practice of literacy within families has existed over the centuries. However, it is only in the past several decades that attention has been given to the interplay of family members in literacy learning (Auerbach, 1995; Hannon, 1996; Morrow & Young, 1997; Neuman, 1996; Purcell-Gates, 1986, 1993, 1995, 1996; Taylor, 1997, 1983). Researchers have documented that what young children learn about written language before schooling is determined by ways in which important people in their lives use print (Clay in Goodman & Goodman, 1976; Heath, 1983; Purcell-Gates, 1986, 1995, 1996; Taylor & Dorsey Gaines, 1988; ). Correlational studies have continually documented the importance of factors in children's reading achievement in school, such as parents' educational level, use of print in the home, number of books in the home, and frequency of parent-child storybook reading events (Anglum, Bell, & Roubinek, 1990; Basic Skills Agency, 1993; Chaney, 1994; Snow, Barnes, Chandler, Goodman, & Hemphill, 1991). So, while the family as a foundation for language and literacy development is defined, it is essentially the parent's role in home literacy experiences that has been examined, with little emphasis on the siblings.

General research on siblings teaching siblings shows there is a teaching-learning process that goes on when one sibling serves as the teacher and the other serves as the learner. Brody, Stoneman, and MacKinnon (1982) found that children with younger siblings can and do teach them; older siblings feel a greater responsibility to teach if the pupil is a younger sibling. Norman-Jackson's (1982) research on children playing school with younger brothers and sisters showed that the younger siblings had an easier time learning to read, and Ervin-Tripp (1989) found that children do a lot of teaching work within the family and that older siblings show a considerable amount of accommodation to the younger child's low level of language competence.

Two seminal studies provide some insight into the role of sibling influence on literacy development. Taylor's (1983) data suggested that both older and younger siblings are active in shaping the literate experiences of each other. Parents in the study spoke of the younger children listening to their older siblings read. Taylor reported,

> The data indicate that although emphasis was given to older siblings reading stories to younger siblings, this did not occur as regularly as the reading of stories by parents. The children read together spasmodi-

cally, and these events were influenced by many factors, including whether the older child wanted to read and the younger child wanted to listen and finding time for such activity in the bustle of daily living. (p. 17)

Regarding siblings and literacy, Durkin (1966) reported that when there was an older sibling, they played a significant role in the younger child's reading development. Durkin suggested that the role of the sibling is very productive and should not be overlooked, especially in the form of playing school. Although there is work in the field on the teaching-learning process between siblings, and a growing body of research on the family's role in literacy development, only Durkin's (1966) and Taylor's (1983) research focuses on the specific role of the sibling.

## Research Design

This was a qualitative, naturalistic inquiry, "a discovery oriented approach that minimizes investigator manipulation of the study setting and places no prior constraints on what the outcomes of the research will be" (Guba, 1978, p. 41). This parent-researcher case study is not the first of its kind. Qualitative research has been conducted by notable parent-researchers such as Bissex (1980), Baghban (1984), Lass (1982, 1983), and Schickedanz (1990). These researchers conducted naturalistic studies on their children's literacy development. Baghban (1984) had this to say regarding the parent as researcher:

While a parent is inherently subjective, a formally trained parent brings to the task the enlightenment that comes from years of training in a particular field. A detailed case study of a child learning language would be virtually impossible for a non-parent researcher. No other person will ever know the child, the contexts of the child's life, and the particular research situation so completely as the parent. No one but a parent would have the opportunity. (p. 8)

## Participants

Hannah, the oldest child, was born on June 5, 1993, and was 5 years and 1 month when the study began in July of 1998, prior to the onset of kindergarten. Her younger sister, Emma, was born 3 years and 8 months later on February 20, 1997. She was 17 months old when this study began and had no formal instruction outside of the home. During the course of the study Emma went from a baby who only babbled to a highly verbal communicator. Hannah progressed from a phase where she understood concepts about print and recognized a few high frequency words to an early reading and writing phase where she could read and retell simple stories, recognize many high frequency words, and write using invented spellings. Although any time period would reveal its own unique developments, this one allowed a peek at Emma's emergence into literacy and Hannah's transition from nonreader to early reader.

Hannah and Emma live with both parents. Their father, a swim coach, works at a local university. At the time of the study I, their mother, was a graduate student and a teacher. Both girls frequented college campuses. They also had a great deal of exposure to educational experiences informally, such as visits to the zoo, story hour at the library, and nature walks and programs in the metro parks.

Hannah has always loved books. In fact, as a toddler they were her favorite toys. She could sit and look at a pile of books for about 45 minutes before she was mobile, and has maintained this love of reading. She attended a nursery school two afternoons a week when she was 3 years old. She attended three mornings a week when she was 4 years old, and entered half-day kindergarten when she was 5 years and 2 months.

In addition to her love of books, Hannah has a special affinity for writing tools. She insisted on a clipboard like Dad's and a grade book like mine. After seeing me write checks, she wanted her own "checkbook" with a fabric cover. She carries a three-ring binder with folders in it and loves stationary, note cards, and tablets of all kinds.

Although read to from infancy, Emma did not spend as much of her free time playing with books as Hannah did. Instead, she preferred to interact and try to keep up with her older sister. As a toddler Emma began to spend more time with books. She sat and looked at books occasionally, enjoyed being read to, and even started to choose a book from the shelf before bedtime and insist that her choice was read, too.

## Setting

This study took place in the children's home; an environment rich with print where they have witnessed both parents read newspapers, books, and magazines. They have seen notes written as well as letters and lists, and have sent and received cards in the mail. Both witnessed their mother research and write papers, grade papers, and prepare lecture notes. Since the family likes to bake, the girls are also familiar with reading recipes. Print is definitely "done" in the environment.

The siblings had easy access to innumerable children's books of various genres and levels as well as an ample supply of pens, paper, pencils, crayons, markers, cards, and envelopes. Each child had her own room with bookshelves filled with books that were at the children's level to allow for accessibility. The rest of the house was filled with print, too. There were shelves of books in the living room, books stacked on nightstands, cookbooks in the kitchen, magazines and books in the bathrooms, and an office filled with professional books for each parent. The refrigerator was covered with pictures of family and always has snippets of print: quotes, reminders, cartoons, Bible verses, and school calendars. There were also books in the car to occupy the children. Books and magazines were highly prized in the home and often given as gifts.

## Data Collection and Analysis

Data were collected throughout all phases of the study using observations, field notes, videotape, and literacy artifacts used and/or produced by the children. Data were collected as it occurred on an on-going basis. Every attempt was made to document literacy events that occurred in the presence of the researcher through observation, video, or field notes.

Because one research question in the original study dealt with how events were initiated, only those captured in their entirety were used for analysis. Therefore, forty-eight literacy events were selected from the data for analysis.

The data analysis strategy used for this study was the constant comparative method (Glaser and Strauss, 1967). Data were coded and examined for groupings and then sub-groupings. Analysis was done in conjunction with on-going data collection, contrasting tentative categories that captured recurring patterns that reflected the focus of the study.

## Results: Hannah Teaches, Responds and Supports

This section highlights the two main groupings of Hannah's behaviors: teacher and responder. Sub-groupings are given as well as vignettes to support findings.

### *Hannah is the "More Capable Other";*
### *She Exhibits Teacher-like Behaviors*

Hannah showed many patterns of behavior that identified her as the "more capable other," almost characteristic of adults who are aware of their role in the literacy development of young children. Figure 1 provides an overview of the behaviors Hannah exhibited throughout the study; Table 1 shows the frequency of the behaviors. A particular behavior could occur once, several times, or not at all during a single event.

**Demonstrates Audience Awareness.** Most patterns of behavior could be classified as "teacher" or "parent" behaviors. This is not surprising, considering that Hannah has attended numerous story hours at the library, had two years of preschool, and was enrolled in kindergarten during this study.

**Figure 1. Overview of Hannah's behaviors.**

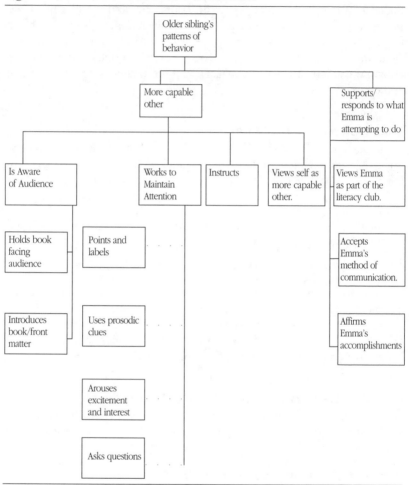

In addition, she has been raised in an environment rich with print with a mother who is a teacher. So it was no surprise that often she would move opposite Emma and hold the book to her "audience" so Emma could see it as she read, even if that meant telling the story upside down! Besides holding the book like a teacher, Hannah would introduce the story like one: When reading together before bedtime, she held the book so Emma could see the cover then said, "*The Foot Book,* by Dr. Seuss" (Seuss, 1968). Next, she read the title page aloud, and then proceeded with the book. Hannah's knowledge of how a parent or teacher introduces a book and then goes over the front matter was evident as she did the same with her "student."

**Table 1.** *Older Sibling's Patterns of Behavior*

| Category | F |
|---|---|
| More capable other | |
| Aware of audience | |
| Holds book facing audience | 10 |
| Introduces book/front matter | 12 |
| Works to maintain attention | |
| Arouses excitement and interest | 19 |
| Uses prosodic cues | 7 |
| Asks questions | 17 |
| Points and labels | 11 |
| Instructs | 13 |
| Views self as more capable other | 10 |
| Supports/responds | |
| Views Emma as part of the literacy club | 14 |
| Accepts Emma's methods of communication | 10 |
| Affirms Emma's accomplishments | 9 |

**Works to Maintain Audience Attention.** In addition to holding her book to the "audience," Hannah also exhibited teacher-like behavior when she worked hard to maintain Emma's attention. The data showed that Emma could be "pulled" back into the event by the use of voice, questioning, and key phrases. She worked to maintain high interest in the story for Emma, her audience. An illustration of this behavior occurred one morning before church. The girls were reading *Puppies Count 1-10!*. After reading a couple of pages Hannah said, "Arf! Arf! Do you like puppies?" Emma nodded positively, and then Hannah continued, "Oh! Look at the stars. Do you want to count the stars?" Hannah proceeded to count the stars, and then pushed the button on the book to elicit the barking sound. When Emma laughed at this Hannah offered, "Do you want to hear that again?" Emma nodded approvingly and then Hannah played it again. The next time she played it, Hannah added tickling to the mix as she barked.

Hannah also used many prosodic cues while reading, conveying more meaning for Emma when she read with expression. One example was the way she read, "Look everyone! Look what I have. (pause) A loose tooth!" Emma's attention was piqued and she immediately looked at the book, because Hannah read it in such a way that it sounded real and exciting. She demonstrated this use of timing again when she read *Chicka Chicka Boom Boom* (Martin & Archambault, 1989), bouncing up and down with rhythm as she read expressively: "A told B, and B told C—Chicka Chicka boom boom. Will there be enough room? . . . Here comes H up the coconut tree . . . I'll meet you at the top of the coconut tree. But wait!—there's more!—W X Y & Z!" Hannah went for the big finish, pleasing Emma and saying in her biggest voice, "CHICKA CHICKA, BOOM! BOOM!" This got Emma's attention, as Hannah explained to Emma that all of the letters "went down."

Another method Hannah used to maintain her audience was questioning. While reading, she stopped and asked questions, like the time she was reading a book on colors and turned to Emma and said, "What color is it?" eliciting a response from Emma. When sharing a book on animals, Hannah turned to a page and said, "Can you find which one has the horn? Which one has the horn?" When Emma did not respond, Hannah offered, "This one" and pointed to the goat. When Hannah asked questions throughout an event, Emma maintained interest.

This use of pointing was another tactic she included in her teaching, using it time and again. When naming objects in a color book she pointed at the pictures as she read to Emma: "Elmo will find lots of red stuff. Can you help him? He found apples, he found sunglasses, he found a truck, he found strawberries, he found a balloon, he found a teddy bear, he found sneakers, he found pencils." Pointing allowed Hannah to match the speech to the picture, making connections and providing a scaffold (Cazden, 1988; Vygotsky, 1962) for Emma.

**Understands Self as "More Capable Other".** In this dyad Hannah was the more capable person. At times she displayed her awareness of this important role by casting a glance my way—a sort of communication between us "teachers." The first time she demonstrated this was when the girls were making birthday cards for a family friend, while waiting to go to the party. They were sitting at the kitchen table with markers, pens, pencils, scissors, and stickers. I was commenting to Emma about her card, noting the scribbles she wrote on the inside of the card for her name. Hannah heard me and said, "Let me see." Emma showed her the card, to which Hannah responded, "Oh!" And then looked at me and smiled a knowing smile and said, "She sort of has a V, doesn't she?" Hannah supported Emma as a writer, capable of signing her name on her card. She turned to Emma and proudly said, "Good job, Emma!"

**Offers Instruction.** Many times Hannah exhibited the behavior of teaching appropriate book handling and the value of books to Emma. One night when Emma was in bed with a pile of books next to her she tore the flaps off the pages of a flap book. The next day Emma showed the book to Hannah and confessed, "Hannah, I tore this." Hannah responded, "Aw—Emma. EMM-MA! We don't rip books!" She proceeded to take the book from Emma, put it in her closet on a shelf, close the door, and say to me, "There. She can't get it." Next, she walked over to Emma and sat down beside her, saying very seriously as she looked her right in the eye: "Emma, let me tell you some-thing. You can't rip things, ok? It's sad." Emma nodded.

Hannah often taught Emma how to do things. Sometimes it was how to accomplish a task, such as the time Emma needed assistance with a flap on her book. Emma asked, "Can you help me?" Hannah responded by showing her how to bend the page a bit to pop the flap open and said, "See? Here is what you do."

While trying to teach her a song, Hannah realized that her technique of singing the song and hoping Emma would simply catch on was not work-ing, so she decided to try a different method: "Wait. Wait Emma. I'll sing it first, then you sing it back to me." In addition to teaching her things, Hannah would often attempt to explain difficult concepts to Emma. On one occa-sion the girls were discussing Curious George's plight of being locked in jail. Distressed at this, Emma said, "Uh oh. George in there." Hannah explained, "Yeah. George is in jail." Emma: "Oh poor George." And when told the mice were eating his food, she said, "Uh oh." Hannah explained, "They'll give him more. They always feed you when you're in jail. They'll find you . . . But sometimes it's like rotten bread, and rotten milk."

When Emma noticed Hannah's name embroidered across her sweatshirt she said, "Hannah, I like your ABC's." Hannah explained, "Those aren't ABC's, Emma. That spells 'Hannah.' See—H-A-N-N-A-H. If you had one of these it would say E-M-M-A. Emma." Hannah repeatedly offered explanations, help-ing Emma to understand the how and why of certain situations, and to ex-plain how literacy works.

### Hannah Supports and Responds to What Emma is Attempting to Do

In addition to serving as the more capable peer, Hannah also supported and responded to what Emma was trying to do.

**Accepts Emma's Methods of Communication.** At the onset of this project Emma was just 18 months old with minimal language, although she knew language had a purpose and demonstrated this with her utterances. She also appeared to know that language was a tool that could be used to inter-act with her sister. When Hannah was 5 years old, she continuously accepted Emma's utterances and nonverbal gestures as communication, and appeared to see them as intentional. For example, one day when both girls were sitting on the couch, Emma picked up a book and said, "Mmmm" as she handed the book to Hannah. Hannah accepted the book and began reading it to Emma. Emma responded to this by rocking back and forth on the couch excitedly. Later, in this same session, Emma pointed at the book and said, "Zeee." Hannah enthusiastically responded, "What color is it?" to which Emma replied, "Eeee" as she rocked back and forth. Hannah affirmed, "Yellow."

Hannah often interpreted nonverbal communication from Emma, too. When Hannah offered, "I'll read to you!" Emma answered and accepted her invitation by bouncing excitedly and waiting for the story. Hannah chose a book and began reading.

**Views Emma as Part of the Literacy Club.** During many literacy events, Hannah showed behaviors that revealed her belief that Emma was part of the "literacy club" (Smith, 1985). Often times Hannah demonstrated this belief by supporting Emma as a literate person; other times, it was the response that Hannah made to Emma. At 20 months old, Emma took a book and went in the kitchen and sat on a chair. She was playing with the flaps on the book when Hannah came in and said, "Are you reading, Emma?" Emma nodded "yes."

Another time Hannah offered, "Do you want me to read that to you?" to which Emma responded, "I read it." Hannah said, "OK." And then got her own book. The two sat together and read.

**Affirms Emma's Accomplishments.** One of the endearing findings of this study is the pride Hannah showed in Emma's literacy development. Some standout examples of this included the time the girls were watching a children's television program. She was apparently unaware that Emma had learned to sing the alphabet song. We were on vacation, and the girls were in front of the television one morning, eating their cereal and watching Barney. As Barney and his friends sang the alphabet song, Emma joined in. Hannah, surprised, looked up and squealed, "Emmie!!" as she looked over and smiled. Then she got up and walked over to Emma, and after giving her a hug said very lovingly, "Emma, you know your ABC's." She seemed touched and proud when she discovered that Emma knew the alphabet song. Emma kept right on singing.

One day when the girls were writing at the kitchen table, Emma showed her writing to Hannah. Hannah encouraged, "Good job, Emma!" And when Emma made what looked like an "A" after Hannah held her hand and helped her, Hannah not only showed pride in Emma by excitedly squealing, "EMMIE!!" but pride in herself when she acknowledged her role in it by shouting, "I helped her! I helped her!" These comments show the affirmation both girls experienced when they expressed their pride in and shared one another's accomplishments during literacy events.

## Conclusions

Limitations in this study did occur and must be taken into account. The first limitation was the researcher's close relationship with the subjects, which could effect objectivity. Nevertheless, this relationship also provided a unique perspective that was only available to a parent. Data and investigator triangulation (Denzin, 1978) and interraters were used to insure that the boundaries of the data were not overstepped.

A second limitation addresses the generalizabilty of the whole population due to the sample size selected. While a single case was purposely selected, further research with many different siblings across cultures needs to be conducted to gain a deeper understanding of the role and impact of the siblings in literacy learning.

A final limitation is that it is probable not all events were captured because there were times when I was simply their mother, enjoying the moments or not aware of their impact.

In this study the older sibling was instrumental in including the younger sibling as a member of the "literacy club," Frank Smith's (1985) metaphor describing the social nature of literacy learning. She also established her role as the more capable other, being an important first teacher for the younger sibling. Her teaching had constructivist qualities (Vygotsky, 1978) because she took cues from the learner and worked at the appropriate level of understanding. This study showed that older siblings intuitively know much about supporting literacy development and share that knowledge with younger siblings when given the opportunity and appropriate environment.

Hannah knew to encourage Emma's membership in the club. F. Smith (1985) said the only requirement for membership is a mutual acknowledgement of acceptance into a group of people who use written language. To be in the literacy club, children must perceive themselves as readers and writers as Emma did, and in turn be perceived as readers and writers by others in the child's community. Hannah revealed her acceptance of Emma into the literacy club when she accepted her babbling, utterances, and gestures as communication and then acted on them, assuring Emma she was understood. She also demonstrated this when she would see Emma with a book and ask her if she was reading, or when Emma said, "I'm reading" she would reply, "OK" and then read her own book. When Hannah did this, she sent the message that Emma was a reader, too. Although she would sometimes sneak a "knowing" glance at me, revealing she knew Emma was not actually reading the words on the page, somehow she knew never to discourage her attempts or approximations.

The older sibling knew a great deal about literacy learning and played an important role as one of the younger child's first teachers. The findings in this study support Durkin's (1966) early research. In her study siblings reported helping by reading to the younger sibling, talking about letters, and helping with printing and spelling. The present study showed that the older sibling helped the younger sibling in many of the same ways Durkin reported over 30 years ago when she suggested the role of the sibling was very productive and should not be overlooked. The value of this study is how strongly it reinforces the vital role of sibling as literate mentor.

Hannah taught Emma many things, demonstrating that along with the parents she, too, was one of Emma's first literacy teachers. Directly, she taught Emma that books are of value and should be treated as such. She explained things to her, and taught her how to accomplish hard tasks, often breaking them down into manageable components. Hannah was a willing teacher, eager to bestow her knowledge on Emma. Not only did Hannah accept the role of teacher, she relished in it, holding the book facing her audience, and even reading the pages upside down. She was always willing to read to Emma or include her in the event with me if the two of us were reading and Emma walked in. She worked hard as a teacher to maintain her student's interest and attention, using expression, asking questions, pointing, and varying her voice.

When Hannah worked hard to understand Emma's babbling or nonverbal communications, she showed a considerable amount of accommodation. This conclusion correlates with Ervin-Tripp's (1989) study that found children do much teaching within the family when they try to understand the communications of a younger sibling. According to Ervin-Tripp, older siblings seem to be more ready than adults to decipher gestures, paraphrase in simpler terms, and reduce information for younger siblings. This study extends Ervin-Tripp's findings by including a focus on siblings and literacy.

The idea of the older sibling teaching the younger sibling is compatible with the previous research on siblings as teachers. Cicerelli (1972, 1973, 1975) found that older siblings who were girls were the most effective teachers of younger siblings and that younger siblings were most likely to accept direction from an older sister. Abromovitch and her colleagues (Abromovitch et al., 1979; Abromovitch, et al., 1980) found that older siblings often assume the role of "manager" and "model." Hannah, as manager, gave Emma instruction. As a model, she demonstrated the literacy functions in their world by the authentic ways in which reading and writing were used daily. The present study highlights how the more capable older sibling was a powerful and effective literacy model.

Emma was not the only one who benefited from Hannah's teaching. Zajonc and Markus' (1975) confluence model was designed to explain the effects of sibling positioning on intellectual ability and achievement. One of the ideas on which the model was based was the idea that teaching a younger sibling adds to the intellectual development of the older sibling. Based on this portion of the model as well as the present study where Hannah was Emma's literacy teacher, the conclusion can be drawn that teaching Emma enhanced Hannah's intellectual ability. In order for Hannah to teach Emma what she knew about literacy, she had to internalize the concepts. She showed this when she made ideas or processes explicit by demonstrating, explaining, or modeling for Emma. The present study not only supports the idea that teaching younger siblings promotes intellectual development of the older sibling but also extends it into the field of literacy.

Not only was Hannah knowledgeable about literacy learning, as the more capable peer or teacher she facilitated cognitive growth and knowledge acquisition by creating zones of proximal development for Emma and scaffolding her learning (Vygotsky, 1978). She did this when she encouraged approximations ("Good job, Emma!"), paraphrased in simpler terms ("Wait. Wait Emma. I'll sing it first, then you sing it back to me."), or provided assistance ("Here. I'll make one for you to trace.").

An important aspect of Vygotsky's (1978) theory is the idea that the potential for cognitive development is limited to a certain time span known as the "zone of proximal development." According to Vygotsky, the best role for the teacher is to mediate between what students are able to do on their own and what they are able to do with support, prompting, and encouragement. In this study the older sibling served as the teacher, facilitating cognitive growth and knowledge acquisition in the younger sibling. Hannah interacted with Emma, provided a scaffold, and served as a model and encourager—all important ways to support learning.

Much of the older sibling's teaching was constructivist in nature (Vygotsky, 1978). Hannah engaged in constructivist practice when she encouraged Emma's efforts and attempts at literacy and when she tried to teach or explain something to Emma at her level of understanding, considering how Emma learned. Several times she would start a task, realize what she was doing was too hard for Emma, and then begin again with a new approach, making the task simpler.

One of Piaget's (1959) main principles is that learning materials and activities should involve the appropriate level of motor or mental operations. He believed that teachers should avoid asking students to perform tasks that are beyond their current cognitive abilities. Although obviously oblivious to Piagetian stages, Hannah appeared to sense Emma's appropriate level of mental operations and then work with her at her current cognitive capability, a complex concept. Hannah also showed signs of constructivist teaching when she acknowledged Emma as a learner whose efforts had a purpose and when she engaged her in real life situations, sometimes extending the book into their world.

## Implications

Although the field has broadened extensively in the last 15 years, family literacy educators need to expand their study to include the role of the sibling. From this study we learned that the older sibling played an important role in teaching the younger sibling about reading and writing. But this is just a beginning. Researchers need to focus specifically on siblings, a powerful context, so we can begin to learn about the potential of the sibling's role in family literacy as well as implications for peers in the classroom environment.

Those involved in working with families would be wise to find ways to help parents understand the value of sibling interactions. This study concluded that siblings play a significant role in the literacy development of one another. Prior research reports that children need to live in environments rich with print from birth.

Preschool and primary grade teachers should set up opportunities for children of various levels to read and write together. This study demonstrated the power of literacy interrelationships among siblings that could be translated to peers in classroom settings.

---

# References

Abromovitch, R., Corter, C., & Lando, B. (1979). Sibling interaction in the home. *Child Development, 50*, 997-1003.

Abromovitch, R., Corter, C., & Pepler, D. (1980). Observations of mixed-sex sibling dyads. *Child Development, 51*, 1268-1271.

Abromovitch, R., Corter, C., Pepler, D., & Stanhope, L. (1986). Sibling and peer interaction: A final follow-up and a comparison. *Child Development, 57*, 217-229.

Anglum, B. S., Bell, M. L., & Roubinek, D. L. (1990). Prediction of elementary student reading achievement from specific home environment variables. *Reading Improvement, 27*, 173-184.

Auerbach, E. (1995). Deconstructing the discourse of strengths in family literacy. *Journal of Reading Behavior, 27*, 643-660.

Azmitia, M., & Hesser, J. (1993). Why siblings are important agents of cognitive development. *Child Development, 64*, 430-444.

Baghban, M. (1984). *Our daughter learns to read and write*. Newark, DE: International Reading Association.

Basic Skills Agency. (1993). *Parents and their children: The intergenerational effect of poor basic skills*. London: Adult Literacy and Basic Skills Unit.

Bissex, G. L. (1980). *Gyns at wrk: A child learns to read and write*. Cambridge, MA: Harvard University Press.

Brody, G., Stoneman, Z., & MacKinnon, C. (1982). Role asymmetries in interactions among school-aged children, their younger siblings, and their friends. *Child Development, 53*, 1364-1370.

Cazden, C. B. (1988). *Classroom discourse: The language of teaching and learning*. Portsmouth, NH: Heinemann.

Chaney, C. (1994). Language development, metalinguistic awareness, and emergent literacy skills of three-year-old children in relation to social class. *Applied Psycholinguistics, 15*, 371-394.

Cicirelli, V. G. (1972). The effect of sibling relationships on concept learning of young children taught by child teachers. *Child Development, 43*, 282-287.

Cicirelli, V. G. (1973). Effects of sibling structure and interaction on children's categorization style. *Developmental Psychology, 9,* 132-139.

Cicirelli, V. G. (1975). Effects of mother and older sibling on the problem solving behavior of the younger child. *Developmental Psychology, 11,* 749-756.

Denzin, N. K. (1978). *The research act: A theoretical introduction to the sociological methods.* New York: McGraw Hill.

Durkin, D. (1966). *Children who read early.* New York: Teachers College Press.

Ervin-Tripp, S. (1989). Sisters & brothers. In P. G. Zukow (Ed.), *Sibling interaction across cultures: Theoretical and methodological issues* (pp. 184-195). New York: Springer-Verlag.

Glaser, B. G., & Strauss, A. L. (1967). *The discovery of grounded theory.* Chicago, IL: Aldine.

Goodman, K., & Goodman, Y. (1976, April). *Learning to read is natural.* Paper presented at conference on Theory and Practice of Beginning Reading Instruction. Pittsburgh, PA.

Guba, E. G. (1978). Toward a methodology of naturalistic inquiry in education evaluation. *Monograph Series in Evaluation, 8,* Los Angeles, CA: University of California Center for the Study of Evaluation.

Hannon, P. (1996). School is too late: Preschool work with parents. In S. Wolfendale & K. Topping (Eds.), *Family involvement in literacy* (pp. 63-74). London: Cassell.

Heath, S. B. (1983). *Ways with words: Language, life, and work in communities and classrooms.* New York: Cambridge University Press.

Lass, B. (1982). Portrait of my son as an early reader. *The Reading Teacher, 36* (1), 20-28.

Lass, B. (1983). Portrait of my son as an early reader II. *The Reading Teacher, 36* (6), 508-515.

Morrow, L. M. (1983). Home and school correlates of early interest in literature. *Journal of Educational Research, 76,* 221-230.

Morrow, L., & Young, J. (1997). A collaborative family literacy program: the effects on children's motivation and literacy achievement. *Early Child Development and Care,* 127-128, 13-25.

Neuman, S. (1996). Children engaging in storybook reading: The influence of access to print resources, opportunity, and parental interaction. *Early Childhood Research Quarterly, 11,* 495-513.

Norman-Jackson, J. (1982). Family interactions, language development and primary reading achievement of black children of low income. *Child Development, 53,* 349-358.

Piaget, J. (1959). *The language and thought of the child.* New York: Humanities Press.

Purcell-Gates, V. (1986). Three levels of understanding about written language acquired by young children prior to formal instruction. In J. Niles & R. Lalik (Eds.), *Solving problems in literacy: Learners, teachers and researchers* (pp. 259-265). Rochester, NY: National Reading Conference.

Purcell-Gates, V. (1993). Issues for family literacy research: Voices from the trenches. *Language Arts,* 70, 670-677.

Purcell-Gates, V. (1995). *Other people's words: the cycle of low literacy.* Cambridge, MA: Harvard University Press.

Purcell-Gates, V. (1996). Stories, coupons, and the TV Guide: Relationships between home literacy experiences and emergent literacy knowledge. *Reading Research Quarterly, 31*, 406-428.

Samuels, H. R. (1980). The effect of older sibling on infant locomotor exploration of a new environment. *Child Development, 51*, 607-609.

Schickedanz, J. A. (1990). *Adam's righting revolutions*. Portsmouth, NH: Heinemann.

Smith, F. (1985). *Reading without nonsense*. New York: Teachers College Press.

Snow, C. E., Barnes, W. S., Chandler, J., Goodman, I. F., & Hemphill, L. (1991). *Unfulfilled expectations: Home and school influences on literacy*. Cambridge, MA: Harvard University Press.

Taylor, D. (1983). *Family literacy: Young children learning to read and write*. Portsmouth, NH: Heinemann.

Taylor, D. (Ed.). (1997). *Many families, many literacies: An international declaration of principles*. Portsmouth, NH: Heinemann.

Taylor, D., & Dorsey-Gaines, C. (1988). *Growing up literate: Learning from inner-city families*. Portsmouth, NH: Heinemann Educational Books.

Vygotsky, L. (1962). *Thought and Language*. Cambridge, MA: MIT Press.

Vygotsky, L. (1978). *Mind in society*. Cambridge, MA: Harvard University Press.

Weinberger, J. (1998). Young children's literacy experiences within the fabric of daily life. In R. Campbell (Ed.), *Facilitating preschool literacy* (pp. 39-50). Newark, DE: International Reading Association.

Zajonc, R. B., & Markus, G. B. (1975). Birth order and intellectual development. *Psychological Review, 82*, 74-88.

## Children's Books

Henkes, K. (1996) *Lilly's purple plastic purse*. New York: Greenwillow Books.

Martin, B., & Archambault, J. (1989). *Chicka Chicka Boom Boom*. New York: Simon & Schuster.

McGill, N. L. (1996). *Puppies count 1-101*. Lincolnwood, IL: Louis Weber.

Rey, H. A. (1941). *Curious George*. New York: Houghton Mifflin.

Seuss, Dr. (1968). *The foot book*. New York: Random House.

Wilhelm, H. (1999). *I lost my tooth*. New York: Scholastic.

# PARENTS AS PARTNERS: IMPROVING CHILDREN'S WRITING

## E. Francine Guastello

St. John's University

## Abstract

*This study examined the effects of parental involvement on students' writing ability and scores. Parents attended a training session where they received instruction in new English Language Arts Standards, the stages of the writing process, strategies for developing writing as a recursive process, and in the criteria of a scoring rubric used to evaluate their child's writing.*

*The study consisted of three phases. In Phase 3, parents scored their child's writing sample and discussed areas of improvement with their children based on the information shared in the training session and using a writing rubric. Students in the experimental groups represented three socioeconomic classes. Results indicated that when students had an understanding of the criteria for evaluation, their writing scores improved. Moreover, when their parents became knowledgeable of the writing process and the criteria for evaluation, they were better able to interact with their children to discuss areas in need of improvement. As a result of this study, parents gained a more thorough understanding of the school's expectations for quality writing and parents expressed greater confidence in their ability to be a supportive audience for their child's writing.*

Former Secretary of Education, William Bennett stated, "The single best way to improve elementary education is to strengthen the parents' role in it" (U.S. Dept. of Education, 1986). There is a considerable body of research to support Bennett's statement that points to the connection between parental involvement and students' achievement (Coleman, 1987; Epstein, 1991; Henderson & Berla, 1994). A synthesis of 2,575 studies revealed that parents directly or indirectly influence the cognitive, affective, and behavioral learning of their children (Walberg, 1984). There is a strong positive correlation between parents communicating their expectations to the child and academic achievement (Duke, 1992; Gyles, 1990). The home environment is one of the major influences on student learning (Walberg, 1984). Several researchers have documented the positive effect upon language skills when parents perform the role of home instructor (Becker & Epstein, 1992; Bermudez & Padron, 1988; Bloom, 1986; Chavkin & Williams, 1989; McLaughlin & Shields, 1987).

Parents often ask, "How can we help our children?" Most parents, regardless of economic status or cultural background, care about their children's education and provide substantial support if given specific opportunities and knowledge (Fruchter, Galletta, & White, 1992; Muller, 1993). Research has shown that parents' participation and involvement improves students' learning (Coleman, 1987; Epstein, 1991). Without the school's assistance however, parents' knowledge and approaches toward helping their children are heavily dependent on their social class and/or their educational background (Epstein, 1995). The ability to help their children often comes from knowing what is involved in the teaching/learning process and what is expected in terms of evaluation and expected learning outcomes.

Although the positive effects of parental involvement upon reading achievement have been documented (Clark, 1988; Rowe, 1991; Rowe & Rowe, 1992; Slaughter, 1987), there is insufficient research on the role of the parent in students' acquisition of writing skills.

## What Prompted This Study?

In January 1999, all fourth-grade students in the State of New York were administered the new English Language Arts Exams. The exam assessed student performance based on the new New York Standards (Board of Education, City of New York, 1997). Sixty-seven percent of the students in the New York City schools failed this exam. These results sent shock waves through the educational community. Educators at every level realized the urgency of examining the instructional strategies and literacy programs in their schools.

The greatest surge in the educational process came from parents who questioned educators from the universities to the classroom teacher as to how they could help their children to improve the quality of their writing. Parents sought out the answers to questions that would provide them: (1) with a clear understanding of the English Language Arts Standards and expected learning outcomes; (2) knowledge of the developmental and reflective aspects of the writing process; and (3) knowledge of a writing rubric to guide them and their child in the recursive process of writing while conferencing with their children. While interviewing teachers and students, the researcher discovered that in most instances, teachers used a rubric for scoring children's writing but the children were not always aware of the criteria on the rubric nor did they fully understand how their writing was being evaluated. This led the researcher to examine similar studies that addressed these factors.

## Supporting Research

In their discussion of difficulties encountered by young writers, Dahl and Farnan (1998) suggest that a lack of specific standards or a scoring rubric severely compromised students' ability to write – especially when attempting to make revisions. Students need to work independently during writing time to monitor and assess their progress. Power (1997) experimented with collaborating with her students to create writing rubrics. These rubrics were based on the needs she and her students identified as important for them to use as a guide to produce quality writing. Setting expectations and designing scoring rubrics in this manner may have more positive results than those (Mabry, 1999) imposed by State or local standards. Boyle (1996), in her research with fourth graders, was concerned with students achieving an acceptable level of competency with persuasive writing. She hypothesized that if students had a better understanding of the criteria for persuasive writing presented in the form of a scoring rubric, they would compose more effective writings and that the gap between the teacher's evaluation and the student's evaluation would narrow as the students became more familiar with the writing expectations. Bratcher (1994) and Spandel and Stiggins (1997) advocate and provide several models of holistic scoring rubrics to guide students in their revisions and rewriting. It is their contention that using a scoring rubric for evaluating writing gives the students a clearer understanding of the writing task and expectations. Another important aspect of consideration was the role of conferencing. Gere and Abbott (1985) studied the effects of peer discussion and interaction during the "writers' talk." What do teachers say to students, what do students say to their peers? They believe that the sharing that takes place during these conferences helps writers to understand and remain on task and to focus on the content and process of their writing (McCarthey, 1994; Newkirk, 1995). If this is the case, can parents be helped to interact more effectively with their children to improve the quality of their children's writing?

## The Purpose of the Study

This study was designed in response to parents seeking information from educators as to how they could help their children with writing and as a result of interviewing teachers and students about what they believe improves or hinders their progress with teaching/learning how to write. The results of six months of initial research provided the impetus to enable classroom teachers to work with parents in an effective partnership to enhance the children's writing skills.

In a preliminary meeting with the parents involved in this study, it was revealed by responses to several questions posed by the researcher, that parents were often unaware of: (1) how their children were being taught writing, (2) the stages in the writing process and how writing is recursive (Hillocks, 1995), and (3) how a writing rubric is used to evaluate their children's writing assignments (Sperling, 1993). It was the contention of this researcher that when parents become knowledgeable in these areas and were involved in helping their children meet writing standards, greater achievement in written expression would be possible.

The researcher investigated the effects of parental involvement in the writing performance of their children. The focus was on the effects of the parents' influence upon the writing achievement of the student.

## Will Training of Parents and Students Make a Difference?

The purpose of the research was to analyze the effects of training parents as an aid to improving the writing skills of fourth grade students. The researcher sought an answer to the following questions: a) Will teaching students how to use a writing rubric as a guide for writing, improve their scores from phase one to phase two?; b) Will teaching parents the writing process and the use of a writing rubric enable them to conference more effectively with their children to improve the writing ability of their children?; and c) will there be significant differences in the writing scores of the students based on socioeconomic status?

## Research Assumptions

For the purpose of this study the following hypotheses were created: There will be significant positive effects upon the writing scores of fourth-grade students in the experimental group from phase one to phase two after having been taught how to use the scoring rubric. There will be significant improvement after each writing sample for the students in the experimental group after parents have been taught the writing process and the use of the writing rubric to conference with their children. There will be significant differences in writing scores based upon socioeconomic status.

The dependent and independent variables for this model were as follows: The dependent variable is the average score on each of the three incremental writing samples. The independent variable is the instructional treatment of in-service to parents on the writing process and the training of students and parents on the criteria of the writing rubric.

# Method
## Subjects
Participants for this study consisted of 167 fourth-grade students attending various elementary schools. Students were enrolled in one of three schools: (1) an affluent suburban school on the south shore of Nassau County, NY; (2) a low socioeconomic multi-ethnic school located in Brooklyn, NY; and (3) a middle-class school in Queens, NY. Eight classes were randomly assigned to either the experimental or control group. The experimental group consisted of 97 students, 50 female, and 47 male. The control group contained 70 students, 34 female, and 36 male. The discrepancy in the number of students in the experimental and control group was due to the varying class sizes in the different schools. It is important to note that all student participants in this study had been formally instructed in the steps of the writing process that they used with their previous writing samples. Parents of the students in the experimental group were provided with an initial formal two-hour workshop at which time they were informed of the new English Language Arts Standards and taught the steps of the writing process. The writing process is an approach to teaching writing that allows students to take charge of their own writing and learning (Calkins, 1994; Graves, 1983; Hillocks, 1987). It involves five steps (1) pre-writing or selecting the topic; (2) drafting or composing; (3) revising; (4) editing or proofreading; and (5) publishing. While Hillocks (1995) explains writing as a recursive process, his text is geared toward the older child in junior high and secondary education. Young children must begin with an understanding of a linear process and the different types of skills that are required of narrative and expository text. Parents and students received direct instruction as to the criteria contained in the scoring rubric (Appendix A) and parents were given a series of questions to use when conferencing with their children, (Appendix B).

## Materials
The topics selected for writing for this study were taken from discontinued 5th grade writing competency tests. The scoring rubric was developed by the Reading Department of St. John's University and was consistent with the new English Language Arts Standards. The rubric contained six components: topic focus, organization, content, sentence structure, language, and mechanics. Students were evaluated in each area using a scale from 1 (low) to 4 (high), based upon descriptions of the type of writing that reflects each component at each level of proficiency. The parents were taught the steps in the writing process as follows: (1) Pre-writing, (2) First draft, (3) Revising, (4) Editing, (5) Second draft and final revision, and (6) Publication. Parents were shown samples of students' writing at each of the stages in the process. Activities for each step will be discussed in the procedure section.

## *Procedures*

The students were given three writing samples that were designated as Phase 1, Phase 2, and Phase 3. The development of each phase is discussed below. For each aspect of the writing rubric, a different writing sample was analyzed by students and the teacher during the student and parent training sessions.

**Phase One:** All students were given the first topic, *A Time When I Felt Special,* to write over a period of three weeks. Each day, students developed their composition engaging in the different aspects of the writing process. However, none of the students in the experimental or control groups were exposed to the writing rubric, nor were they given any formal instruction as to how to use the rubric to improve their writing. At the end of three weeks, the writing samples were scored. The two researchers who scored the samples were trained to use the rubric and were familiar with it having used it for over two years. A third rater was available in the event that there was a .5 discrepancy between the two raters. The scores were recorded for analysis.

**Phase Two**: In Phase 2, both groups were given the second topic, *My Hero,* to develop. But before the experimental group began to write, they were given formal instruction on the criteria and the use of the writing rubric. Over the course of two weeks, the students were given a separate piece of writing for each component of the rubric. As a class and with the teacher's guidance, the students practiced analyzing and evaluating different writing samples. For the first writing sample, the students were asked to determine whether the author developed the assigned topic in an interesting and imaginative way—**Topic Focus**. After discussing several pieces with each other and their teacher, the students scored the writing samples on a scale of 1 to 4 with 4 as the highest. As each component of the rubric was introduced, it was discussed and analyzed until students came to consensus on the score within a .5 range.

A second writing sample focused on **Organization.** Students were asked to determine if the piece had a logical plan of organization and coherence in the development of ideas. Again, the students discussed, analyzed, and scored the several writing samples on the same scale.

The third writing piece was subsequently examined for **Content**. Did the author use supportive material that was relevant and appropriate for the purpose and audience?

The fourth aspect of the rubric, **Sentence Structure**, focused on the skillful use of sentence variety. Students specifically noted the length and kinds of sentences that were used in the writing sample. The next writing pieces challenged students to determine the evidence of specific and vivid **Language**.

The last writing samples called upon the students' editing skills. Students examined the pieces for errors in **Mechanics** which included punctuation and capitalization. Their rating was based on whether these errors interfered with the communication of ideas from the author to the reader. The students added their ratings of the six components of the rubric and divided the total by six, which yielded a holistic score.

Finally, the students were given yet another sample and were asked to score the writing samples based on the six aspects of the writing rubric. After this training period was over, the two groups of students were given their second writing assignment to complete over a period of three weeks following the same procedures as in phase one. This time the students in the experimental group were aware of the criteria for scoring their composition. They self-evaluated their writing piece based on the rubric and made frequent revisions to their work. The control group students were given the second topic, *My Hero,* and proceeded to develop their writing piece following the same procedures as in phase one. The students' writing samples were scored by the same two raters and recorded for analysis.

**Phase Three:** At the same time that the students were given their third topic, *Making Something That I Enjoyed,* the parents attended a formal two-hour training session. First, they were informed of the English Language Arts Standards, then taught the steps of the writing process. This procedure was followed to enable parents to understand that writing is a gradual and recursive process that develops in stages from pre-writing to publication with many opportunities for revising and recreating. During this time the researchers shared with the parents many practical ways of helping them to enhance their child's ability to think about, talk about, and share with their children experiences that were meaningful to them. Parents were given samples of their child's work and asked to comment on the areas they thought were in need of improvement.

The second hour of the training session involved the same procedures that were used with the children to acquaint them with all six components of the writing rubric and how to arrive at a holistic score. Parents were given a script to guide their interaction with the students. They were taught how to critique their child's work, not their child.

Parents responded to each composition based on the specific component of the writing rubric. Finally, they were given three samples and were asked to score the samples on all six criteria. A discussion followed each scoring until parents arrived at a consensus. It was explained to parents that their child would be coming home in the next few days with a composition for them to score. After parents scored the writing piece, they were to discuss with their child the areas of strengths and those needing improvement on the writing sample. No additional writing or corrections were to take place at home. Parents were only to discuss the child's writing piece based on the criteria in the rubric.

Over a period of another three weeks, the students wrote their third composition, *Making Something That I Enjoyed,* and used their scoring rubric to self-evaluate their writing piece. The writing sample was taken home where parent and student discussed the sample based on the criteria of the rubric and the strategies for "sharing" discussed in the training. The child returned to school the next day and began to revise the composition. The two raters scored the third writing piece to determine whether or not the parental knowledge of the rubric and input may have improved the quality of the students' writing.

The control group also received three writing samples, however, unlike the experimental group, they did not have instruction in the use of the writing rubric, nor was there any parental involvement. These students had knowledge of the writing process, and revised and edited their work accordingly. They spent the same amount of time working and revising their composition as did the experimental group.

## Results

In order to assess rater reliability, a Pearson Product Moment Correlations was computed to assess the degree of correlation between raters in each phase of the study. The Pearson Product Moment Correlations between raters in Phase One was .85, for Phase Two, it was .88, and for Phase Three, .92. Therefore, it was appropriate to average the two raters' ratings for each phase to form composite scores.

In order to assess whether there were differential increases in performance during each phase for each group, a two-factor repeated measure analysis of variance was performed. The first factor treatment involved between-subject factor with two levels: an experimental group and a control group. The experimental group had 97 students and the control group had 70 students. The within-subjects factor was "Phase" consisting of three phases. The means of the groups within each phase are presented in Table 1.

**Table 1. Means and Standard Deviations Within Each Phase**

| GROUP | | PHASE 1 | PHASE 2 | PHASE 3 |
|---|---|---|---|---|
| Experimental | **Mean** | 2.45 | 2.76 | 3.22 |
| **(N=97)** | **(SD)** | (.42) | (.36) | (.37) |
| Control | **Mean** | 2.45 | 2.37 | 2.47 |
| **(N=70)** | **(SD)** | (.28) | (.21) | (.30) |
| Total | **Mean** | 2.45 | 2.60 | 2.91 |
| **(N=167)** | **(SD)** | (.37) | (.39) | (.51) |

Table 1 shows that the means for both the control group (2.45) and experimental group (2.45) began at the same approximate baseline for Phase One. However, after Phase Two, the experimental group had an increase to 2.76 while the control group actually had a reduction in its mean to 2.37. It was at this point that the students in the experimental group wrote their composition using the writing rubric as a guide. In Phase Three, after the parents received their training and they interacted with the students, the results were even more striking with the experimental group realizing a mean of 3.22, however, the control still remained close to its baseline mean with 2.47.

Mauchly's Test of Sphericity indicated that sphericity assumptions could not be retained. Therefore, the tests have been adjusted for violation of sphericity through the use of the Huynh-Feldt corrections. Table 2 presents the results of the analysis of variance. As can be seen in Table 2, there were significant main effects for phase, a significant main effect for group, and most important, significant main effect for group by phase interaction. The partial Eta squared or correlation ratio were computed, indicating a strong effect (.27). Any correlation over a .25 is considered a strong effect.

## Table 2. ANOVA of test Scores by Experimental Group and Instructional Phase

| TEST OF BETWEEN-SUBJECT EFFECTS* | | | | | | |
|---|---|---|---|---|---|---|
| FACTOR | SUM OF SQUARES | DF | MS | F | SIG | ETA SQUARED |
| GROUP | 17.96 | 1 | 17.96 | 60.24 | .000 | .267 |
| ERROR | 49.21 | 165 | .30 | | | |
| **TEST OF WITHIN-SUBJECT EFFECTS*** | | | | | | |
| PHASE | 13.59 | 1.89 | 7.20 | 181.84 | .000 | .52 |
| PHASE BY GROUP | 11.97 | 1.89 | 6.34 | 160.12 | .000 | .49 |
| ERROR | 12.33 | 311.46 | 3.96 | | | |

*Huynh-Feldt        $p < .05$

In order to further examine the statistical significance of group by phase interaction, simple main effect tests were computed. There were two such sets of tests. The first set of tests compared groups within each phase. As can be seen in Table 3, there were no significant differences between the experimental group and the control group within the baseline Phase One. However, there were significant differences between the groups in Phase Two and Phase Three. In order to assess if there were significant increments from phase to phase within each group, a second set of simple main effect tests were computed.

**Table 3. Simple Main Effects Tests for Groups within Instructional Phase**

| TRIAL | GROUP | GROUP | MEAN DIFFERENCE | SIG. |
|---|---|---|---|---|
| 1 | Control | Experimental | 6.47 | .911 |
| 2 | Control | Experimental | -.397 | .000 |
| 3 | Control | Experimental | -.760 | .000 |

*$P<.05$

Within the experimental and control groups there was a significant change from phase to phase. However, it should be noted that in the experimental group there was continuous improvement. In the control group there was a slight decrement in the second phase from the baseline score and then a slight improvement from Phase Two to Phase Three.

A graph of the means can be seen in Figure 1. It illustrates that there is no significant difference from Phase One to Phase Three for the control group. This group remained close to the baseline score in Phase One. However, the experimental group improved with each phase.

**Figure 1.  Means of Measure**

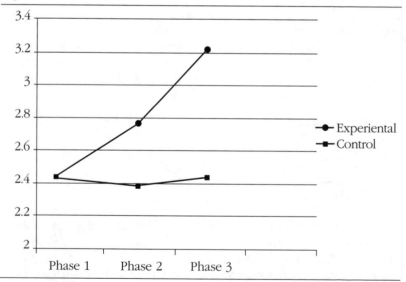

The hypothesis comparing scores by socioeconomic status was tested. Table 4 reports the Means and Standard Deviations for each school (SES). While the results indicate that all three subgroups of the experimental group improved their writing scores, the students in the more suburban affluent school scored higher than their counterparts in the urban schools.

**Table 4. Means and Standard Deviations Each School (SES)**

| School (SES) | | Phase 1 | Phase 2 | Phase 3 |
|---|---|---|---|---|
| Nassau | Mean | 2.41 | 2.67 | 3.18 |
| (N=30) | (SD) | (.48) | (.45) | (.37) |
| Brooklyn | Mean | 2.44 | 2.60 | 2.88 |
| (N=54) | (SD) | (.39) | (.39) | (.53) |
| Queens | Mean | 2.46 | 2.57 | 2.84 |
| (N=81) | (SD) | (.31) | (.37) | (.51) |
| Total | Mean | 2.44 | 2.60 | 2.91 |
| (N=167) | (SD) | (.37) | (.39) | (.51) |

A simple main effect test revealed that there were significant differences within the subgroups of the experimental group from phase to phase as noted in Table 5.

**Table 5. ANOVA of Test Scores by Phase and School (SES)**

**Test of Between-Subject Effects***

| Factor | Sum of Squares | Df | MS | F | Sig | Eta squared |
|---|---|---|---|---|---|---|
| School (SES) | 1.99 | 3 | .67 | 1.66 | .177 | .030 |
| Error | 65.18 | 163 | .40 | | | |

**Test of Within-Subject Effects***

| | | | | | | |
|---|---|---|---|---|---|---|
| Phase | 2.26 | 1.50 | 1.51 | 16.58 | .000 | .09 |
| Phase by SES | 2.08 | 4.49 | .46 | 5.08 | .000 | .09 |
| Error | 22.22 | 244.12 | 9.10 | | | |

*Huynh-Feldt          $p < .001$

Further analysis compared scores by gender. There was no significant difference between the scores of the males and females in either the experimental and control groups within or between phases.

## Discussion

The findings of this study are presented in relation to the three original research questions: (a) Will teaching students how to use a writing rubric as a guide for writing, improve their scores?; (b) Will teaching parents the writing process and use of a writing rubric enable them to conference more effectively with their children?; and (c) Will there be a significant difference in the writing scores based upon socioeconomic status?

Although all the students had been developing the stages of the writing process in their writing since first grade, at the time of the study, they did not have knowledge of a writing rubric nor did they know how to use the rubric as a means of improving the quality of their writing. During Phase Two, the students in the experimental group interacted with the trainers and with each other when evaluating separate writing pieces based on the criteria in the rubric. When scoring a sample, each student had to justify the score thus explaining the significance of the score. Students commented that now that they knew the criteria used in evaluating their writing, they could use the rubric to help them self-assess and subsequently engage in the recursive process of writing. The data indicates that there was indeed an improvement in their scores from phase to phase. The difference from the first phase to the second phase appeared to be contributed to their understanding and use of the writing rubric. Coupled with the interaction with their parents, students' scores improved again from Phase Two to Phase Three.

In response to the question, "How can I help my child with writing?," the response of the parents was overwhelming. Ninety-seven percent of the inner-city school parents attended the in-service and asked for additional training from the researcher and the classroom teachers. In a follow-up session with these parents whose children were in the experimental group, parents talked about their own writing ability and how engaging in discussions about their child's writing pieces enabled them to be more reflective with their own writing. Parents saw how over a period of six months, their child's writing improved. They remarked how the "sharing" that took place between parent and child became more open, supportive, and constructive. While in the past most of these parents admittedly focused on the mechanics of the composition, they now had a broader understanding of the quality of good writing. Overall, parents expressed a greater confidence in their ability to help their child with writing. Comments from parents after the study seemed to indicate that there was a better understanding of the writing task and the school's expectations for their child's writing. By their responses to scoring their child's writing sample, it seemed that many were able to recognize the elements of quality writing. Parents also indicated by their interaction with the trainers that they felt they now had an effective tool for assisting their child with writing. These are similar to the kinds of positive effects Howard (1996) reveals as a result of including parents as part of their children's writing audience.

The teachers were stunned by the parents' enthusiastic response to this project and created opportunities that enabled parents to become more involved in the writing experiences with their child. Students commented that now that their parents were aware of the writing process and the criteria for evaluation, their discussions about the writing were more directed and constructive. Students seemed to feel more comfortable about sharing their ideas with their parents and reported that over a six-month period of time, their parents spent more time with them and they enjoyed the interaction with their parents

Within the experimental group, there were three subgroups. The experimental group consisted of students from affluent, middle, and low-socioeconomic families. The analysis of data revealed that although all students in the experimental group improved their scores as a result of the treatment, the students from the affluent suburban school had a greater increase in the scores. This finding substantiates previous research in SES and student achievement (Walberg, 1984; Coleman, 1988; Comer, 1988). One can speculate on the reasons for these differences. Several factors may be considered: (a) the educational background and professional experiences of the parents; (b) the ability to understand completely the criteria presented in the training sessions; (c) the amount of time and quality of interaction with the child; and (d) language differences or limitations of parents in families where English is not the primary language. However, despite the language difficulties some parents experienced, they did not dampen the parents' enthusiasm for learning how to help their child. Additional training or a different type of training session may need to be developed for parents of bilingual backgrounds. But the fact remains, that despite these factors, the potential for improvement exists.

The results of this study point to the need to include parents in the teaching/learning process and to provide parents with opportunities to help their children. Quite often, parents are criticized for not being involved in their child's education. Perhaps the truth is that sometimes parents, though willing, don't always understand **how** to help their children. This study has initiated similar projects in other school districts where educators continue to foster parents as **partners** in their child's education.

Although this study was conducted with elementary school students in East coast, urban and suburban schools, it is suggested that follow-up studies should be initiated in sites in other parts of the country to determine if the results can be replicated. It is recommended that the training of the parents may include a follow-up session with more comprehensive feedback and that the procedures of Phase Three be repeated over a prolonged period of time to monitor improvement. This study can be replicated for any grade level and perhaps, the earlier the better. These results have initiated similar studies currently being conducted in several schools in New York City especially in schools with diverse student populations. This study emphasizes the importance of students and parents knowing the criteria when learning to improve writing and is indicative of the power connecting the school and home to create more proficient writers.

# References

Becker, H., & Epstein, J. (1992). Parent involvement: a study of teacher practices. *Elementary School Journal, 83*, 85-102.

Bermudez, A., & Padron, Y. (1988). University-school collaboration that increases minority parent involvement. *Educational Horizons, 66*(2). 83-86.

Bloom, B. S. (1986). *The home environment and school learning.* Paper commissioned by the Study Group on the National Assessment of Student Achievement (ERIC document Reproduction Service No. ED 279 663).

Board of Education. (1997). Performance standards: New standards. New York City, NY.

Boyle, C. (1996). *Efficacy of peer evaluation and effects of peer evaluation on persuasive writing.* Unpublished master's thesis. San Diego State University, San Diego, CA.

Bratcher, S. (1994). *Evaluating children's writing: A handbook of communication choices for classroom teachers.* New York: St. Martin Press.

Calkins, L. M. (1994). *The art of teaching writing.* (New Ed.). Portsmouth, NH: Heinemann.

Chavkin, N. F., & Williams, D. L. (1989). Low-income parents' attitudes toward parent involvement in education. *Journal of Sociology and Social Welfare, 16*(3), 17-23.

Clark, R. M. (1988). Parents as providers of linguistic and social capital. *Educational Horizons,* (Winter 1988), 93-95.

Coleman, J. S. (1987). Families and schools. *Educational Researcher, 16*(6), 32-38.

Coleman, J. S. (1988). Social capital in the creation of human capital. *American Journal of Sociology., 94*, 95-120.

Comer, J. P.(1988). Educating poor minority children. *Scientific American, 259*(5), 42-48.

Dahl, K. L., & Farnan, N. (1998). *Children's writing: Perspectives from research.* Newark, DE. International Reading Association.

Duke, D. G. (1992). *Parental expectation and its relationship to achievement in algebra 1.* Doctoral dissertation, Memphis State University.

Epstein, J. (1991). Effects on student achievement of teacher practice of parent involvement. In S. Silverman (Ed.), *Advances in reading/language research. Literacy through family, community and school interaction.* Greenwich: JAI Press.

Epstein, J. (1995). *Family-school links: How do they affect educational outcomes.* In A. Booth & J. Dun (Eds.) Chapter 14. Hillsdale, N.J.: Lawrence Erlbaum Associates. 209-246.

Fruchter, N., Galetta, A., & White, L. (1992). *New direction in parent involvement.* New York: Academy for Educational Development Inc.

Gere, A. R., & Abbott, R. D. (1985). Talking about writing: The Language of writing groups. *Research in the Teaching of English, 19*, 362-385.

Graves, D. H. (1983). *Writing: Teachers and children at work.* Exeter, NH: Heinemann.

Gyles, R. (1990). *Learning mathematics: A quantitative inquiry on parental involvement as reported by urban, poor black parents and their fourth-grade children.* Doctoral dissertation, New York University.

Henderson, A., & Berla, N. (1994). *The family is critical in student achievement.* Washington D.C.: National Committee for Citizens in Education.

Hillocks, G. Jr. (1995). *Teaching writing as a reflective practice.* New York: Teachers College Press.

Hillocks, G., Jr. (1987). A synthesis of research on teaching writing. *Educational Leadership, 45*, 71-82.

Howard, K. (1996). When parents serve as writing critics. *Teaching Pre-K to 8, 27*(2), 58, 61-62.

Mabry, L. (1999). Writing to the rubric: Lingering effects of traditional standardized testing on direct writing assessment. *Phi Delta Kappan, 80*, 73-79

McCarthey, S. J. (1994). Authors, text, and talk: The internalization o f dialogue from social interaction during writing. *Reading Research Quarterly, 29*, 200-231.

McLaughlin, M., & Shields, P. (October 1987). Involving low-income parents in the schools: A role for policy *Phi Delta Kappan. 56-60.*

Muller, C. (1993). Parent involvement and academic achievement: An analysis of family resources available to the child. In B. Schneider & J. Coleman (Eds.). *Parents, their children, and schools (pp. 77-113).* San Francisco: Westview Press.

Newkirk, T. (1995). The writing conference a performance. *Research in the Teaching of English, 29*, 193-215.

Power, B. (1997). Teaching writing. *Instructor, 106*, 24-33.

Rowe, K. J. (1991). The influence of reading activity at home on students' attitudes towards reading, classroom attentiveness, and reading achievement: An application of structural equation modeling, *British Journal of Educational Psychology, 61*, 19-35.

Rowe, K. J., & Rowe, K. S. (1992). The relationship between inattentiveness and reading achievement (Part B): An explanatory study, *Journal of the American Academy of Child and Adolescent Psychiatry, 31*, 357-368.

Slaughter, D. T. (1987). The home environment and academic achievement of Black American children. *Journal of Negro Education, 56*(1), 3-20.

Spandel, V., & Stiggins, R. J. (1997). *Creating writers: Linking writing assessment and instruction.* (2nd ed.). New York, NY: Longman.

Sperling, D. (1993). What's worth an "A"? Setting standards together. *Educational Leadership, 50*, 73-75.

U.S. Department of Education. (1986). *What Works.* Washington, DC.

Walberg, H. J. (1984). Families as partners in education productivity. *Phi Delta Kappan 65* (6) 397-400.

## Appendix A. Teacher's Holistic Criteria For Evaluating Student Papers (Nys & Nyc Procedure)

For each of the six components listed, assign a 1, 2, 3, or 4 dependent on criteria. Add your six scores and average. This is the holistic score for the paper.

### *Criteria for Rating Student Responses*

| | Scores for Writing Component | Level 4 | Level 3 | Level 2 | Level 1 |
|---|---|---|---|---|---|
| **Topic Focus =** | ____ | Develops the assigned topic in an interesting and imaginative way. | Develops the assigned topic in an acceptable but unimaginative way. | Attempts to develop the assigned topic but includes digressions. | Minimally addresses the assigned topic. |
| **Organization =** | ____ | Demonstrates a logical plan of organization and coherence in the development of ideas. | Has a plan of organization a satisfactory development of ideas. | Demonstrates weakness in organization and the development of ideas. | Shows lack of organization and development of ideas. |
| **Content =** | ____ | Uses support that is relevant and appropriate for the purpose and audience. | Uses adequate support material. | Uses little support material. | Uses no support material or uses irrelevant material. |
| Sentence **Structure =** | ____ | Shows skillful use of sentence variety. | Uses some sentence variety. | Demonstrates sentence sense but has little sentence variety. | Demonstrates a lack of sentence sense. |
| **Language Use =** | ____ | Uses specific, vivid language. | Uses appropriate language. | Uses trite and/or imprecise language. | Uses immature and/or appropriate language. |
| **Mechanics =** | ____ | Makes few or no mechanical errors. | Makes mechanical errors which do not interfere with communication. | Makes mechanical errors which interfere with communication. | Makes mechanical errors which seriously interfere with communication. |

**Total Holistic Score =** _____ ÷ 6 = _____   **Passing (3.0 to 4.0)**

## Appendix B. Questions Parents Might Ask to Help Their Child With the Writing Task.

**Topic Focus:**  Did you write about the topic in an interesting and imaginative way?
What would make someone want to read your composition?
Did you stay on the topic?
Will the reader understand what you have written?
Have you left out information that belongs with your topic?
Did you include information that **does not** belong with your topic?

**Organization:**  Do the events in your composition follow in the right or logical order?
Have you arranged your ideas so that they can be followed from one step to another?
Do you have a strong beginning, an interesting middle, and a good ending?
Have you used a new paragraph as you wrote the beginning, middle, and end of your story?

**Content:**  Have you written your composition with your purpose in mind?
Have you written your composition with your audience in mind?
Did you include enough information in your composition?
Do you have enough details to support your main idea?

**Sentence Structure:**  **Look at your sentences.** Have you tried to use different kinds of sentences? (Interrogative? Imperative. Exclamatory! Declarative.)
Have you used sentences that include dialogue? ("Quotation marks")
Are your sentences long enough...or are they too long to understand?

**Language Use:**  Look at the words you have used.
Have you used the same words over too many times?
Did you use interesting words, replacing the ordinary with more colorful and descriptive words?
Did you use your thesaurus to replace ordinary words?
Were the words you used appropriate for your audience? Will they understand them?
Did you proofread to determine if your verb tenses were in agreement and consistent?

**Mechanics:**  Did you proofread for errors in spelling, punctuation, and capitalization?
Did you indent your paragraphs?
Did you begin every sentence with a capital letter?
Did you use quotation marks correctly?